# Journey to the Ragged Islands

## Sailing Solo Through The Bahamas

By
Paul Trammell

**ISBN:** 9781726888721

This book is dedicated to my nieces and nephews: Meriwether, Antoinette, Virginia, Winston, and Gus. May you all find adventure and wisdom in your wonderful lives!

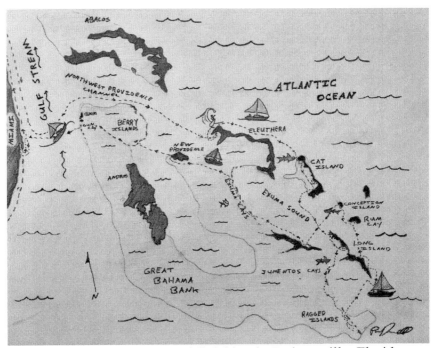

The journey, starting and finishing in Jacksonville, Florida

**TABLE OF CONTENTS**

# INTRODUCTION

What follows is a non-fiction account of a sailing voyage that was the realization of a dream three years in the making. While on the surface it is a book about sailing, this is also a book describing the unique experiences that only come from dreaming big and chasing the dream to its conclusion, voyaging into the unknown alone, and facing the raw essence of nature and the depths of one's soul.

While I often use plural pronouns, I am only referring to myself and *Sobrius*, my 30' 1972 Dufour Arpege. No other person set foot on *Sobrius* until Miami, when my friend Cristina sailed with me back to Jacksonville.

I named my boat *Sobrius* to remind myself of my commitment to sobriety, and as a testament to the fact that sailing helped pull me out of a life of debauchery and into a life of adventure (and vastly improved health). My father gave me the gift of sailing as a child, and this experience sat dormant until I was in my forties, when it came back gave me a new life.

I speak a lot in this book about coral reefs and fish. I studied marine biology in college and earned a BS in Biology at Florida Institute of Technology, and an MS in Biology at West Virginia University. The book I used to identify fish is *A Field Guide to Atlantic Coast Fishes of North America* (Peterson Filed Guide Series) by C. Richard Robins and G. Carleton Ray. This is the same book that I studied in college, and although the pages are falling out and have been stuffed back in, the book remains relevant.

I hope that this book inspires others to step outside of their comfort zones, chase their dreams, and achieve greatness, or at least to rise above mediocrity. As you read this book, I encourage you to start planning your next adventure, and if you have the opportunity to take children sailing, or to introduce adults to sailing, please consider doing so.

I've included a glossary in the back of the book for those who need sailing terms defined.

If you would like to watch videos from this journey, please look up the "Journey to the Ragged Islands" series on YouTube, on

my channel, "Paul Trammell."
https://www.youtube.com/watch?v=fQCaTsFITSY

Color versions of all the photos in this book can be found on YouTube in the video "Color Photos from the book Journey to the Ragged Islands."

If you would like to follow my future adventures and writings, like my Facebook page "Paul Trammell."

I've also included GPS coordinates of all the places I anchored. If you sail to these places, please treat the islands and the coral with the utmost respect. Observe the coral, but don't touch. Never allow your anchor or rode to have any contact with coral, and this requires visually checking the bottom for small young coral. And finally, don't let the beauty go unappreciated!

*Life thrusts upon us a constant barrage of challenges, choices, options, and decisions we all must face. The meek will stare at the ground, looking at the feet of the masses nearby, running down the path of those before them like a herd of sheep. Each new runner widens the path, and all those behind more clearly see this path with each new sheep.*

*The brave will stand and face the challenge, recognizing it as a choice, and will perhaps casually walk off in a new direction, leaving the herd wondering where their friend is going and why. The sheep all relish the comfort of the herd to their own detriment, because the herd knows not where it runs, only that it must be the right way because it's the way all the sheep run, and run they must, because the wolves are sure to be close behind. If a pit is what lies ahead of the herd, then the pit must be the place to go.*

*The brave don't run, but rather stop and observe, think, decide, and plan. All the world is open to the brave, while the world is a trap to those who simply follow.*

*One way is the way of the masses, and the other way is the way of ourselves.*

*Sobrius*, my 1972 Dufour Arpege, freshly painted before the journey

*"Be alone, that is the secret of invention; be alone, that is where ideas are born."* Nikola Tesla

**DEPARTURE**

Wednesday, March 7, 2018

The air is cool for March and high cirrus clouds scatter across the otherwise bright blue sky as I stand in the cockpit, smile and wave goodbye. If all goes well my ship and I will return in two months, *Sobrius* only in need of some fresh varnish and me with darker skin, longer hair, and tales of adventure for any who might listen. However, I have tried to mentally prepare myself for disaster – to lose her to a reef, a storm, a mistake, or pirates. With great adventure comes great risk, and without an element of the unknown, there is no adventure. Worries of disaster have haunted me, but have not overcome my desire to execute the plan.

However, my plan is vague and my destinations are flexible. But I do know that for the next week or more I will be sailing non-stop from Jacksonville, Florida, to somewhere in The Bahamas, and for the next two months I will live on my boat while sailing wherever the weather dictates, at the mercy of the wind, the sea, and the creatures within. I hope to coexist peacefully with all, but am willing to suffer whatever consequences the journey may have in store for me.

I've spent the last year preparing for this trip – saving money, studying charts, working on *Sobrius*, and getting myself into shape. I have onboard what I hope is a two-month supply of food and water. Ready or not, the time is now, *Sobrius* is heading out to sea; the voyage has begun!

The little one-cylinder diesel engine hidden below rumbles and pushes *Sobrius* across the dark brown water of the Ortega River, through the picturesque little bascule bridge at its mouth, and into the equally dark water of the wide and still St Johns River. The back yards and patios of stately houses that line the banks fade into the distance as I stand at the mast and raise the mainsail, then move to the bow and watch for the little colored floats that mark crab traps while the tillerpilot steers.

I spend the next six hours sailing down the river, underneath bridges, and past the city of Jacksonville, its various neighborhoods, industrial monstrosities, and gigantic ports for container ships. As we cruise along, I daydream about uninhabited islands, like Water Cay and Conception Island, and freediving in the blue holes at Cat Island, Long Island, and the Jumentos Cays. I've never been to these places, but I've studied them so much that they seem to live and occupy space inside of me.

The weather continues to improve, and a wonderful feeling is washing over me like the sunlight from above. All is exactly as it should be. The weather is fine, the boat is well-prepared, I feel fantastic, and the adventure is just now starting. I have no obligations other than to sail wherever I want to sail, for the next *two months*, and I couldn't be more thankful to be here.

The ocean calls to me and I crave the vast wilderness of the Atlantic, the endless expanse of deep water, and the raw nature that only an ocean can provide. However, it's going to be cold; it's supposed to get down to the thirties tonight, which, as a Floridian, I wasn't really expecting (we never expect cold weather, and often forget what season it is). So be it, the "warm stuff" locker is still stocked from last year's adventure with sweaters, jackets, hats, gloves, long johns, and various other warm clothes to keep me comfortable in cold weather. I've also got good foul-weather gear and two backup rain jackets. I fear the cold, and I have neither bimini nor dodger, so I will be fully exposed to the elements. Thus, I stock lots of gear to help me deal with the weather. A wise man once told me "There is no bad weather, only inappropriate dress."

As we approach the inlet, Mayport Naval Station passes to starboard, the final bastion of civilization I will pass before entering the ocean. Battle ships, drab grey and stationary, with odd structures rising up from their decks, sit still as *Sobrius* and I enter the Fort George Inlet. A helicopter flies overhead, another joins and the two of them fly all about like noisy birds at play. Waves crash and send whitewater flying above a long stone jetty to port.

The water near the mouth of the great river is surprisingly flat, calm, and friendly. The wind is behind us, the current is with us, and the ease of the first day of the journey does not escape me. I start the engine as we enter the wide inlet. We really don't need it running and I generally try to sail as if I don't have an engine. But when in an inlet, good seamanship, I feel, dictates running the engine. However, the wind pushes us faster than the current and the diesel engine idles, waiting patiently in case the unexpected happens and necessitates its use.

Outside, a six-foot swell is running, but since the swell comes from the north, I suppose it's not affecting the conditions in the inlet much, and I appreciate the unexpected calmness of the water, which continues as we enter the mighty Atlantic Ocean, turn south, and trim the sails for a beam reach towards South Florida and The Bahamas. The serenity of the scene and the exhilaration of the beginning of the long journey mix inside my chest and flow through my extremities. The ocean, my friend, mysterious and powerful, is master here, and I venture out alone.

Before nightfall I reef the mainsail and take down the jib, which is blanketed by the main (the main is blocking the wind from the jib). The wind seems like it's northwest (*coming from* the northwest, wind is always reported as the direction from which it comes – waves are reported this way too), probably blowing in the low teens. Swell pushes us forward as *Sobrius* tries to surf. We accelerate as the waves pick us up, riding briefly on the crests, then decelerate in the troughs, varying between 4.5 and 6.5 knots.

*The first two days of the journey were very cold and the seas were lively, but the sailing was fine and downwind. Here the sun is setting for the first time on this journey. Notice the aloe plant hanging from the stern pulpit. I took this from my yard at home to treat sunburn while in the islands. Miraculously, it survived the entire journey and is still alive and growing as I write these words.*

The first evening of my journey has settled, and the beauty of the dark ocean captivates me. But the air has gotten surprisingly colder, so I go below and make a pot of chicken noodle soup while the tillerpilot steers. The warmth of the soup is so pleasing that I follow it with a cup of hot peppermint tea. I'm wearing my big red coat, with a turtleneck sweater underneath, full-finger gloves, and the Mad Bomber hat, with its fuzzy forehead and big fur-lined ear flaps. This is the warmest hat I've ever owned, and I used to wear it only on the coldest days when I was a snow skier. I even have a towel draped over my legs to keep them warm. Despite the cold, I feel incredibly content. Properly dressed, the conditions are quite tolerable, pleasant even.

Winds are about 15 knots out of the west, the seas are calm, and we head just east of south (160 degrees) at about 4.5 knots. Between nearly invisible clouds, stars shine in the otherwise dark sky. The only sounds I hear come from the water stroking *Sobrius'* hull, and the rig creaking with the movement of the boat; together they compose an entrancing song that speaks directly to my soul and coaxes me into a state of deep serenity.

The unexpectedly peaceful disposition of the Atlantic Ocean is both surprising and welcome. I expected the weather and seas to be scary, rough, uncomfortable, somewhat miserable, and I think because of that, I appreciate these docile conditions even more so. I'm sure that one path to happiness is to set expectations low and then try to appreciate all that is good. Appreciating all that is good is no struggle today as I sail south, with the whole ocean to myself, and the level of relaxation within me builds with each passing wave.

My solitude is briefly interrupted by the sighting of a ship in the distance, and I check the AIS, but it registers no ships within its range of 24 miles. The mysterious ship is moving quickly in the opposite direction, a few miles away, and I wonder if it is a Naval vessel, since it is not transmitting on the AIS. All commercial ships above a certain size are required to transmit, and most private boats do as well. The Navy does not. Pirates don't either. *Sobrius* transmits on the AIS, as I want all other vessels to be able to "see" me.

Seeing a boat not transmitting on AIS worries me, as I rely on this system to warn me of potential collisions while I sleep. This is the main reason I only allow myself 20 minutes of rest at a time. I need to be looking out at least this often should a boat approach and my AIS not know of its presence; I have to see it before we collide. Suddenly I wish *Sobrius* was equipped with radar.

Earlier today I unintentionally gybed twice while looking at my phone when I should have been paying attention. Unintentional gybes can break things, important things like the boom, or me. So, to prevent this from happening again, I tie a line to a carabiner, clip it to the aft end of the boom, lead the line to the block I installed near the bow, then take the line back to the cockpit via the other side of the mast, pull it tight and cleat it off. Now I have a preventer rigged and unless it is freed the boom cannot gybe.

As we approach the waters of my home town of St Augustine, I hear an airplane flying overhead to my left and I imagine all the passengers warm and comfortable in their airplane seats. They probably left an hour ago from somewhere farther away than my destination, which will take me about a week to reach. For a brief moment, I envy them. However, tomorrow they will be back at work and I will still be sailing.

After a few hours of sailing in the darkness and looking at the shining stars, my eyes become heavy and I feel the undeniable need for rest. Neither my eyes nor the AIS detect any ships or other lights on the water, land is five miles away, and the chartplotter shows no obstacles ahead. I start the countdown timer on my watch, which is set for 22 minutes, then go below and lie down in all my clothes and lifejacket. I fall asleep almost immediately.

I'm cold when the vibrating then beeping alarm on my wrist shakes me from my sleep. After a moment of disorientation, I remember where I am and stick my head up through the companionway hatch into the brisk night air and look about in the darkness. But there is nothing to see. I check the AIS and it has nothing to report, the chartplotter shows that we still travel in the same direction as we did before I went to sleep, and the mainsail appears to be properly trimmed. All is well in the dark ocean world and I decide to sleep for another 20 minutes.

But the jeans I wear under my big yellow bibs are damp and cold and this situation demands a prompt solution. I dig into the warm-stuff locker and find my black long johns, which are actually cycling tights from my days as a mountain biker. In the dark swaying cabin, I take off the lifejacket, the red coat, my neoprene boots, the big yellow bibs, and finally my damp and cold jeans, which I replace with the tights, then put everything back on and lay down for another rest. The 22-minute timer resets itself as soon as the alarm goes off, so there is no need to restart it. I pull a blanket over me and fall asleep as *Sobrius* gently rolls and pitches across the deep water.

March 8, 6:45 am

It is a unique and priceless experience to sail through the night and then watch the gradual rising of the sun. Darkness very slowly gives way to twilight, followed by the colors of the sunrise, and finally the full brightness and warmth of the sun. This morning I appreciate the warmth it brings almost as much as I appreciate staying afloat. It was a very, very cold night, probably in the thirties. I now have on all the warm clothing I can fit on myself: the mad bomber, neoprene gloves and booties, long johns underneath my bibs, shirt, turtleneck, sweater, and my big red jacket with my lifejacket on top. I slept with all of this on so as to be ready to go on deck at a moment's notice, and was kept company by the green blinking light on the SPOT tracking device (this device communicates with a satellite to let family and friends know where I am).

The sun, which somehow looks bigger this morning, shines both in the sky and on the water, through illuminated sprays on the tops of the waves. Little glowing, shimmering crests cover the seascape and command my attention while the sky above is bright blue with a few cirrostratus clouds hanging motionless to the north. The south sky is clear.

Daytona Beach and Ormond Beach pass just within sight as we sail 5 miles offshore. We should be going around Cape Canaveral this afternoon and hopefully will be all the way around it before dark. In these conditions, with north winds, the cape could be rough and have breaking waves, which worries me. But the wind might shift to the west and if so I'll be tempted to cross the Gulf Stream today and enter The Bahamas through the Little Bahama Bank and the Abacos. Otherwise we'll continue south and cross either Friday or Saturday and enter the Northwest Providence Channel, south of the Abacos. The weather shall have the final say in all of my decisions.

March 8, 1:20 pm

As we sail away from the mainland and out towards the Cape Canaveral safe-water buoy, I'm reminded of the very uncomfortable and difficult night I had the last time I was here. Interestingly, the conditions today are very similar to what they were then – NW wind at 15 knots and 5-8' seas – when I was first sailing *Sobrius* home after I bought her in St Petersburg. It's infinitely more pleasant this time. The main differences are that today we are sailing downwind, on a broad reach, instead of upwind, and the other is that the sun is out. Going downwind and down-wave is vastly more comfortable, while the sunlight brings an enhanced mood.

Today we sail at 5 knots, under just the reefed main, with no problems. No water is coming over the bow as the waves push us from behind. *Sobrius* rolls from side-to-side, but is not consistently heeling, so it's very easy in comparison to last year when I was beating against the wind and waves, unsure of how much *Sobrius* could take.

While considering taking a nap, I realize that I should first check the chartplotter for any obstacles that might be in the area, and sure enough, after zooming in, something on the chartplotter catches my attention – "exposed wreck, hazard to navigation." The existence of an exposed wreck sticking up out of the water somewhere in front of us shocks me. We certainly do need to go out and around the red buoy to avoid this obstacle. There will be no cutting corners at the cape, and I delay my nap; I am wide awake now.

There is an important lesson here: chartplotters do not show all of their information, like exposed wrecks, unless they are zoomed in. I almost ran aground on a reef last year south of Miami because I had the chartplotter zoomed out. This is a good argument for always reviewing paper charts before a journey, and for constantly zooming in to check for details on the chartplotter.

I took two naps earlier today, in the late morning, but now I'll have to wait until we get around the cape before I sleep again, on account of the exposed wreck and some shoals in the area. An hour later I'm beginning to feel fatigued again, but I remain in the cockpit, sitting upright and steering, alternately watching the ocean, then the chartplotter, staying on course and getting past the cape.

I am captivated by the changing colors in the sky as the sun sets when whitewater leaping up over the surface of the dark ocean far off ahead and to the right catches my attention. I check the chart and see a jetty there, on the north side of Port Canaveral Inlet. A power boat comes out of the inlet and passes in front of us, safely about a mile away. But I get nervous every time a boat is moving in our general direction.

The waves are larger now, but thankfully travelling in roughly the same direction as we are, lifting and pushing us forward. Still I'd like some relief from all the movement. I think if I turn west after passing the inlet I'll find calmer water as the swell should be blocked by the cape and the jetty. I'd like to heave-to and take a break.

Finally I see the inlet and we pass it and its jetties. I set the autopilot, creep to the mast, and with legs spread in safety stance I haul down on the jib halyard, and the jib raises like the wings of a bird about to take flight. It goes up without resistance since the mainsail is blanketing it. My tethers keep me attached to *Sobrius*, and the carabiners slide along the jacklines, obediently following me as I return to the safety of the cockpit. *Sobrius* bounces in the waves; I walk crouched way over, as carefully as possible, always holding on to something with one or both hands. A sense of relief always follows returning to the cockpit. I unclip from the jackline and clip a tether to the big stainless steel padeye in the center of the floor of the cockpit. I like to remain attached to the boat, it feels like wearing the seatbelt in my truck.

Staying tethered to the vessel is essential for a singlehander. If I fall overboard, the best-case scenario is that I survive but lose the ship. But it's more likely that neither of us will survive. She will continue sailing under autopilot, powered by the solar panels, until she hits something, or perhaps do endless laps around the globe, and I will bob around in my lifejacket until I die from dehydration or hypothermia – unless I am within a few miles of shore, in which case I might be able to swim to safety. To void such a fate, I always clip my tethers to the jacklines when I leave the cockpit, and I usually clip in to the big padeye on the floor while in the cockpit. I also never relieve myself overboard, but instead use a plastic fruit-juice container with a handle and the top cut off. It's tied to a rope and I simply empty it and toss it overboard to rinse it out. Many dead sailors have been found bobbing in the ocean with their pants down, or so I have read.

With gloved hands, I haul in the sheets of the jib and the mainsail and turn us into the wind, towards the shore, hoping to find sheltered waters. *Sobrius* accelerates and heels as we sail fast into and across the dark grey waves that are no longer directly behind us. We rise and fall as we charge through the seas; spray flies off the bow sending waves of airborne water over the deck and into my face – and the rest of me. Without my foul-weather gear I'd be miserable, but properly dressed, the action enlivens me.

Closer to shore, and in the lee of the jetty north of us, we heave-to. But the mainsail is luffing violently, and I'm worried it's being damaged by all this, so I trim it in a little. Although we are hove-to, we still move forward at 2 knots. I make dinner, get a little bit of rest, and then return to the cockpit, tack the jib across, and get moving again, in the dark of the night.

We head south on a broad reach, fast, making 6-7 knots in the dark of night.

I sleep again for twenty minutes, then check the AIS, which shows a ship ahead, the *Brooke Chapman*, moving north, in our general direction. However, when I look across the water to the south, I think I see two boats. I watch the bearing of the *Brooke Chapman* on the AIS, which is slightly increasing, so I bear off to port. But then I am shocked and nearly blinded as a powerful spotlight shines on us, immediately followed by the loud beeping of the AIS alarm.

"One whistle" a New York accent comes across the VHF radio.

I gather myself, then pick up the microphone and ask him to clarify. He says he wants to pass port-to-port (on each other's left). The captain asks me to change course to the west, so I do this. He also says something about towing a long line, which makes me think it might be a fishing boat.

It's very strange to look at, this vessel, and I don't understand its navigation lights. I need to study commercial vessel lights; I should be able to interpret them, but can't. It looks like two boats, and further investigation of the information displayed on the AIS reveals that the *Brooke Chapman* is a towing vessel, and now I realize that what I thought were two boats was actually a tugboat and a barge being towed behind it. This is critical information because one can't go between the two without facing total destruction from the towing line. I should have checked this information on the AIS sooner – I'm still learning about and getting more accustomed to this crucial piece of equipment.

I try to stay very far away from the boats, but It's impossible to tell distance in the dark. The barge could be big and far away, or small and close, or even big and close. I keep getting the sickening feeling that these two vessels are dangerously close to my fragile little ship, but I relax a little when it's clear that we are safely past the duo.

March 9

We heave-to again in the morning, just to get some rest, then sail downwind all day under the reefed main with a preventer holding the boom fast.

I am tempted to go in at Ft. Pierce, but don't see anywhere to anchor on the charts, and now I am considering going in at Lake Worth Inlet to anchor for a day or two. I could stay in there until Sunday (today is Friday) and then cross the Gulf Stream into the Abacos. It looks like a low-pressure system is going to pass just north of us on Monday so it shouldn't bring much bad weather, but it might.

We sail downwind in about ten knots of breeze, heading towards Lake Worth Inlet, where the temptation to go in and anchor is strong. If I don't go in I'll be out in a high-traffic area tonight, and it will probably be difficult to get any sleep. I suppose I should wait out Saturday, so I'm not quite sure what the best plan is, but for now, I sail.

Originally, I wanted to set out on the ambitious journey of sailing east from Jacksonville, crossing the open ocean north of the Abacos and Eleuthera, and sail all the way to Cat Island (an idea which was called "wrong-headed" by an older and more experienced sailor). I had to abandon this plan due to the weather. Ironically, it turns out I'm doing nearly what everybody else does, which is sail south, then wait for a good time to cross the Gulf Stream at an anchorage in the Intracoastal Waterway (ICW). However, most boats sail south through the ICW to avoid the ocean. I prefer the ocean; there's much less to run into out here and I can sail at night and occasionally sleep, which we can't do on the ICW. And on the ocean, I can make two to three times as much distance per day as I could on the ICW.

A mast to the right catches my eye, and it's a sailboat passing me to the west, with no sails up, motoring downwind. *Why isn't it sailing?*

We are just north of Lake Worth inlet when the approaching evening finds me still debating whether or not to go inside and anchor somewhere, but I'm leaning towards continuing south and crossing tomorrow morning, putting me in the Northwest Providence Channel by nightfall. If I stay here tonight I would be crossing tomorrow morning and ending up on the Little Bahama Bank tomorrow night. I really don't want to cross the Little Bahama Bank in darkness because the water there is shallow. The NW Providence Channel is deep, and I could be in the Berry Islands by Sunday. Sunday the weather is supposed to deteriorate here, with rain and thunderstorms. There might be rain tomorrow too, and I'm going to try to avoid all that by getting as far south as I can.

I certainly have had quite a bit of anxiety about this Gulf Stream crossing. The coming rain throws a whole new curveball into the equation. I wonder why I don't have a bimini or a dodger and feel like I should have invested in one or the other, which would make a huge difference in the rain. I'll have to be getting one soon. It's next on the list of things I want for *Sobrius*. But I do have an umbrella.

I've been napping on and off throughout the day, trying to get as much sleep as I can before the evening, in anticipation of encountering shipping traffic tonight. However, I don't really foresee too much traffic this close to shore; I'm only about a mile offshore, trying to stay out of the northward Gulf Stream current.

Giant cruise ships lumber out of Lake Worth inlet, 1.5 nm ahead, making me happy to be out of their path. The breeze has been light all day, the sails have been annoyingly flapping around, and I'm only making about 2 knots to the south. The wind varies between northeast and east, stopping sometimes. I put my next larger headsail up, but it's not long before I drop it to the deck, as it is not contributing to forward progress.

I see on the chart an area just north of Lake Worth Inlet labeled "anchorage area." I think it's odd to have an anchorage area in the ocean, but there are no waves tonight and very little breeze, and this seems a lot easier and less time consuming than going into the inlet to rest. Minutes later we drift into the anchorage area and I take the sails down.

I drop the Fortress anchor, which has been riding in the anchor locker near the bow, and all its 250 feet of rode, as we are in 50 feet of water and this gives me an acceptable 5:1 scope. This anchor is aluminum and very light. My new, heavy Vulcan anchor and its 50 feet of heavy chain are stored below, near the keel, keeping *Sobrius'* center of gravity low and centered. The Fortress sets, as confirmed by the 0-knot speed displayed on the chartplotter. I set the anchor-drag alarm for 500 feet.

For the first time in three days I can fully relax, and the feeling washes over me like a warm shower after a hard day of work. I make a pot of soup and eat it in the cockpit, looking out across the calm dark water at the beach and the lights of condominiums and hotels. I imagine what all the people there are doing. Two worlds are laid out before me, separated by less than a mile of water.

March 10, 4:00 am

In the dim light of the morning, I make coffee and oatmeal on the little alcohol stove, then get out jib #3, hank it to the forestay, and tie on the sheets. I raise the mainsail, sheet it in tight, then move to the bow and start pulling in the 250 feet of anchor rode.

The breeze has come back and we sail away from the ocean anchorage fast on a close reach – into the wind. The sun is up and its light feels warm in the cold air. My feet are braced on the opposite seat of the cockpit, as we are heeling 15-20 degrees. I'm hand steering and looking forward, sailing and enjoying it. But it's not long before the wind becomes too strong for the sails I have up; we heel beyond the point of efficient sailing and comfort, and I need to reef the main.

I set the tillerpilot, clip in to the jackline, and move to the mast. I release the halyard from its cleat on the mast, pull the sail down just a couple feet – enough to attach the steel ring of the first reef to the hook on the boom, then I raise the halyard and tighten it with the winch on the mast. With my feet spread apart wide to keep my balance on the dancing ship, I pull on the reefing line and the boom rises to the foot of the sail; I cleat it off and the reef is in – the mainsail is now considerably smaller. I crouch low and carefully return to the safety of the cockpit, keeping my right hand between the boom and my head, just in case it swings across and tries to kill me.

We sail on, but it's not long before it becomes clear that we still have too much sail up and I need to replace the headsail with a smaller one – a necessary but rather unenjoyable task.

I go below and get out jib #4, the small one, take it to the bow, and hank it on below jib #3, which is up and working. I roll out jib # 4 on the windward rail, one tether clipped to a jackline all the time. I move to the leeward side, clip my second tether to a shroud, then, leaning and reaching out over the moving water, I untie the lazy sheet from jib #3. This is the most exciting part of the job.

I take the sheet to the other side of the boat and tie it on to jib #4, then go back to the cockpit and pull the lazy sheet tight and cleat it off. Next, I push the auto-tack on the tillerpilot's control head.

As *Sobrius* turns to starboard, I move back to the mast and drop the jib as it comes across, using the downhaul to pull the sail to the deck. I move back to the bow, unhank jib #3 from the forestay and transfer the halyard to jib #4. I move back to the mast, careful on the rocking deck, always holding on, always clipped in. Falling overboard is unacceptable. I pull on the jib halyard and raise jib #4, then move back to the cockpit and trim the sail. I return to the foredeck and untie the lazy sheet from jib #3, which is now laying on the deck, then transfer it to jib #4, which is now up and working. Finally, I roll up jib #3, bag it, and stash it below.

All this take about 20 minutes and it is exhausting because *Sobrius* is charging ahead the whole time and moving in all three dimensions. I could have hove-to and changed the headsail while *Sobrius* lay relatively still, but I want to keep moving.

I open a LaCroix as a reward for the hard work and sip the mango-flavored soda water in the cockpit, back at the helm, and enjoy the lively sailing.

*POP!*

I hear it above my head, followed by the sound of the mainsail luffing as the wind chaotically shakes the loose sail, two sure signs that something is very wrong. A broken line hangs from the boom. The reefing line has broken and the clew of the main is free, the bottom aft end of the sail luffs in the strong breeze, shortening the life of the sail and quickening the pace of my thoughts. *What to do?*

I have to put in the second reef, then improvise a repair. I feel foolish because I've never put in the second reef. Out here on the ocean in time of need is not the time to be working out something new. I should have practiced this before; now I'm sure to make a mistake or two. So be it, it must be done. I go to the mast and go through the reefing process again, putting in the second reef and thus further reducing the size of the mainsail.

While sailing along under the second reef, I find a line and tie it to the reefing-line attachment padeye at the end of the boom. I feed it up through the first reef cringle and take it down and through the reef block on the other side of the boom, then along the boom to its cleat. This is a good bit of work, balancing all the while, holding on with one hand and feeding the line through various bits with the other, interpreting where the line goes and making a mistake or two before I get it right. When the new line is in, I take out the second reef and put the first back in.

I feel good about the repair; it was a lot of work, but it had to be done. However now I'm worried about all of my lines. The reef line broke without warning, probably just because of its age. This could happen to any of the lines. I think to myself – why didn't I replace all my running rigging (the lines)? I could have done this instead of painting the hull bright red. There are so many things a sailboat needs, or might need, and just as many things a sailor wants but doesn't need. Putting all these wants and needs into their proper categories and prioritizing them is a constant affair.

As we beat into the SE wind, *Sobrius* steers herself with the tiller tied off. The beach slowly passes by to starboard and I can almost make out the faces of the people on the sand. I've stayed as close to the coast as I deem safe all day, in order to stay out of the Gulf Stream current. I figure that if I can get close to Miami then I can tack to the southeast, cross the Gulf Stream, and make it to the Northwest Providence Channel. The wind is supposed to shift to the east at some point today, bringing with it thunderstorms; the farther south I get, the more likely I am to avoid them. The radar app on my phone shows a huge orange patch moving across all of South Florida right now, and I hope it passes north of me.

Port Everglades is just ahead, the busiest port in Florida. I'm about two miles offshore and four big container ships are anchored ahead of me. A huge cruise ship is coming out of the inlet. I tack *Sobrius* to the east and get further offshore, wanting to pass them all to the outside and give the entire inlet plenty of room. Another cruise ship comes into view and I wonder if I need to alter course to avoid it. They're so big, like large floating buildings – skyscrapers laying on their sides – and it's hard to tell how far away they are. But this one passes well ahead of me. As big as they are, they are also fast, at least compared to me.

Two more are coming, still inside the inlet but towering over the landscape. It's a strange view, these large boats rising up over the houses and hotels on land.

We slowly approach the inlet while a cruise ship is coming out with another large commercial vessel behind it. Behind the landscape is yet another cruise ship. I feel like a turtle about to attempt crossing a busy street. I call the Carnival cruise ship on the VHF and ask which way it would like to pass.

"Port to port" is the answer, and I steer to starboard. I also let the next ship pass while I start the engine. As soon as I'm past the second vessel, I throttle up *Sobrius'* little 10-horsepower engine and speed across the inlet (at 5 knots), before the next behemoth comes out.

When we are safely past the inlet, I shut off the engine. A family in a little fishing boat is motoring alongside me to starboard. I wave and the captain waves back as they pass.

I tie off the tiller on a close reach and try to relax. I can't nap right now, but tying off the tiller, leaning back and shutting my eyes is the next best thing, and I feel rested soon after.

It's funny how I've never napped before. I never did at all until I started singlehanding. I knew I'd have to learn how in order to sail by myself, and I wondered if I could, but I've found that napping comes easily when I'm at sea for days at a time.

*"Life shrinks or expands in proportion to one's courage."* Anias Nin

## CROSSING THE GULF STREAM

All day the wind blows at about 20 knots out of the ESE, and we sail almost all the way to Miami before the wind shifts to east, and this is the change I've been waiting for. Finally, we turn southeast into the Gulf Stream. It's time to cross!

We sail into the great northward current for three hours before the wind changes again, and unexpectedly comes from the north. I respond by changing course to east-north-east and we make 5-6 knots as the South Florida skyline descends into the horizon behind us.

The sun sets in a cloudy grey sky and darkness falls across the deep water. The thunderstorms that my all-knowing phone predicted are on my mind and I hope they will all pass to the north and leave me in peace. However, I'm in the powerful and unpredictable Gulf Stream, and there is nothing to do but take whatever comes my way. But for now, the sailing is fine and the stars are beginning to show themselves, coming out by the handful, covering the portion of the sky not obscured by clouds. This is surely what I came for, sailing across the ocean, enjoying the peace and quiet of the night, the solitude of the sea, and the beauty of the heavens shining down on me from above.

My tranquil musings of the dark sky and the bright stars are rudely interrupted by a loud beeping noise, and it takes me a moment to recognize the collision alarm on the AIS. I check the instrument and discover that we are on a collision course (or close to one) with a cargo ship, and I watch the bearing between us slowly decrease on the little orange screen. I alter course to starboard slightly, to give us more room.

The boat is miles away, and I decide to take the reef out of the mainsail. I'm working at the mast when the jib becomes backwinded and *Sobrius* turns all the way around through a wide circle.

As we turn, I am shocked to see a huge container ship passing behind us, seemingly way too close (although it's hard to tell at night). *I can't let that happen again. I thought the ship was much further away.*

It was a cheap lesson that could have cost the ultimate price. Everyone says that these ships can't be expected to keep a lookout for little boats like mine, and they certainly can't turn quickly to take evasive action. I've got to keep myself from becoming distracted whenever the AIS warns me of a ship nearby – lesson learned, I hope.

The invisible night wind calms, then begins shifting southeast. I tack and continue sailing northeast, in this beautiful and warm night. So far, the formidable Gulf Stream has been agreeable and all is going according to plan.

The beeping of the AIS alarm alerts me to the presence of C___, a sailing vessel crossing my bow within a mile. I see its green starboard light, then it disappears across the black southern horizon.

An hour passes and the alarm goes off again, and again it is C___, now headed north, again across my bow. This makes no sense to me and leaves me with a sense of foreboding. *Is it running from something?*

The stars disappear; clouds must be covering the sky, and the night darkens.

Rain – I feel it and I can smell it. Somehow rain has a slight scent noticeably different from the clean ocean air. I go below and quickly put on my foul-weather gear: yellow bibs and my big red jacket. I cinch the wrists and the neck closed to keep out the rain.

Back in the cockpit, rain is falling in heavy, big drops and soon the air becomes dense with falling water as it batters everything below. The sound of the rain begins in a high treble tone as small drops hit the water and the fiberglass deck, then develops into deep bass as the drops get bigger and more numerous, trouncing the boat like loads of gravel and making it reverberate like a giant drum.

As quickly as I can, I install the sliding hatch boards and close off the companionway. This keeps the rain out of the cabin, but also prevents me from seeing or being able to access the instruments; the VHF radio, the AIS, and the chartplotter are all cut off from me now. I clip one tether to the big padeye on the floor and the other to a padeye on the bulkhead, doubly clipped in, so whatever the weather does, I will remain attached to *Sobrius*.

The wind increases quickly, as do the waves. I brace myself with my feet against the opposite side of the cockpit as we heel further and further. I pull my reading glasses over my eyes to shield them from the ferocious rain pelting me in the face as I steer into a dark wall of water, and soon I can't see anything beyond the water in my face.

All is water – saltwater below, rising and falling with the waves, freshwater above, filling the air, blown by the wind. I steer by feel and sound, left hand on the tiller, right hand holding on firmly to a cleat; with nothing else I can do, I just sit here, take it, and steer.

I have too much sail up for the worsening conditions, causing *Sobrius* to heel dramatically. Each gust pushes her perilously close to the water. I try to pinch into the wind to keep *Sobrius* from broaching and to keep the bow pointed into the oncoming waves, which seem to have become angry. The adventure level is high!

I hope the AIS alarm doesn't go off now, although I might not even be able to hear it – that would be more than I could take. I need for nothing else to happen; I am right at the edge of my ability. I can do this, but no more.

*It's OK, this can't go on forever,* I tell myself, and I get some small comfort from the thought.

I steer blindly into the dark squall before the rain lets up and then stops, although the sea state remains agitated. I tack to accommodate the changing wind, which is now coming from the southeast again. I open the companionway so I can see the chartplotter and the AIS. All clean from the rain, *Sobrius* is moving right along making about 5 knots at 75 degrees towards the south edge of the Northwest Providence Channel. I set the autopilot and go below.

I sit in the dark on the step below-deck, my feet braced against the cabinetry on either side of me as *Sobrius* rolls with the waves, taking a rest, soaking wet, cold, and exhausted from the squall. I need to change clothes and go back in the cockpit, but the rain storm has me rattled. I've never been in conditions like that, blinded by rain, with the ship overpowered.

I suppose I should have hove-to and just gone below to wait it out. At least that way I could have monitored the AIS and the VHF, and stayed warm and dry. Heaving-to is a classic and standard heavy-weather practice, but seems counterintuitive. Instinctively, I simply want to continue steering the ship as the weather worsens.

Tacking into the wind and back-winding the jib seems like it would be dangerous, yet this is an acceptable tactic when conditions get bad enough for it to be dangerous in the cockpit, or in my case, blinded by rain and unable to hear the AIS alarm or the VHF radio. If a ship would have been on a collision course with us, I would not have known. If a ship would have called me on the VHF to warn me of imminent collision, I would not have heard. Once again, an important lesson is learned, I hope.

I eat a luxurious piece of chocolate which immediately brightens my mood, then take off my wet red jacket and put on the big yellow PVC coat with a hood that I found at the marina hanging next to the dumpster, where sailors leave the things they no longer want for others to take. It seems like a fine foul-weather jacket, and I'm ready to give it a try. But first I lay down for a twenty-minute rest as the autopilot steers us ahead.

*"The sea, once it casts its spell, holds one in its net of wonder forever."* Jacques Cousteau

## THE NORTHWEST PROVIDENCE CHANNEL

The rising sun on Sunday, March 11, shines down on *Sobrius* as we sail through the Northwest Providence Channel – The Bahamas, at last! The Gulf Stream has been crossed and I have officially sailed into foreign waters; my ego swells with pride at the thought. We might even be able to make landfall in the Berry Islands before nightfall, and what a treat it would be to drop the anchor and feel the stillness of a calm bay and eat a hot meal in the cockpit while gazing at the lights of a small Bahamian town!

The water is a dark sapphire-blue; it doesn't have the green tint of the water around Florida. No land is in sight. The seas are 4-6 feet, the wind is in the mid-teens, and the dim morning sky is grey. We are making 5.5 knots at 123 degrees, charging ahead and leaping off the backs of waves. *Sobrius* feels alive as she moves with the water, running like a deer through the forest. She accelerates up the face of a wave, moving to the left, then falls off the back and angles to the right, then up the next wave, faster now, heeling with the wind, I at the helm, countering the turning forces of the waves, riding the bull, five days into the journey and in-sync with the rhythm of the ocean. *This is surely what I came for.*

Now that we are in the waters of The Bahamas, I need to fly the American flag off the stern, so I leave the helm to the tillerpilot and go below and fetch the flag I bought over a year ago in St Petersburg when I was originally fitting out *Sobrius* before I sailed her home. I take the flag from the locker to the stern rail and attach it with two black zip ties when a strange sight in the water snaps me to attention. A green line appears to be trailing behind us, off to starboard. I lift my glasses, and I can still see it. I put them back on, and it is still there.

*Is this some trick of the lighting?*

I go and get another pair of sunglasses, the more expensive pair I bought just for this journey, to help me see through the water. The green line is still there. I seem to remember the feeling of hitting something last night, while I lay in the bunk, followed by a new vibration after the impact. I must have collided with some fishing gear and now have its line wrapped around the keel.

I heave-to, and we nearly come to a halt. Now I can clearly see three long bright green lines trailing behind us, obviously wrapped around the keel.

I think.

*Can I let this wait until we get to port?*

No, I can't. As soon as I start the engine, these lines would probably foul the propeller and possibly send us drifting into a reef. *Sobrius* depends on me to fix this now. I have to get in the water, which will not be pleasant, because the seas are still 4-6 feet and the rocking of the boat will make getting back out of the water very hazardous.

I go below and get out the ladder, hang it over the side, and tie it on for safety. I also get out the backup rope ladder and hang it over the other side. And finally, I tie a fender to a long line and toss it over the stern, in case the boat starts to get away from me.

But even hove-to, the sails still propel us forward at about one knot. I take the sails down and we lie ahull. Our speed drops to zero as I put on the mask and snorkel, and strap a knife to my leg, not my usual dive knife, but my new, and very sharp, Gerber survival knife with a serrated back edge for cutting rope. Moitessier would have done this, and now it is up to me.

But as I get to the ladder, I can't see the lines anymore. I take off the mask and put my polarized glasses back on. I look all around for the offending green lines, but they are no longer visible. They must have fallen off when our forward motion ceased. *Thank goodness, I really didn't want to get in the water*. I typically take any excuse to swim, but climbing *out* of the water up the little ladder in these 4-6' seas had me worried, and I am thankful that the problem went away without necessitating a blue-water dive.

The sun is shining bright as I pull on the halyards and raise the sails; *Sobrius* charges on. Flying fish leap from her path and glide off, just above the waves, an amalgam of dragonfly, bird, and fish. They fly; we fly. Water flies from the bow, splashing me; sometimes I turn my head, other times I just close my eyes. It's not cold, so I don't mind the saltwater spray; it brings me closer to the ocean, nature, something I long for not yet found – solitude in a wet kiss from mother ocean.

But the ocean kisses often, and waves crash into the hull and sometimes flow right across the bow, sending rivers of water flowing aft, overwhelming the small scuppers. I hear a mechanical whirring noise from below; it startles me and I wonder what it is. I think as I steer. It's a familiar noise, but I can't place it. The noise stops after less than a minute, and I identify it – the bilge pump. Water must be finding its way into the cabin, from the deck I hope, and not from something below the waterline.

While studying the charts, it becomes clear that we will not make the Berry Islands before dark, and as much as I'd like to stop there and drop anchor, I will not consider entering a strange Bahamian port at night. Here, especially, I need to be able to see. There are no buoys marking the ports and channels in The Bahamas, not like we have in Florida, with red and green lighted buoys nearly everywhere. Here I will have to rely on the chartplotter, the depth gauge, and especially my eyes to safely guide us to our destinations. Eleuthera might make a good landfall. I could be in Spanish Wells, where there is a customs office and a government dock, by early afternoon tomorrow. It is settled, Spanish Wells it is. We sail on.

The sun sets in an explosion of colors lighting up both sky and sea. The stars soon follow and cover the darkness in a brilliant display of lights, making incredible, yet unrecognizable patterns; there are so many. On the dark horizon sit the lights of the Berry Islands, a landfall and rest forbidden to me. No matter, I came here to sail, and we are sailing – and looking at the stars, so all is as it should be.

The lights of ships speckle the horizon. Cruise ships follow each other like giant lighted ducks in a row, all either going to The Bahamas or back to Florida. Their paths are predictable, and I stay further south. The lights of one smaller ship ahead of me I cannot interpret. The AIS seems to say it will pass on my left, but I'm not so sure.

I call the ship on the VHF.

"How would you like to pass?" I ask.

"We *are* passing, *now, port-to-port*" comes the reply.

And indeed, we have already passed before I can say "OK, thank you, port-to-port." It was a small ship, close, not a big ship, far away. It's so hard to tell, and I wonder if I might be getting delirious, on this fifth night of the passage.

I keep steering for another hour or two or three, until I can see no more ships. I can neither see the stars, as clouds have covered the sky. I can see nothing but a misty blackness all around us, and I steer by the compass heading on the chartplotter, which is difficult because this is a constantly changing number. The stars are useful as reference points to steer towards, but the sky map has been taken away. I installed a light on the magnetic compass last year, but it is too weak and now I can't read the compass at all. For hours, all I can do is stare at the fluctuating white numbers in the upper right corner of the chartplotter, the GPS heading, while trying to steer towards the far-off island of Eleuthera. If I get off course to the left, the number decreases, and if I veer to the right, it increases. *Bigger numbers to the right, bigger numbers to the right*, I repeat like a mantra in my head.

The familiar green and red lights that have illuminated the bow pulpit every night suddenly go dark. These are navigation lights and they let other ships know if they are looking at my port side (red) or the starboard side (green). They come back on a minute later, then go out again. I go below and turn them off, then turn on the masthead tricolor. It serves the same purpose, and using one or the other is proper.

But now I notice that the masthead tricolor sways from left to right as we move across the undulating surface of the sea. I'll have to fix both of these when we get to port. I keep looking up at the masthead light, and I hope it doesn't fall on my head, or at all. It's an expensive light and would also be very difficult to replace, being on the top of the mast and thus hard to access.

But I need to rest, and I see no ships, neither with my eyes nor the AIS, and the chartplotter shows no obstacles in our path. I set the autopilot and lay down for a twenty-minute sleep.

A loud beeping wakes me. *Where am I?* I wonder for a moment before it all comes clear – I'm sailing to The Bahamas, and the AIS is alerting me of a potential collision. I hop up, check the instrument and see a giant mass of moving lights approaching from behind.

"Sailing vessel *Sobrius* sailing vessel *Sobrius*, *Carnival Elation*" comes a calm voice over the VHF radio. I like this about transmitting on the AIS; other ships can call me by name.

"This is sailing vessel *Sobrius*"

"Good evening, what are your intentions?"

"I intend to maintain speed and course. Do you need me to change course?" I ask this out of my habit of being polite, even though I have right-of-way over the massive ship, because I am under sail.

"If you will maintain speed and course, we will turn to starboard"

"OK, thank you, and have a great evening."

I look outside and see the enormous floating party of the *Carnival Elation*, complete with giant spotlights shining up into the night sky, panning, rotating, creating huge beams of light searching the heavens, for what purpose, I've no idea. The lightshow turns to starboard and drifts off into the darkness, leaving me once again in complete blackness, sailing into open and invisible sea, I can only hope. I rely on the chartplotter to know what lies ahead. Should there be a huge rock or an island just ahead I would not know until we hit it. I hand steer in the blackness for an unmeasurable time, staring at the white numbers on the dark blue screen.

Monday morning brings cloudy skies and winds out of the southwest at about 15 knots, propelling *Sobrius* forward through the waves rolling over the grey sea. The sky ahead of us is light on the horizon, but dark clouds hang low, promising more rain. I have on my yellow dumpster rain jacket, which hangs down to my knees. I'm also wearing yellow bibs and neoprene booties, which keep my feet warm even in these wet conditions. Rain comes and goes. The wind slowly increases.

We are sailing on a broad reach, with the reefed mainsail out and the #4 jib sheeted in to keep it from flogging about. We make 6 knots, sometimes more. The sailing is fun, but I'm excited to reach land and we should be at Eleuthera by noon. I search the horizon for the island, but all I see is varying shades of grey, sky merging with water, water merging with sky.

I set the trusty Pelagic autopilot and fetch the black umbrella from below, which is advertised to withstand 60-mph winds. I strap it to the stanchion behind me and get a little shelter from the blowing rain.

This is the sixth day of sailing, and I'm enjoying it, even though the weather is far from pleasant. I'm reaching a state of symbiosis with *Sobrius*. She moves with the sea, and I move with her. I'm thankful that I haven't gotten seasick or even a bit queasy on this journey, as I have on every other sailing trip in the past. Perhaps I haven't on this journey because I've spent so much time living aboard *Sobrius* in the past year. My body has gotten used to the constant movement of the ship, and she rocks me to sleep as I lay on my air mattress while *Sobrius* dances through the waves, slowing and rising, accelerating and falling, gently swaying side-to-side all the while.

I hear a howling, *Sobrius* heels to port, pressure on the tiller increases, and I allow her to turn a bit to starboard. The gusts bring the apparent wind more aft, so we must accommodate the shift by turning into the wind. We accelerate through the sea and water leaps out of the ocean and rolls across the bow. Again, I hear the ominous whirring of the automatic bilge pump below.

I pick up my left foot and place it on the backrest of the bench opposite me. My left arm pulls on the wooden tiller, my face stares ahead into the grey. My mind is completely occupied with steering through the waves and adapting to the wind. Steered properly, *Sobrius* dances across the waves, negotiating them like cyclist rides over terrain, like a surfer pumping for speed; she dances, I lead. Properly focused, she and I work together and the vessel is at one with the constantly changing sea surface. Lapses of concentration cause us to slam in the troughs between the waves, to decelerate, plowing into the back of the next wave, or to lose the wind and luff the sails.

A wave in our path ahead breaks, and as the whitewater hits the bow with a dull thud, spray is thrown up into the wind, which sends an airborne wave of seawater across the entire boat. I turn my body aft and take the unwanted dousing to the back, while my left arm continues to steer.

*The sailing was quite lively for most of the journey from Jacksonville to Eleuthera. Here the camera captures me turning my head to avoid flying spray sent skyward from the bow as it collides with a broken wave. We were sailing in light rain on a beam reach between 6.5 and 7 knots, about as fast as Sobrius can go.*

Thankful to be wearing waterproof clothes, I turn forward and refocus on the horizon. I wipe off my glasses, a futile gesture more out of habit than utility, and pull up my hood to cover my wet head, wishing I had done this a minute ago.

"Land Ho!" I shout to the sky as a dark mass forms on the horizon. I've been sailing for six days and now I can finally see my destination. I smile. It's hard to imagine it's possible, that I sailed this little boat, alone, all the way here from Jacksonville, Florida, where I've been working for the past year to save up enough money to be able to make the journey. Yet here we are, and Eleuthera is in sight. It's almost disorienting.

I had never planned on making landfall at Eleuthera. My first plan was to go to San Salvador. But after doing some research, I read that there are no safe anchorages there, unless the conditions are very calm. There are only two marinas where a sailboat might find shelter, but even these can only be entered and exited in calm conditions. My next plan was to clear customs at Cat Island. But both of those plans depended on approaching The Bahamas from the north, which I decided against because of the big swell all last week. And finally, I thought the Berry Islands would be my landfall, but reaching them at night canceled that plan. So, as they should be, my plans are as fluid as the sea on which we sail.

A long shallow reef scattered with coral and the exposed wreck of an unlucky ship guard the bay on the northwest coast of Eleuthera. I must sail way around all this to safely approach the protected waters of the bay, and I stay well away from the danger. The chartplotter shows the reef and the wreck, but looking at the real world, it all just looks like water. I'm reminded of the difficulty sailors must have faced when navigating a place like this before the advent of modern navigation technology.

Nearing the waypoint where the charts suggest entering, I heave-to and drop the headsail, just to simplify things as I pass, downwind, through a narrow channel in the barrier reef. I start the engine for safety, in case I need to take evasive action. It's my first time making landfall in The Bahamas, with no navigational aids (buoys, channel markers, lights) to help me avoid the reef. I feel anxiety. My senses sharpen. My mind focuses on the task ahead. There is no room for error. I feel incredibly alive and alert, even though I've been sailing for six days with only sparse bits of rest. I move slowly, deliberately, thinking everything through before acting.

We sail in with no problem, for the passage is wide; the water changes from dark grey to light blue as the depth decreases from 500 meters to 5 meters. I feel a change in me, a quickening. I've made it to The Bahamas, and another dream has become reality.

*"In the end, the greatest victory we can know is the result of all of our hard work, discipline, and dedication: the realization of our dreams"* Cheryl Burke

## ELEUTHERA

As we sail across the shallow bank towards Spanish Wells, the rain and the grey sky work together in an attempt to lull me to sleep, and I consider going in to Royal Island Harbor, the first safe anchorage I'll come to. It's a protected cove in front of a defunct resort that never opened. I could stay here before clearing customs as long as I don't set foot on land. I sail close to the entrance, let my focus lapse, and something hits me with great force in the left elbow, spinning my entire body clockwise. I gybed unintentionally, and the boom swung across the cockpit, pulling the mainsheet assembly with it, which is what hit me. My elbow hurts, but seems uninjured, for now.

The incident causes me to change my mind and instead try the government dock, where I can clear customs.

I call the customs office on my phone, and am given directions to a large concrete dock next to a yellow building. I feel nervous about docking, and even sailing into the narrow channel that leads to the town of Spanish Wells. The customs officer has a strong Caribbean accent and I find him hard to understand, adding to my anxiety.

When I get within sight of the channel leading to Spanish Wells, I drop the mainsail and motor towards the tiny opening. A small floating ball is the only marker, and it's in the middle of what appears to be the channel. It's up to me to decide which side of it is the deep water, and which is the shallow. My eyes and the chartplotter both suggest passing it to the left, very close to shore. We do so and all is well, but while in the inlet, the chartplotter shows my boat on the beach, and my heart beats fast.

Inside is a narrow canal of calm water leading left and right. We turn right and pass a variety of docks, some wooden, some concrete. Fishing boats, both pleasure and commercial, are tied up at varying angles and configurations. Houses in pastel colors decorate the shore. A fancy black speedboat slowly passes to port, just as I look at my depth gauge, which alarmingly reads 3.8'. My draft is 4.8

feet. I wave the speedboat on and turn left. What a shame it would be to run aground here, so close to my destination. I haven't yet calibrated the depth gauge, so it is probably reading the depth below itself, and it is about a foot below the surface of the water, so my keel was likely just scraping the sandy bottom.

A wrecked sailboat lies in the mangroves to my right, next to the shallow spot, a startling reminder of the consequences of mistakes.

I see the yellow building and the concrete government dock. A huge commercial fishing boat is tied up, but there is ample room behind it for my little ship. I pass the dock and turn around, surveying the situation. I pass the dock again, then turn around and pass it a third time, turn around, and approach, slowly, with the dock to starboard. We approach at a 45-degree angle. I turn left only a couple feet from the dock, shift into reverse, and the prop walk pulls the stern to the concrete wall as *Sobrius* comes to a halt. I step off with a long line in hand. One end of the line is tied to the bow, and the other to the stern. I wrap it around the huge bollard on shore, and pull *Sobrius* to the dock, her fenders cushioning her and protecting her from the hard concrete. I tie two more lines from the bow to another bollard further forward, and two more from the stern. She is secure.

We are here, and I'm standing on land for the first time in six days, king of my own world.

Location: 25° 32.54'N, 76° 44.78'W

*Sobrius sits comfortably at the Government Dock at Spanish Wells, tied to massive bollards intended for much larger vessels. Landfall in the Bahamas was a glorious moment, and the town was charming. When I took this picture, I realized that I had never seen my boat from this view, and was surprised by how wide she looks.*

I stand for a while, simply taking in the view and enjoying the moment. It's absolutely amazing to be here, to have travelled to another country on my little 30' sailboat, to have travelled hundreds of miles at no more than a jogging pace, to be on land for the first time in six days.

I walk to the yellow building labeled "Customs" and enter the small office, which seems to move like a ship at sea, swaying and rolling all about. It's disorienting, and I hope the officer doesn't think I'm drunk.

Clearing customs is easy, a simple matter of filling out forms and paying $150. The customs officer has to come out to *Sobrius* to confirm the serial number on my firearm, a 357 magnum, the same handgun my father carried when we came to the Bahamas in the 1980's, when I was a young teenager. He also counts the 25 rounds of ammunition.

"Would it be OK if I stayed at the dock while I walk around town and get something to eat?" I ask the customs officer.

"No problem."

"Could I stay there overnight? I have some chores to do that would be much easier while tied to the dock, like climbing the mast to fix the masthead tricolor."

"That's no problem, as long as you leave early in the morning, a supply ship is scheduled to be here at 7:30."

"Great, thanks. I'm an early riser, so I'll make sure I'm gone before then."

Hunger and curiosity compel me to walk in search of a restaurant, but before I get 100 yards down the road, a man driving a golf cart and wearing suspenders, a bow-tie, and a dapper straw hat from a different time period stops to asks if I need a ride.

"Well, I'm looking for a place to get something to eat."

"Hop in" he says.

Chris is a friendly man and he takes me to a place called The Gap, where I order a grouper sandwich and two chocolate-chip cookies. I devour the food like a starved man, and the satisfaction it brings is boundless.

Back aboard *Sobrius* I need to fix the masthead tricolor, and thus I need to climb the mast, although I'd much rather lie down and take a nap. But I need to do this while tied up to the dock; otherwise, at anchor tomorrow, the boat will be swaying and climbing the mast and working at the top would be much more difficult.

I get out the canvas mast ladder and take the mainsail off. The mast ladder has slugs that ride in the mast track, the same track that the mainsail slugs ride in. While taking the mainsail slugs out of the track, I remember that two of them are broken. This happened, I think, when I put the second reef in after the first-reef line broke, off the coast of Florida. I'll have to address this next, I tell myself.

I attach the main halyard and the jib halyard, as a backup, to the mast ladder and slowly hoist it while feeding the slugs into the mast track.

I climb, with a tube of marine caulk tucked in my harness.

When I'm above the spreaders (about halfway up) I loop a tether around the mast so I can't fall backwards. At the top, I clip the second tether to a ring at the very top of the mast, then take a moment to enjoy the view of Spanish Wells: green palm trees, houses of all colors, boats, blue water all around.

I squeeze out a big mess of black polysulfide caulk under the light and hope this works for the duration of this trip. It's an amateur repair at best, but it's all I can think to do for now.

Back on deck, I remove two slugs from the mast ladder and use them to replace the two broken mainsail slugs. While I'm working, a car stops and a boisterous man with a gold necklace and a big smile leans out the window and asks about my boat and where I'm from.

"I sailed here from Jacksonville, Florida. I left Wednesday and just got here" I answer, proud of my accomplishment and more than willing to share the details with any passerby.

"Jacksonville!" he says. "Then you're a lucky man! I used to have a girlfriend from Jacksonville, and she was a *mighty pretty* one. Lots of fine women in *Jacksonville*!"

"Yes, I suppose there are."

"You came all the way from Jacksonville in that little boat? What size is that boat?"

"Thirty feet."

"If I sailed here from Jacksonville I'd be in a forty-footer with an *all-girl crew*!"

I can't help but notice there is a woman sitting in the car next to him and I wonder what she thinks of all this.

"This boat's all I need. It's a fine sea boat."

"I guess it must be! Where are you going?"

"Oh, wherever the wind takes me, but I'd like to see Cat Island, Conception Island, the Jumentos Cays and the Ragged Islands."

"The *Jumentos*! That's a long sail. You'll have to go around Long Island. When I go there I like to go to *Flamingo Cay*." He pronounces this "FLAH-me-EEN-go KEY."

He drives off, waving a big hand and wishing me good luck, and I get back to work.

Next, I replace both reefing lines with thicker line that can't escape the reefing blocks. The original lines were small enough in diameter that they often came out of the blocks, which were designed to allow for this (I've no idea why).

Another car pulls up, and this man is the opposite of the previous guy. He asks where I'm from, but says nothing after I respond, yet he keeps looking at me. I feel like it's up to me to keep the conversation going. I ask him some benign question, just to be polite. He soon leaves me to my work.

Finally, I take my new Vulcan anchor and its 50' of 5/16" G4 chain out from under the settee in the center of the cabin and move it to the anchor locker. I wanted it to be low and in the center of the boat for the passage here, to keep *Sobrius'* center of gravity low and to keep weight off the bow.

A couple pulls up on bicycles and asks where I'm from.

"I just got here from Jacksonville, Florida."

Catherine, an American woman, and Bjorn Jordan, a Norwegian man, stay and chat for a while. They are sailors too, but arrived here by plane and water taxi. He tells me about sailing his Vindo, which he pronounces "Vind-UHH."

I tell them about my other book *Becoming a Sailor, a Singlehand Sailing Adventure* and give them a business card, hoping they'll stay in touch, and buy my book.

I do a few more small chores, feeling mighty energetic for someone who has only slept 2-4 hours a night in twenty-minute increments for the last four out of five nights.

My phone alerts me of a text, and it's Catherine and Bjorn, letting me know they are at The Shipyard restaurant around the corner if I'd like to join them, and I do.

Immediately after arriving I regret having eaten at the other place. While the food there was fine, the atmosphere at The Shipyard is what I really wanted for my first meal after six days at sea. We sit on a patio overlooking an expanse of shallow blue water, sailboats at anchor, and another island in the distance. Families on vacation and couples in love fill the tables around us and the sound of jovial chattering fills the air, both pleasant contrasts to my previous week.

Sleep comes easy while tied up to the government dock, but I dream of sinking. There's a hole in the boat, and I'm frantically trying to improvise a solution, when a loud noise wakes me. I'm confused for a moment, until I hear the sound of the umbrella skidding across the deck. I left it sheltering the forward hatch with its handle hanging inside and its canopy over the hatch and resting on the deck. I leap out of my bunk and climb to the cockpit, hoping to find the umbrella caught in the lifelines, but the umbrella is gone, and I never see it again.

I wake up early and make coffee and oatmeal, just like I do back in Jacksonville at the marina. Afterwards I start the engine and untie all but one line, the same line I started with when I docked. I coil these lines carefully and hang them from the lifelines. Then I step back to the dock, release the final line and step aboard as the wind pushes us away from the concrete structure. We motor out the little channel past the various docks, boats, and pastel-colored houses.

Again, I think I'll go to Royal Island Harbor, and I set sail under reefed main alone. Sailing with just the main feels very casual, with no jib to tack; all I need to do is steer and trim the main.

But I feel drawn towards two small islands nearby, Meeks Patch. They're labeled as an anchorage on the chart, and a group of sailboats is anchored on the north side of the islands, as the wind was south yesterday. But today the wind comes from the north, and I sail to the south side to take a look. In the lee of the first island is a quiet and serene cove of glassy water where no boats are anchored. Even though Spanish Wells is right around the corner, a sense of peace and the promise of solitude emanates from these little islands.

We sail in and survey the perimeter, checking the depth and looking for obstacles. The two islands almost meet in the little cove, but remain separated by a narrow and shallow cut, strewn with rocks and showing some visible coral underneath. The island is painted green with short trees and shrubs, and the water is still and smooth, reflecting the blue-grey sky, still cloudy but clearing. There are no houses or any other signs of civilization on the tiny islands, and I think to myself that this is just what I came to The Bahamas for – uninhabited and picturesque islands to anchor behind and explore.

I move to the middle of the cove and, trying to remember all I read in Fatty Goodlander's book *"Creative Anchoring,"* drop anchor in 7' of water. We've reached the first anchorage of the trip, and it feels like success.

Location: 25° 30.30'N, 76° 46.58'W

I stand on the deck of my little ship and take in the tropical scene, still marveling at the distance we travelled in order to get here. The small island to my left is rimmed with rock and topped with green scrubby vegetation bent with the prevailing wind, which must come from the northeast. In the distance, I can see through the shallow cut between the two islands and the other sailboats resting peacefully on the north side, which is now the windward side of Meeks Patch. Beyond the boats, the tops of the colorful houses of Spanish Wells rise above the trees. Directly ahead of me is a small rocky outcropping in the water, which promises to have fish below. To my right is the other of the two islands, with a pristine sandy beach, some dark brown rock strewn about the shore, and low green vegetation in front of a few short trees. Further to the right, in the distance across the water of the bay, is Eleuthera Island, its green and brown color is partially obscured by mist, yet some houses are visible. One other small island sits alone to the southwest.

Not only is this little spot protected from the wind, but it is an extraordinarily beautiful place, and offers exactly what I wanted from The Bahamas: *nature, seclusion, serenity…*

The sun is shining and nearly everything below is damp from the arduous journey. I pull out my sleeping bag and all my damp clothes and hang them on the lifelines to dry. I too stand in the bright light and all the trials and ordeals of the last week seem to dissolve in the bright sun. Mind and body relax and time seems to fade away as I take in the magnificent setting.

However, my relaxation is interrupted by thoughts of needed maintenance, and there's no time like the present to fix everything that needs fixing. Good seamanship dictates punctuality, and the sea punishes the procrastinator. I slowly pull myself out of my musings and get right to work.

The female connector of the tillerpilot has become detached from the cockpit. Apparently the four screws I chose for its original installation were of insufficient length, so I replace them with longer ones. *Fixed.* On to the next project.

The situation with navigation lights at the bow has hung over my conscious like a sword since they went out by the Berry Islands. But I dread getting into what I know will be a long and arduous project; I'd so like to relax and take in the scenery for the rest of the day. But I tell myself to just go look at the lights and then take some time to think up a solution. This is a trick to get me to start the job; I'm tricking myself into doing what needs to be done, even though I don't want to wade into this can-of-worms project. Just looking at it seems much easier than fixing the whole problem – *just go look at it* – and I do.

I turn the lights on and then wiggle the wires at the lights on the bow. They try to come on, but only do so a little bit, and only intermittently, indicating a bad connection. These lights have an incredibly tough life, living right out front, taking the full force of waves and blasts of saltwater for days at a time. They come with short little wires, necessitating wiring connections outside and exposed to the harsh elements.

I have an idea. I get out my wiring toolbox, ratchet set, my big drill, and the marine caulk. I cut the wires and remove the lights and the wood support they sit on. I see that the supply wire is not marine grade and is corroded. I cut out this short piece of wire that connects the lights to the main supply wire below-deck. But this wire runs inside the steel tubes that make up the bow pulpit to the inside of the boat, and I can't pull the wire out through the tubing. No matter, I leave it where it is and drill a hole in the deck, cut the wire below and pull the main supply wire out through the hole and connect it to the lights with waterproof DC connectors and rubber electrical tape. I seal everything with thick globs of black marine caulk and bolt it all back together. *Fixed and improved.*

*Repairs are not what I had in mind for my first day in The Bahamas, but the passage from Florida was rough on Sobrius, so repairs are what I needed to do, and the ocean can be unforgiving to one who does not keep the ship's systems in good working order.*

Work is over, the water calls, and finally I can swim. The underwater world of The Bahamas is perhaps the main attraction to me and now is the time to experience it in all its glory: clear water, coral reef, fish, and the otherworldly silence and weightlessness of submersion.

I put on my snorkeling gear, deploy the ladder, and slowly climb down into the sea. Neutrally buoyant in the silent blue world, I hover like a great bird riding an updraft over a mountain, surveying the terrain below.

I swim all around the little cove, following the coral that lines the shallow banks. I'm surprised to see some live staghorn coral, which I haven't seen in a long time; I've seen lots of dead staghorn so seeing it alive is a pleasant surprise. A Nassau grouper looks at me from behind a rock; a yellow and blue angelfish welcomes me to the islands. The bizarre scrawled filefish, which hardly looks like a fish, swims by looking at me sideways with one eye, sculling with its dorsal and anal fins while its tail fin remains still. I see two stunning juvenile blue angelfish. These fish are yellow with blue accents when adults, but are dark blue with brilliant vertical white stripes when young. Many species of reef fish are like this, with different color patterns when young.

I look in a little cave and see my old friend, who's always there, the red and white squirrelfish, looking back at me with big black eyes. Grey angelfish display territoriality and fearlessness when I invade their space, swimming at me and turning broadside to encourage me to move on. A little yellow and blue honey gregory sits still near the bottom, too pretty to move. The odd-looking porcupine pufferfish hides in a little cave, and fears me not. Their defense is not to run, but to inflate themselves with water, changing from their usual pear shape to that of a basketball with spikes.

As I swim and the bottom passes below me, the first shark of the trip comes into view, but it's just a nurse shark lying on the bottom. Nurse sharks are easily identified by their little moustache – barbels protruding down from the corners of their mouth. Their head is rather flat, the upper lobe of the tail fin is long and droopy while there is no lower lobe, and the body is a yellowish brown. They are typically found lying on the bottom in a cave or some other protected spot. Nurse sharks feed on small fish and shellfish, and have flat teeth adapted to crushing shells.

A friend of mine speared one once, while I was in the water with him, in the Abacos, during a college summer class – Tropical Ecology – with Florida Institute of Technology. He speared the shark, which turned and bit him in the arm. He held the spear in one hand and the shark's tail in the other, while the shark held his arm that held the spear. Blood filled the water. I was shocked by the scene of two predators battling for life. The shark finally gave up and died, and miraculously, my friend's arm was only scratched. There is no need to fear these animals, and they give me little notice.

While swimming back to *Sobrius*, I see a line on the bottom and follow it to a small float. I follow the line in the other direction and see a large engine block sitting on the bottom, encrusted with various marine organisms. A few fish have made a home here, not caring that their home is a discarded man-made object.

I return to *Sobrius* and make a dinner of chili with sardines, onions, and chipotle peppers, an avocado and a sleeve of crackers. I eat in the cockpit, as I always do – to keep the inside of the vessel clean. But today's dinner view is a dramatic and welcome change from the usual view of the marina back home. The air is warm and pleasant, low cumulus clouds dot the sky, and I marvel at the beauty that makes me want to sit here and eat chili forever.

I really am amazed to be here, both with the fantastical and tropical setting, but also by the fact that my little boat floated across the ocean, pushed by the wind, all the way here from Jacksonville, Florida, which seems forever away. When I started this journey, I was not entirely convinced that I would make it, and that makes being here even sweeter.

*Sobrius* amazes me. It's hard to imagine what she does, moving through the ocean for days at a time, putting up with foul weather and my inexperience and mistakes. She was built in 1972, and I wonder if Michel Dufour, who designed her, thought she would still be making ocean passages in 2018.

I spoke to my parents last night. They are both thrilled with my journey, and follow my progress via the SPOT tracking device, the Garmin inReach satellite communicator, and the Marine Traffic website, which relays my position via the AIS. Sharing my adventure with them gives me great pleasure. In the past I would only have words to describe my adventures afterwards, but in today's world, my adventures can be interactive, and I love thinking about my family watching my progress on a computer in the comfort of their homes.

I've taken this endeavor of becoming a sailor very seriously, and treated it like a college class, reading books constantly, taking notes, practicing, taking a one-week sailing class, staying sober. Although drinking alcohol is traditionally a part of sailing, I can't imagine how a heavy drinker (like I was) could also sail. I have enough trouble keeping my balance while sober.

All the hard work has paid off marvelously. There is nothing we can't do if we put our minds to it and follow through with action. Too often we let our fears and our lack of confidence in ourselves prevent us from achieving our dreams. Too often we let the norms of society dictate what our lives will become. Rather we should dream big and plan our lives accordingly, doing what we love to do, chasing happiness instead of money.

I love being deep in nature, and the ocean certainly delivers. This is where I feel I belong. Today, my ideal location is on a sailboat anchored at Meeks Patch, and here I am. Here and now are very, very good.

As beautiful as this place is, I can't help but think of moving on, and I check the weather forecast on my Garmin inReach satellite communicator. It looks like the winds will be NNE – NW for a couple of days, then become light, which should make for prime conditions for a two-day sail to Conception Island and then maybe three days of very light winds there, which would be perfect. I first heard of Conception Island two years ago while sailing in the Abacos, and it's been a place I've wanted to go to since then. The island lives in my mind as a symbol of the remote, wild, and pristine. It is one of the main goals of this voyage, and my restless nature compels me to make haste.

The sun is beginning to set, and I suddenly have the urge to get out on the water on my surfboard, a 12-0 Softop (12' 0" – surfboards are named like this, by their length, in feet then inches – Softop is the brand, and is an epoxy board with a rubber skin on top, which is peeling off in places, giving the board a battered look). The 12-0 is not only a surfboard, but also my dinghy and life raft. I want to take some pictures of *Sobrius* from the water of her first Bahamian anchorage.

I pull out the 12-0, which dominates the interior of *Sobrius*, and carefully lower it into the water by its leash, which I strap to my leg. I climb down the ladder and step from a 30' vessel onto a 12' vessel, upon which I sit and propel myself across the still water with a cheap kayak paddle.

I'm photographing *Sobrius* from the water when a man on a beautiful two-masted catamaran anchored nearby waves me over to his boat. I paddle to the vessel and meet the captain, Ray, and his friend, Peter, and step aboard the stately *Tempus Fugit* (time flies). The boat was designed by Chris White and made in Chile. Ray tells me he got the name from the Rocky and Bullwinkle cartoon.

The catamaran has two self-tending jibs and wing-foils over both masts. There are no mainsails; the wing foils act as sails and can be trimmed (rotated) via winches at the base of each. It's a beautiful vessel and it looks comfortable and fast. Ray and Peter are friendly and offer me a drink.

"What do you drink?" asks Ray.

"Anything non-alcoholic."

"That's going to be difficult" Ray answers, but then pulls out a LaCroix, one of my favorites, and the beverage that I used as a substitute for beer when I was getting sober. They show me around the fine catamaran, which seems incredibly spacious compared to *Sobrius*, and we trade sailing stories until nightfall. Peter lights up *Sobrius* with a spotlight while I paddle back in the darkness.

The following morning, I wake up anxious to sail somewhere else, even though yesterday I was ready to sit here forever. Sitting still seems wrong, moving from place to place seems right, so as the sun rises, the anchor rises, the sails rise, and *Sobrius* slips out across the calm water in the light wind.

But as we approach the edge of the bay and the deeper water, the wind dies, and the Southeast Reef, clearly labeled on the chartplotter, calls my name. I steer us south, towards the reef, find it, and find some sand in which to drop the anchor.

Location: 25° 26.41'N, 76° 52.03'W

I gear up and swim 200 yards to the reef, then dive to the bottom in 30' of water, and casually take in the patchy reef and its colorful inhabitants. I frequently look around for sharks, but see only a barracuda or two following me from a safe distance. These are curious fish with a menacing look, swimming with their mouths slightly open and showing their long pointy teeth. But they do me no harm and I'm used to seeing them. They are not known to bother people unless one is cleaning fish in the water, or perhaps wearing something shiny in murky water, tricking the barracuda into thinking the jewelry is a small fish. They don't like to be fooled.

Two orange filefish swim near the bottom and I go for a closer look. I don't think I've ever seen these before. Their bodies are vertically flat, orange and yellow, and their lips protrude as if the fish are desperately trying to kiss something in front of them that's just out of reach. I also see two queen angelfish, some blue chromis, a spotfin butterflyfish, a royal gramma, blue tang, a glasseye snapper, and a black grouper.

Back aboard my vessel, the wind comes up and we sail north, trying to go around the north end of Eleuthera. But now something else catches my attention: whitewater lines in the distance. The chartplotter reveals that Egg Reef lies ahead, and as we get closer, bright blue waves standing up and breaking come into view. I quiver with excitement at the thought of getting good surf at an offshore reef.

Sailing in the islands and finding surf is another dream, and it looks like this one is about to come true. I get out the binoculars and find what appear to be large surfable waves breaking to the right along a point, a mile or two offshore. It's hard to tell the size with nothing to scale the waves, but judging from the swell around me, I expect them to be at least head high.

I motor along the edge of the reef in 65'-deep water and survey the situation. It looks good, and I drop anchor – my new anchor, the 35 lb Vulcan with 50' of heavy 5/16" chain and all 300' of line – and the Vulcan quickly grabs hold of the unseen bottom.

Six-foot seas roll underneath us and large waves stand up and break off to the right, but *Sobrius* is held firmly in place, and I take a minute to confirm that she is not moving before I get in the water.

Location: 25° 31.02'N, 76° 54.04'W

*Surfing Egg Reef was certainly one of the highlights of the voyage. The waves were big and challenging, the reef was a mile or two offshore and accessible only by boat, nobody else was around, and the adventure level was high!*

I change into my board shorts, get out the 12-0, and consider wearing a hat to block the sun, but decide against it. Land seems very far away and the adventure level is high as I paddle the long surfboard across deep water, away from my vessel and to the edge of the offshore reef, then along its edge while watching and studying the waves and looking for any exposed rocks or reef that might present obstacles to surfing. When I reach the point, I try to gauge how far outside of the breakers to sit in order to catch the set waves, then pick a spot, based only on intuition and reading the way the smaller waves break. Looking back, I can only see land when lifted by one of the larger waves.

It's not long before I realize I've chosen the wrong place to sit, and that not wearing a hat was the right call. A mountain of water rises over the horizon, and I scramble towards it, hoping to get there before it breaks. I don't, so I turn and face away from the wave and let the whitewater hit me from behind, hoping to belly surf and direct myself to the right and back out into deeper water. I ponder the fact that I really don't know anything about this point, such as how deep it is, and if there are any exposed rocks or reef in front of me. The mass of whitewater picks me and the board up, rolls us over, and gives us a good thrashing while dragging us on hundred yards towards shore, and I'm thankful, as I'm dragged underwater, not to hit anything hard. When the powerful wave lets go, I grab the leash at my ankle and pull the board to me, surface, breathe, and climb back aboard.

*Welcome to the point!*

I paddle back across deep water around to the point and position myself further out this time – or so I hope – it's hard to tell when I'm the only surfer in the water, and this far from shore the beach is no use in gauging how far out I am, as I can't even see it.

More waves rise on the horizon. I let the first one go, then paddle hard to get the second wave. I accelerate as it lifts me from behind, and I've got it!

I drop in, stepping way back to weight the tail of the 12' board so as not to nose-dive. We skip across the water accelerating as we fall down the steep blue face of the powerful and smooth wave. I point the board just a bit right, because the wave breaks almost straight, not at all like I'm used to, having spent most of my time surfing over Florida's sandbars. This wave is well overhead, the water is clear blue, and I'm flying – skipping across the water, negotiating odd steps in the wave. My knees are deeply bent and my arms are pointing straight out to keep balance, fully in "safety stance." I am totally focused on not falling, as the reef is still completely unknown to me and could be shallow in places or even have exposed reef, which I watch for as my board is propelled forward.

I ride the wave for what seems like a great distance, and end up on the edge of the reef where I kick out of the wave, which by now is only a fraction of the size it was when I caught it. I paddle back out through deep water to what I hope is the same spot where I caught the wave, but again, it's hard to tell.

I catch two more waves similar to the first one, but I haven't caught a really big one yet. So I sit further out and wait patiently. Finally, the wave I've been waiting for comes. It's the third wave of the set, and considerably bigger than the other three I've caught, but it's also standing up and getting very steep as I paddle for it, looking over my shoulder. It's going to be a late drop, on a vertical face and therefore it's questionable whether or not I'll be able to manage it on the 12-0. It's not a board designed for waves like this, but I go for it anyway. *This is what I came for!*

At the top of the wave, my big blue board is pointing almost straight down the face, which is longer than the 12' surfboard. I stand up as quickly and smoothly as I can, but only to a deep crouch and all the way on the tail of the board. I put all my weight on my back foot, and as we fall down the face I feel the tail of the board leave the water for a moment as we air-drop. The board lands back on the wave with an audible smack, and with both my arms out and waving about to keep my balance, I hang on and fly down the line as my entire body buzzes with adrenaline. I ride all the way to the end and the wave gets small and shoots me out into the deep water at the edge of the reef – a perfect ride on which to end the session.

The sky is lit in warm colors as I paddle back to my little ship after this fabulous and first surf-session from *Sobrius*, feeling grand and showing respect to Egg Reef. Adrenaline is still pumping and I savor the bliss of nature and the natural high that comes from such a fantastic event. It occurs to me that this session was so good as to be worth everything that it took to get here: all my years of surfing, the sailboat, the journey, and the risk of surfing alone at such a place.

After putting the surfboard away, I start the engine and put it in forward at idle speed, then move to the bow and with gloved hands start pulling in the 300' of ½" nylon anchor rode. I wear full-finger gloves when I deal with the anchor now because back at the Marina at Ortega Landing in Florida, where *Sobrius* lives, my neighbor Brian told me how his wife lost part of one of her fingers while sailing off anchor. The doctor said she might not have lost the digit had she been wearing full-finger gloves. I have lots of full-finger gloves on board anyway, so why not wear them and keep my fingers attached to my hands?

But after getting nearly all of the line in, and before I can see the beginning of the chain, I can pull no more. The swell is lifting the bow six feet every 15 seconds or so, and I'm very careful with the line, now under a lot of tension. If we get directly over the anchor and it is stuck, a wave could put incredible pressure on the line and pull the bow underwater. I pull as hard as I can, but cannot raise the anchor. I have to try something different.

I assume the anchor is stuck on the bottom so I go back to the cockpit and motor forward to try to dislodge the anchor, then put it in neutral, hurry to the bow, and pull hard on the anchor rode, which does not yield. I try motoring forward again, more aggressively this time, but still without success. I try motoring to the left, and then to the right, but the rode remains taught and the anchor immoveable.

Looking at the western horizon ahead, I estimate that the sun will set in about an hour. As far as I can tell I have three choices: 1) sit here overnight 2) cut the rode and divorce the anchor 3) dive on the anchor and free it from the bottom. I'm in 65 feet of water and exposed to the six-foot swell. I could stay here but conditions would be uncomfortable, and the large breaking waves just 200 yards to the right would provide quite an ominous setting for an evening on a sailboat. I think about the money I recently spent on the new anchor and chain. I know I can dive to 65', however, wrestling an anchor 65' down after surfing and already having worked hard trying to pull it up will certainly push me to my limit, and I shouldn't be freediving this deep without a dive buddy. There's also the fact that I'm over a reef next to very deep water, which is prime habitat for big sharks. But I feel compelled to dive and free the anchor. I don't want to lose it; I just bought it, the chain, the shackle, and the 300' of nylon line, and I need it for the rest of this journey.

I put on my mask and snorkel, climb down the ladder into the clear, deep water, then put on my new long freediving fins. I don't jump in because I don't want to attract any unwanted attention to myself. Quietly I swim past the anchor rode to the point above where I think the anchor is, about 30' in front of my boat, and hover on the surface for just a minute, trying to meditate and prepare for the deep dive. Mind and body relax; all thoughts cease; nothing exists but the water and myself. Silence.

I start swimming down, following the chain, which is almost vertical. I can't see the bottom, even though the water is relatively clear, and I continue swimming down, down into the blue-grey water as the air in my lungs compresses, making my chest smaller. Eventually I can see the anchor way down below me in a crevice. As the volume of the air inside my lungs decreases with depth, I become negatively buoyant and start sinking without having to swim down, finally reaching the anchor.

The anchor is stuck, and *Sobrius* tugs on it as each passing swell lifts her. The rode is getting tight, then loose, tight, loose, the anchor poking into the rock, then falling back. I brace my finned feet on both sides of the heavy steel anchor, behind its direction of pull, and grab ahold of the curved shank of the Vulcan to wrestle it out of the crevice. It's heavy, 35 pounds, and I can just get it up over the rim of the rock. But it starts bumping across the hard bottom and grabbing at it. I pick it up again and I have it in my arms when I remember how deep I am, and the fact that I've been working underwater. I need to get to the surface *now* and I drop the anchor and start swimming up, but looking at the light above, the surface looks really far away and I'm thinking to myself *man, you are risking your life, for an anchor!*

As the surface gets closer, I'm really running out of air, but I can feel myself starting to float, and I relax for the last ten feet and let my own buoyancy pull me the rest of the way up as my mind threatens to wander off. I breathe deeply in the air, then swim back to the boat, hastily toss my fins aboard, and scramble up the ladder.

Seated at the bow with my feet braced on the gunwale, I pull with everything I've got, yet the anchor will not rise. I have to dive again. I don't want to do it, but I am resigned to the fact that it must be done. No other solution comes to mind (besides cutting the line, and this is not acceptable).

I put my mask and fins back on and dive again. And *again* I pull it out of a crevice and swim for the surface, this time a little sooner. And *again* I hastily toss my fins aboard and scramble up the ladder and across the deck to the bow, where *again* I pull with all my might, and *again* the anchor does not budge.

I'm thinking about how much money I spent on the anchor and how much I'm risking in order to get it, risking my life, essentially, but somehow the momentum of the effort compels me to continue the struggle. It's now me versus the anchor and I feel that I must solve the riddle.

The situation calls for a different approach; I sit and think until I realize another option. I need a tripping line. The anchor has a hole for a tripping line drilled into the back of the fluke – a place from where if pulled will dislodge the anchor, pulling it backward, and allow me to bring it up. So I tie my preventer line to my barber-haul line (just two lines that happen to be on deck) and the preventer already has a large carabiner tied to it, which I could quickly hook to the anchor.

I reluctantly get back in the water a third time, and swim all the way back down, line in hand. However, when I am five feet from the anchor, the line I hold becomes taught and will not reach the anchor. It's too short.

I let go of the line and, instead, unhook the anchor from the rocks before making the long swim back to the surface. Hoping that the anchor is still unhooked from the rocks, and imagining that hurrying back aboard will improve my chances, I hastily toss my fins aboard and climb the ladder in a rush, sprint to the bow, sit down, brace my feet, and pull with all my strength. But, much to my dismay, it feels like pulling on a rope tied to a tree, and does not move at all.

Exasperated and resigned to a fourth dive, I add a third length of line to the tripping line and gather mask, snorkel, and fins. But one of my fins, that I hastily threw onboard, is gone. I bought these fins specifically for this journey, for freediving. Now I only have one. I briefly consider looking for the fin, but quickly dismiss the idea.

I get my old spare fins out of the forward locker, grateful for their presence, and dive again. On the way down, I notice that the chain is absolutely vertical, whereas before it was at a slight angle. Before I reach the bottom, I can see that the anchor is hanging free, suspended about five feet above the bottom. *It's free!* I rejoice at the thought as I swim for the surface, propelled not by my new modern freediving fins, but my very old SCUBA fins from the 1980's. I think of my friend, David Smith, who traded me these fins for mine when we were in high school. Sadly, he died of cancer recently. *Rest in peace old friend. I'll think of you every time I use these fins.*

I scramble aboard a fourth time, quickly make my way to the bow, sit down, grab a hold of the anchor rode, brace my feet against the toe rail, and pull with arms, legs, and back. And yet it does not move, and the real problem is revealed. *I'm not strong enough* to pull up my new anchor when it is fully deployed with all 50 feet of chain hanging straight down in water over 50' deep. The anchor wasn't stuck, I just couldn't lift it.

Humbled by the revelation, I stand up and look in the direction we drift. Deep water lies downwind, at least for a mile before the island, so we are safe for now.

I need a new strategy. *What would Moitessier do*, I think to myself. He'd break out a block and tackle, tie it to the rode with a rolling hitch, and lift the anchor up a little at a time. But that's only because in that story he didn't have winches on *Joshua*, his 40' steel ketch. I have winches right behind me, on the mast. I pull the anchor rode (1/2" nylon 3-strand line) from behind the cleat to a mast winch, wrap it on and cleat it off. I then release the rode from the cleat on the deck by the bow, and proceed to winch up the anchor, until the chain reaches the winch. I've only got about ten feet of the fifty-foot chain up, yet I can now lift the anchor, but I must use all my strength to do so.

I've got to remember not to use this anchor in water over 40' deep.

It's ironic that after surfing, I was thinking about how the Egg Reef session was so good that it was worth whatever I had to sacrifice in my life to have gotten to do it. I felt like it was worth risking anything and everything. And in the end, that's exactly what I did – I risked my anchor, my life, and lost a fin.

Egg Reef delivered on the surf, but took its toll otherwise.

We motor away from the breaking waves of the reef and towards the warm and brilliant sunset, then turn to starboard to round the northern end of Eleuthera. After the sun sets and darkness falls, we turn starboard again and begin sailing southeast, at 126 degrees, a few miles off the island. I kill the engine as we are no longer going upwind, and the immediate silence is powerful and serene. This never gets old or loses its charm, shutting off the engine and continuing on under sail, powered by the invisible wind, a magical experience so unlike the transportation we have all grown accustomed to with the sound of an engine rumbling whenever we move in a vehicle; to do so with a silent, invisible, natural power, is mesmerizing and otherworldly.

The distant and lonely lights on the island to the west merge with the stars above, connecting heaven and earth. The invisible wind is north at ten knots, and we sail comfortably on a broad reach as the waves lift the stern and gently rock us from left to right, aft to fore, as they quietly pass. The tranquility of the night is deepened by the contrast from the events at sunset, and I feel as relaxed as I can be, gently rocked by the sea like a baby in the womb.

I go below and make a pot of chili for dinner; there are no other boats out here tonight, and the water is deep and safe. Into the little black pot goes a can of chili, a can of sardines, fresh onion that I chop with a big black survival knife, and half a can of hot chipotle peppers. The air is cold, the night is dark, and the warm chili cannot be improved upon.

I eat dinner from the pot in the cockpit while looking up at the stars, which are fabulous tonight. This unobstructed view of the sky is one of the very few advantages to not having a bimini. Here in the Bahamas, far from light pollution, stars fill the heavens, so many more than what I am used to seeing at home, and they cover the sky like glowing grains of sand from horizon to horizon. *This is surely what I came for*!

My father asked me how often I sleep when we spoke on the phone at Spanish Wells, and I really didn't have an answer for him. It's hard to keep track, sleeping only 20 minutes at a time and at odd times throughout the day and night. When done consecutively, they blur together in memory. Tonight, I'm going to try and keep track.

After dinner, I lay down and let the tillerpilot steer. When my alarm goes off twenty minutes later, I get up, look around, check the sail trim, the horizon for boats or any other lights, the chartplotter for course and any obstacles, and the AIS for ships. All is well, so I lay back down. It's quiet out here, on the Atlantic just north of Eleuthera. There is no ship traffic; my little sailboat seems to be the only vessel out here.

After my second nap, I sit in the cockpit and steer for two hours, steering by the stars and watching the instruments. I set course by watching the compass readout on the chartplotter, then pick a star ahead of us and steer towards it, occasionally checking the compass reading to make sure we are still on course. Sailing under the stars is fantastical, and much easier than steering on black starless nights, when I typically end up staring at the compass readout on the chartplotter. Tonight, the sky map is available for use.

I take two more naps, steer for an hour and a half, then take three naps in a row.

In the morning, I take note that I slept for seven 20-minute naps last night, for a total of two hours and twenty minutes. It doesn't sound like much, but I feel fine. It certainly is strange that this system works. I always try to sleep for eight hours when I'm home.

My original intention was to sail to Conception Island, but after considering that we will make Conception Island in the middle of the night, tomorrow night, I decide to go to Cat Island instead. We can be there by this afternoon, and Cat Island looks interesting. There's no need to "stay the course," rather, my plans should be flexible. Each landfall should be as safe and practical as possible, and this means in the daytime, especially for a place like Conception Island, where the charts show reefs that need to be seen to be avoided.

The chart shows that the north point of Cat Island looks like a beautiful place to stay, with much to do: there's a blue hole and reef for diving, a reef that might provide good surf (the swell is still running and aiming right at this point), and there's a big cave on the beach.

The cruising guide says it's a great place to anchor, and I hope to prove it right.

I take another nap at 9:22 am.

*"It is dangerous to exist in the world. To exist is to be threatened. We must live with threats."*
Adam Levin
*"There is safety in the very heart of danger."* Vincent van Gough

## CAT ISLAND

"Land ho!" I shout to the fish and the birds as the distant hills of Cat Island rise above the horizon and present themselves. Another island that before today existed only on maps has proven itself to be real, and the transformation is pure magic.

The misty grey mirage of the island turns green, then bright horizontal turquoise lines appear beneath it. *Waves! Perhaps I'll get to surf again.* A yellow line depicting a sandy beach forms below the hill, and now I can see the waves breaking, the same waves that have been lifting and pushing *Sobrius* forward all night and day.

The symbols and drawings on the charts that I have been studying for months now come alive: the "cave," the "breakers," the "conspicuous house" on the hill. For a moment it is not clear if the chart depicts the geography or if the geography depicts the chart. Regardless, Cat Island is now full size, risen from the horizon like an animal in a pop-up book – no longer a two-dimensional map, but a solid three-dimensional island towering over the ocean that caresses its shore.

I sail close to the point to get a good look at the waves. The ocean floor at the point rises from over 1000' to 6' very quickly, causing the six-foot swell to stand up, changing color from dark blue to bright turquoise blue, and then break into white foam.

Movement in the water catches my eye. The squared-off black tip of a fin slices the water just below the surface, moving fast in the opposite direction, a large and unknown sea creature, and an ominous sight right before I want to surf.

In another area further to starboard, indicated on the chart as "breakers," I can see whitecaps from breaking waves. I turn *Sobrius* to starboard and pass outside of the coral reef that makes these smaller waves break. A blue hole is marked on the chart on the other side of this reef, which separates the shallow bay inside from the very deep water on the outside. This is one of the many blue holes I found in the charts while studying at home, and I hope to find it and explore its contents while freediving.

After passing the reef, I start the engine, heave-to, and drop the sails. We then motor into the bay and survey the area in front of the cave, which seems satisfactory for an anchorage. The cave is indicated by the word "cave" on the chart, but in real life it is quite a spectacle, like a big dark mouth on the beach daring visitors to step inside. To the right (south) of the cave is a curved beach behind which sits a collection of small buildings – a resort, the chart says. To the left of the cave is a rocky beach terminating at a jagged and undercut rock at the north point of the island, where the large waves break next to deep water. All around *Sobrius* is bright blue water with white sand on the bottom. It looks like a happy place, inviting us to stay. I like it here, and I let the anchor dig into the sand.

Location: 24° 40.25'N, 75° 45.59'W

Immediately after setting the anchor, I take the 12-0 out to the point for a surf. The waves are not nearly as fun as Egg Reef, but I catch one good ride, then start working my way back into the bay, riding a few very small waves that wrap around the point and break right next to the rocky shore.

The scenery here is spectacular – bright blue water in the bay, dark blue water outside, grey and black rocky cliffs rising out of the water, topped with green trees, the cave, the beach, and no other boats in sight – just what I came for: nature; adventure; solitude.

The sun sets behind the island, and I sleep a deep sleep, then get up in the middle of the night to look at the myriad stars lighting up the otherwise jet-black sky. There is no electric light visible here, and I forgot to turn on my masthead anchor light, so the night is even darker. The stars cover the sky completely, the likes of which I never see on land. I want to stay and stargaze all night, but I'm tired and I soon go back to sleep below.

Coffee and oatmeal with honey, dried fruit, and nuts make breakfast, just like when I'm home at the marina. While eating I listen to the Chris Parker weather forecast on my shortwave radio receiver.

My tentative plan is to stay here today and look for the blue hole labeled on the chart, and maybe explore the beach on the north point too. Then I'll move around the corner to Orange Point and anchor for the night, move to New Bight the following day, and hike to the fabled hermitage of Father Jerome. Southwest winds should be coming Monday through Wednesday, so I'll either seek shelter on the south end of Cat Island or go to the Exumas, or somewhere else...

The time has come to go find my first blue hole and freedive to its bottom. I've read about the legend of Lusca, a sea monster with the head of a shark and the body of an octopus, said to live in blue holes and attack people. While I'd rather not see a legitimate sea monster, I would like to get an octopus on video, and they live in caves, and blue holes lead to caves.

The blue holes are sinkholes that formed when these islands were above sea level, during an ice age, similar to the sinkholes in which I dive in Florida, except that these are in the ocean.

This summer, while doing carpentry on the *Barcelona Explorer*, a 100' wooden schooner that was docked in St Augustine, Robby, the captain, told me the story of his octopus tattoo. He was freediving in a blue hole in the Abacos, and he saw what looked like a tree in front of him in the dark water, about 60' down. But when he went to investigate, the tree reached out and grabbed him – it was no tree but rather a giant Atlantic octopus! Calmly, he peeled the tentacle off his arm and swam to the surface before running out of breath. The experience changed his life and thus he got the tattoo.

I pack all my dive gear on the 12-0 and set out for the blue hole by the reef labeled as "breakers" on the chart. I didn't see the blue hole on the way in, but it shouldn't be too hard to find, I think as I happily paddle away from *Sobrius* sitting on the surfboard and stroking the clear water with my kayak paddle. My dive gear is all in front of me, strapped down with a single blue bungee cord. The GoPro video camera is ready for action in case a dolphin or a turtle or some other interesting wildlife makes an appearance. I don't want to miss any such opportunities (I have in the past).

As I paddle along the edge of the shallow water where the bay meets the deep Atlantic Ocean, I hear a splash behind my board. The water here drops off quickly from six feet to six hundred feet, and is as much as 4000 feet deep just a couple miles out. I am on the edge of a plateau at the top of an undersea mountain.

I quickly turn and see a boil in the water right behind my board, on which I sit just an inch above the surface of the water.

Behind the splash, as I drift away, an animal looks back at me from the water; it's grey, white, greenish perhaps – a sea turtle, a ray? No, it's a *shark*; I see it clearly now as it turns broadside to me, both of us observing the other. I see its fins, which are long with rounded and white tips, and its whole body, unmistakably a shark. I hope it's a small one; I can't really tell. It moves quickly and disappears as my heartrate quickens.

I turn my board towards where I saw it and paddle that way, to let it know that I'm not afraid and thus not prey, the same way I would treat a menacing dog – turn and run and it will chase you; running away triggers the predator/prey reaction. But fear slowly flows through my mind and body, trying to take hold. I get out my video camera and hastily turn it on.

The shark remains out of sight, and I have a moment of hopeful relief, but this is short-lived. A dorsal fin rises from the water ahead, tall, rounded on the top, slicing the water. Well behind the dorsal fin swishes the tail fin, back and forth, slowly propelling the animal directly towards me. The dorsal fin is at least a foot out of the water when the head starts to appear just beneath the surface, and then it too breaks the surface, only a few feet in front of the 12-0, moving slowly towards the front of my surfboard.

Its head is enormous and it seems too big to be a shark; I momentarily think it may be something benign, like a whale shark or a basking shark. It reminds me of a salamander, smooth and curved, with small beady eyes; yet it's not the eyes I see, rather I see the shark's nostrils. But my hopefulness is not based in reality; my mind is trying to make the problem go away; it's not going away, it's coming right at me. I put the camera in the water thinking I'll at least get some shark video out of this ordeal.

The head is broad, ridiculously broad, as broad as my shoulders, and flat on top, nearly straight across the front, but slightly rounded as viewed from above. The skin is light grey, smooth and glistening wet. Its small dark nostril breaks the surface as it bumps my board. I'm sitting with my legs out of the water, as if I were in a kayak. My right hand is holding the camera and with my left I reach out with the paddle and poke the offending sea monster in the head and try to push it away as it rubs the side of its great head along the edge of my surfboard.

At this point, I remember hearing an interview on NPR with a diver who sought out tiger sharks to study and film. He said we need only to "push them gently away with our hand" should a shark approach a diver. So I push, hard, but not with my hand, I use the paddle.

The shark resists at first, which surprises me, but then swims down and away. For a brief moment, I see its entire body, which is similar in length to my board, and then if fades away. I sit still and hope it's gone.

Not a minute passes before the dorsal fin breaks the surface again. I can hardly believe this is happening, but it most definitely is. The shark slowly swims parallel to my board and again rubs its head along the side of the 12-0. I assume the shark is trying to get a little taste of the unfamiliar thing in the water to determine what it is, and whether or not it is edible.

I jab it in the head with my paddle, hard this time, not gently pushing at all, as it makes contact with my board, the top of its head again slightly out of the water, nostrils and mouth visible. It jerks away and swims down and to its left. I hope it's gone this time. I really hope it's gone.

*Remain calm, don't run, and next time push it away gently, don't jab it.* I tell myself these things as I wait for whatever comes next, hoping it's not a full attack, against which I would have no defense. I knew this sailing adventure would put my life at risk, and I accept that, but not this early; I'm not ready yet!

The dorsal fin breaks the surface ahead of me, slightly to the right of the front of the 12-0. It's coming at me again, for a third time, and again slowly. I can see its mouth and an eye as it brushes its head against the side of my board. This time I place the blade of my paddle against the side of its head and push it away, hard.

I can see its full length in the clear water as it descends, turns to its left, and disappears. It seems like it might be as long as my board (12'), but it's hard to tell. Judging from the size of its head, it certainly is big enough to eat me.

Again, I hope that the shark is gone for good, and again, I suppress the urge to run. *Show no fear, the shark doesn't know what*

*I am and I can't let it think I'm prey.* I sit still and hope for a good outcome, but I know a full attack is a possibility. I'm scared, but I'm also peaking – on high alert and fully conscious and aware, ready for action, although I know inaction is the thing to do right now. *Sit still.*

I look at *Sobrius* in the distance, maybe a mile away. I long to be back aboard her, safe from the menace below. I turn the board toward salvation and start paddling, consciously at the same pace I was going before the encounter, not wanting to let the shark know how scared I really am.

I look behind me – no shark. The water brightens as I paddle across the shallow bank, leaving the deeper, darker water behind. The sand below is yellow, and the water has a slightly green tint. The surface is rippled by the light east wind into which I paddle.

I look behind me, imagining a large dorsal fin breaking the surface, charging towards me. But there is nothing to see besides water. *Sobrius* is getting closer. I look back again.

I reach up and put my hand on the varnished teak toerail, the toerail that I have varnished twice already, and it feels like home, like salvation, like the hand of a mother to a scared child. I drop my head and just sit there on the board for a moment, taking it all in. Again I suppress the urge to run – to just throw all my gear aboard and climb the ladder in a rush. The shark has defeated me, but from this small act of defiance I feel a saving of face.

Slowly, methodically, I put my paddle, spear, anchor and backpack on *Sobrius*. I remove the leash from my right ankle and attach it to a stanchion, then calmly I stand up and climb the boarding ladder.

I've never been more grateful to be back on my little ship.

[I later identified the shark as an oceanic whitetip, recognized by its long, rounded dorsal and pelvic fins, tipped with white, and the broad rounded snout. It's described as an active, dangerous shark that is pelagic (ocean-going) and rarely comes to shore. They are opportunistic feeders that investigate anything in the water that might be edible. These are the sharks that ate so many of the sailors from the WWII vessel *Indianapolis* after it was torpedoed by a Japanese submarine, in what is considered the worst maritime disaster in US Naval history. Cat Island is the only known place where oceanic whitetips congregate close to land.]

Later in the day I feel like some safe land-based activity is in order. Besides, the shore is inviting, with its green tree-covered hills, and I'd like to explore the beach on the north point. I stand on deck and survey the water for a long time, hoping not to see any large grey masses moving through the water, before stepping down onto the 12-0 for the paddle to shore.

The water is very clear and gets shallow quickly as I paddle away from my floating home, and I'm grateful that no sea creatures trouble me along the way. Tiny waves break on a sandbar nearly perpendicular to the beach, waves that have wrapped around the point and come in moving parallel to the shoreline. I carefully weave through the little breakers, not wanting to take any chance of capsizing, and make a dry beach landing, then pull my board up into the shade of the scrubby trees.

There's a trail right in front of me, probably leading to one of the resorts, and I start along it, stepping carefully over occasional sharp rocks and enjoying the sensation of being in the shade and surrounded by forest.

I come to a hand-lettered signpost pointing to the beach from which I came, the resort, and "Man-O-War," which must be the north point. I turn left to Man-O-War, cross a small hill, and step out into the sun and onto a soft-sand beach looking out at the waves I surfed yesterday. An undercut rock to my left marks the point of the point; waves are running up underneath it, slowly and endlessly carving away its base.

I walk to the right, east, along the beach. The reef is visible, green and yellow and brown, like a great amoeba in the clear blue-green water, stretching beyond my field of view to the east. It looks like a fantastic place to snorkel, but as tempting as it is, there's no way I'm getting back in the water today.

Instead I sit and try to meditate. *Will I ever get back in the water? Will I be too scared to snorkel, to freedive, to surf?* I'm not sure. I hope not. Throughout my life, I've regularly changed sports and activities, adopting new as the old become monotonous. Perhaps the time has come for another change. I ponder what else there is to do and appreciate. I try to clear my mind and think of nothing, just letting the vista in front of me fill my mind and dominate my consciousness.

*Happiness always come from within. External influences are nice, but never necessary. When one activity ceases, others present themselves.*

I need to meditate, and I need to write. I have important life-changing decisions to make. And I need to visit Father Jerome's hermitage in New Bight, on this island. I will meditate in the place he built for just that. I sense I am forever changed by the encounter with the shark.

*The northern point of Cat Island was a spectacular place to anchor with astounding natural beauty and at least one real sea monster.*

The engine is running as I pull up the anchor, ready to leave this place of rugged beauty and sea monsters and see what's around the next corner. The town of Orange Creek is my destination, and it's only about four miles away. On the way out, I pass right by the place where the shark paid me a visit, but he's not showing himself now.

I anchor right off Orange Creek, happy to be somewhere new and away from the deep water and the large predators within.

Location: 24° 38.61'N, 75°43.04'W

I paddle the 12-0 dinghy/surfboard/liferaft to shore, wave to a couple of boys snorkeling in the creek, and set off for a walk. I pass some ruins of stone and mortar houses, rocky shoreline, and a lady on a bicycle who tells me of Periwinkle's restaurant ahead on the right. But when I reach Periwinkle's the kitchen is closed, and only the bar is open. I set out on the road heading back the way I came.

I haven't walked 100 yards from Periwinkle's when a grey sedan zooms by, hits the breaks and backs up. The young black man at the wheel asks if I need any help.

"I could use a ride back to Orange Creek."

"Let's go."

He introduces himself as Adam, and tells me that his family owns the general store, by the creek where my board sits waiting for me.

"Can I ask what you do for a living?" he asks.

"I'm a carpenter."

"Well then" he says, looking at me quizzically "you look like Jesus and you're a *carpenter*."

I laugh. "Yes, I've heard that before."

I marvel at the hospitality of the few people I've met. So far, I've been on two islands, and I've been offered rides on both.

I enjoy the splendid view of *Sobrius* from the water as I paddle back home, with the sunset in the background painting the sky in all the warm colors. I'm so happy to have this little boat, capable of ocean passages and singlehanding, and to be with her, here in The Bahamas.

Since the shark encounter I am now faced with the question of whether or not to continue my pursuit of the dangerous sport of solo freediving. On the one hand, I've already experienced it many times, and seen quite a bit of what there is to see underwater. I could just call it quits and feel ok with that decision. On the other hand, an encounter with a shark like that is extremely rare, and will likely never happen again.

Perhaps I should just get right back on the horse and dive again. Or perhaps I should continue to dive but avoid reefs next to deep water.

As far as surfing goes, the shark encounter will make me want to longboard exclusively, especially when out in remote places next to deep water. That shark might have killed me if I was on a shortboard paddling out to a reef to surf, or if I was swimming when it came to investigate. Or, maybe I'm just overreacting; perhaps there is nothing to fear.

March 17

It's another beautiful day with a very light breeze. I raise the mainsail and sail off anchor, then raise the genoa and turn downwind onto a deep broad reach. But soon it becomes clear that either the main or the genoa should come down, as the former blankets the latter. I decide to take down the main and sail under the larger genoa. This will be a first; so many aspects of sailing are still untried and experimental to me.

The afternoon sun is creating a hypnotic pattern on the water with flashing lights reaching from me to the horizon, the sun reflecting off the crests of wavelets, like a million camera flashes, an army of paparazzi taking my picture.

By noon we are sailing south at only 3 knots, yet this is a lot more than we've been making all day. Light-wind sailing is pleasant, but takes a lot of patience. However, the peace and quiet of sailing slowly across clear water on a beautiful sunny day is all I want right now.

Occasionally, in the incredibly clear water, I see patches of coral reef pass by and am tempted to stop and dive. The big shark is surely nowhere around as we are well away from the deep water where the oceanic whitetips live. I'm watching the depth gauge, sailing through clear water 30-feet deep when we sail right over a patch of reef and the depth drops to 15 feet. *This must be a good one.*

I tack, under genoa alone, sail away from the reef, then tack again to maneuver upwind of it. I tack twice more until I'm about 200' directly upwind of the little reef, and here I drop the anchor, and then the big headsail.

We drift back over the reef, a bit to one side of it but close enough. Since this is to be my first dive since seeing the enormous shark yesterday, I want *Sobrius* to be right there with me.

Location: 24° 31.08'N, 75° 41.93'W

The water calls to me, but another sailboat is approaching from the south, and I hail them on the VHF.

"Sailing vessel approaching Alligator Point from the south, sailing vessel approaching Alligator Point from the south, this is sailing vessel *Sobrius*"

"This is sailing vessel *Muriella*, approaching Alligator Point from the south" comes the voice of a man with a European accent.

"Let's go to 17."

"Going to 17."

"Hi, I'm the red sailboat ahead of you. I don't know if you have any divers on board, but I'm anchored over a nice little reef, about to dive, and it would be nice to have some company in the water, over."

"Oh, thanks, but I can't dive, I can't get down *even one foot*. I'm all by myself and I have to keep moving, but thanks for the offer."

"OK, well then you have a great day, over and out."

I had to try for company; I'm still shaken from the shark encounter, but I feel driven to dive in this clear and stunningly beautiful water. This is, after all, what I am here for, and the underwater world has been calling to me all day.

Very slowly and quietly, I climb down the boarding ladder and into the water, putting my head in to look around before committing to full submersion in the marine wilderness. But the water welcomes me and the scene compels me to investigate. The main reef, thirty yards away, is a dome-shaped mound rising halfway to the surface in thirty feet of water, while directly below sit little clusters of reef on a flat sand bottom. I swim the short distance to the reef and feel surprisingly comfortable in the clear water.

The first fish I see is a beautiful and magnificent queen triggerfish, one of my favorites, and one I don't often see. It swims between purple sea fans, past yellow sponges, then disappears in a dark crevice. A stoplight parrotfish swims away from me, bright green with a yellow band by the tail. Two blue tang seem interested and unafraid. Nobody spears blue tang because they carry ciguatera, a painful and debilitating disease caused by a neurotoxin that comes from the dinoflagellates they eat.

A juvenile yellow and blue Spanish hogfish shows itself to me, then hides in one of the many caves in the reef, like holes in Swiss cheese. Orange fire coral rises like the antennae of insects, reaching out and warning me with its bright orange color not to touch. It stings like jellyfish, which are members of the same phylum as coral – cnidaria.

A cocoa damselfish, brown on top, yellow on the bottom, defends its portion of a cave as I peer in. Another cave reveals a large Nassau grouper; always hiding or swimming away, these fish seem to know that humans want to eat them.

I swim through a maze of hard coral, soft coral, live coral, dead coral… It all looks like curving and twisted rock, antler shaped, covered in strange plant-like animals of various colors, and populated with fish that look like artists created them.

Coral reefs are the most spectacular and beautiful places I've ever been. They're also wild and unpredictable. In the ocean live animals of all sorts, small and pretty, giant and hungry, some with no teeth, and some with wicked teeth. It is a priceless privilege to be able to visit here, and yet the reef only asks for respect as payment.

Much of the reef is covered with algae, a sign of dead coral, but live coral cover about half the reef and is a welcome sight in this age of worldwide coral Armageddon.

The reef is vertical on the sides and is decorated with at least four species of live stony coral, as well as many soft corals – that look like strange plants – sponges and various odd invertebrates. My flashlight illuminates the interior of a small cave, and I'm greeted by a majestic grey angelfish. Red and orange encrusting invertebrates color the ancient walls inside this little cave. Colors all appear grey-blue at this depth, but the flashlight adds the wavelengths necessary to bring out the warm colors.

Seawater filters out different wavelengths of light with depth, and red is the first to go, followed by orange, yellow and green. Blue is last because it has the shortest wavelength, and thus the highest energy. Red light has the longest wavelength of our visible spectrum, and is thus filtered out in shallower water. Note that the order of visible wavelengths from longest to shortest is the same as the order of the colors of the rainbow, which we were taught in school ROY G BIV (red, orange, yellow, green, blue, indigo, violet). All appears grey in deep water.

The reef is essentially a round patch rising like a lone hill from yellow sand. All around appears empty – just blue water in all directions. A forest full of life, an oasis of habitat in the vast ocean, a treasure more wonderful and valuable than anything man made. This is where life comes from, and without it ours may end.

I keep looking over my shoulder for sharks, which probably isn't a bad habit, but the clear blue water feels like home, and I'm glad to be back. I'm also comforted by the near presence of *Sobrius*, right next to me. The thought of having to swim any distance while in a state of fear, as I would be if I were to see another big shark, is unacceptable today.

On my last dive, I turn and see *Sobrius* from below, her bright blue bottom blending in with the water. The keel hangs down, keeping her stable, the rudder on its skeg (like a small keel) points down from the rear. The ladder welcomes me home.

*A grey angelfish and I observe each other on a Cat Island Reef. Live coral can be seen to its right in the foreground, and in the background center, while dead coral covered in algae can be seen to the fish's left in the foreground.*

*I kept Sobrius close during my first dive after encountering the oceanic whitetip shark, and her underbody was a comforting sight.*

4:48pm

The gentle breeze has come back, but now blows from the southeast, and we are doing all of three knots, away from the reef and towards New Bight. It's funny how it seems fast to go three knots after sailing at one knot most of the day. But it sure is nice, I can feel the wind, it's much cooler, *Sobrius* is heeling a bit, the big genoa is pulling us forward. I've got a barber haul reaching from the clew of the genoa to a block on the stern pulpit, leading to a cleat on the windward side, which is keeping the sheeting angle tight, allowing us to go a bit higher (upwind).

The sun is bright, the temperature of the air is fine, and the sky and the ocean are the same shade of blue. I'm standing in the cockpit with the tiller behind me, steering with my left hand, leaning back on it. My surfboard is up on the deck, and under the surfboard is a green net which I found on the beach yesterday. I intend to hang this on *Sobrius* somewhere, but it will more likely be moved from place to place until I eventually decide to get rid of it. All is as it should be.

The green and hilly Cat Island, which is about five miles away, attracts my eye like a magnet. White spots dot the island, which must be houses. In the distance is a hill which I assume is Mt Alvernia, the tallest point in the Bahamas and the site of Father Jerome's hermitage. Smoke is rising in a dark curved line from something burning on the land.

Low fair-weather cumulus clouds decorate the otherwise bright blue sky. The sun is powerful and reflecting off the clear water. The sand on the bottom is about 30 feet down and appears turquoise blue. Little patches of coral show up as dark spots. The dark shadow of *Sobrius* follows us to our left, dancing, undulating with the rhythm of the water.

My sinuses are completely clear, and the air has no scent whatsoever. The only sound I hear is the gentle moving of the water as we push through it, little waves making themselves known. I've only seen one sailboat today, and one very small motorboat. The VHF is silent; there are no other boats in sight. It's a very calm place, a beautiful place. I don't know why there aren't more sailboats here. Most people like to congregate in groups, and maybe most are more social than me. They're probably all over in The Exumas hanging out together.

I like Cat Island. I like sailing by myself.

In light and shifting wind like today, the challenge is to keep the sails full and the boat pointed in the right direction relative to the wind. Lack of concentration sacrifices speed and forward progress. Today I've learned that if I really focus on the wind and watch the shape of the genoa, particularly up front, and attentively steer with the wind, we go a lot faster, 2 knots instead of one, or 3 knots instead of 2. So, I'm working on my sail focus, which requires, and brings on, a meditative state, and this state of mind brings the solitude I seek.

If solitude is what I'm searching for, I certainly have found it, out here in the waters of Cat Island. It's just me and my boat, and a whole lot of clear water. This is just what I came for. Sailing from place to place, letting the wind take me wherever it dictates.

I take in the scene. To my right, the turquoise-blue water stretches off into the distance, darkening at the horizon, making a long, perfect line, showing the curvature of the Earth, where the water meets the misty blue-grey sky, punctuated by purplish clouds. To my left the green island stretches off into the distance, disappearing into the blue water, followed by the mountains behind the town of New Bight, poking up out of the water in a dot-dash pattern not unlike Morse code.

The wind blows gently, then stops, then comes back at a slightly different angle and blows gently again, changing angles all the time. I trim the sails; I steer by the wind. I focus on the shape of the headsail, trying to keep it just into the wind, while slowly, at about a walking pace, we make progress towards our destination of New Bight.

I sail all day, relying on the minimal power provided by the wind in the sails, determined not to start the engine. Sometimes we move as fast as four knots; sometimes we don't move at all.

At sunset, I make a meal of chili and sardines and I notice the two bulbs of garlic that I brought, hiding behind the stove amongst the hot sauce, coffee, and tea. I chop up a clove, toss it in the pot, and the aroma brings back memories of an Italian girlfriend and her lasagna.

I let the constantly whirring and buzzing autopilot steer while I eat dinner. The sun is setting and provides a show of colors in the sky. I watch the sun disappear below the horizon, hoping to see the illusive and fabled green flash which sometimes accompanies the sun in the moment that it sets. There is no green flash tonight, but as soon as the sun sets, a planet, I imagine it's Venus, reveals itself right above the red, orange, and yellow horizon. The colors fade, and the stars increase in brilliance and number, eventually covering the sky. The few familiar constellations I know look like they've been powdered with glitter. There are so many stars, so many that I'm not used to seeing.

I continue steering in the cool darkness, working my way around the invisible Bonefish Point, trying to stay clear of the shallows, constantly checking the charts to make sure there is nothing I might run into. But it looks like this whole bank is wide open for cruising, without any obstacles on which a sailboat might run aground.

I wait until the red flashing light on the Batelco Tower marking New Bight is 100 degrees to my left before I tack East. But the wind decreases as soon as I tack, and my course is too much north, towards the shallow water around the point. I tack again, now travelling parallel to the beach, slowly moving away from my destination. This is a reality of sailing, sometimes progress is made towards our destination by sailing away from it.

Still I am determined not to start the engine, even though we are only moving at 1.5 knots. Eventually we tack back towards the tower, once again headed towards New Bight. At this pace, we will be there in about three hours, which would put arrival at about 3:00 am.

My patience and resolve eventually run out, and I start the engine. I reason that I'll have just enough time before anchoring to take down the sails, bag the genoa, put the mainsail cover on, tie off the boom so it doesn't swing, and put things away. I do these chores in the dark as the diesel engine and the autopilot take us towards the lights of town.

The lights of New Bight look close, even though the chart plotter says we are half a mile away. I try to imagine what a half mile looks like, and I figure this is a safe distance. The depth is ten feet, which I like; the chart says it's all soft sand, and thus ideal for anchoring, with no shallow spots or coral. The wind is calm.

I put the engine in neutral, steer us 90 degrees off the nearly nonexistent breeze, wait until we slow, then point *Sobrius* straight into it. I move to the bow and lower the 15-kg anchor and its 50 feet of heavy chain to the bottom. When the anchor touches the bottom, illuminated by the navigation lights (that I rewired at Meeks Patch) I cleat it off, go back to the cockpit and put us in reverse, at idle speed. *Sobrius* slowly starts moving backwards; the anchor drags across the bottom, aligning itself properly. I then slowly pay out the chain, making sure the anchor is biting into the sand. I let out all 50 feet of chain, then another 20 feet of line, attach the anti-chafing gear, tie off the line, move back to the cockpit, rev the engine up, still in reverse, to pull the anchor firmly into the sand. Finally, I shift into neutral and shut the engine off by pulling on the kill knob and then turning off the key.

I am here, it is now, and here and now are good.

Location: 24° 16.90'N, 75° 25.30'W

March 18

After the encounter with the shark, I spent some time thinking while sitting still on the beach at Man-O-War point, looking out at the ocean and the reef that I would normally have been snorkeling. I pondered about how all of my outdoor activities are both an excuse to be exposed to nature, and to approach a clear and meditative state of mind. While the adventurer in me seeks thrill and extreme exposure to raw nature, the intellectual side of me knows that little external influence, if any, is needed to achieve a clear and peaceful mind. We all live with the keys to happiness contained within our own minds.

This all reminded me of the hermitage of Father Jerome, located on Mt Alvernia at New Bight. The hermitage was surely a site for meditation. I believe prayer is a form of meditation, and I think we all seek this state of mind one way or another. Some pray, some meditate, some play golf, others freedive and sail. However, all we need to achieve a calm and peaceful state of mind is within us already.

I determined, while sitting on the beach at Man-O-War point, to visit the hermitage and meditate there, as Father Jerome intended.

Now I am at New Bight, and need only to paddle to the beach and walk up the hill to see the hermitage. But in the daylight, the half mile to shore looks a lot further away than it does at night. No matter, I mount the 12-0 and start paddling.

The wooden dock on the beach is crooked and dilapidated, and appears to have suffered a severe battery. I disembark on the sand and pull my board up onto the dock where it will be safe, and the first building I see is the Police station, which makes me feel like my board, an absolute necessity to me while cruising, will be there when I get back. A large sign points the way to the hermitage, and I set out, walking in my sandals along the lonely road, which leads through low scrubby forest, to the hill known as Mt Alvernia.

The hermitage comes into view on the hill above and looks like a castle from the road below. A round tower with a pointed top looms over domed roofs below. The paved road ends and an archway leads to a rocky trail. Inside the archway are two inscriptions, one reads "Pius XII Pontifex Maximus." The other reads "Deo Optimo Maximo Et In Honorem Sancti Francisci Assisi Mons Haec Sacra."

The trail steepens and is punctuated by the stations of the cross, carved into four-foot-tall rocks covered in stone and mortar. They lead up the trail, depicting Jesus carrying the cross, falling down, getting back up. These are images of Jesus representing the day of his crucifixion and are typically placed in order along a path that the faithful can walk, pray, and contemplate Jesus' sacrifice to humanity. In the steepest parts of the trail appear stairs, hewn directly from the bedrock.

At the top of the hill the hermitage rises out of the grey precipice. The round tower I saw from below is attached to small stone buildings with domed roofs, and one has a cross on top, looking like a tiny church. The hermitage reminds me of a dollhouse, a miniature version of something one would expect to be much larger. I realize that Father Jerome must not have been a large man – a strong man, to have built all this from stone, but not a tall man. Everything is built from local stone and mortar, except the doors and windows. They are made of wood and old green paint fades and peels from their surface.

The whole structure is perched on a rocky outcropping overlooking New Bight and the bright blue water of the bay. The view is a full 360 degrees, of Cat Island, the Cat Island Bight, and the Atlantic Ocean behind. Bonefish Point is visible, with its inland creeks, the same point that I sailed around last night.

The walls of these little buildings are not vertical, but they rise up at an angle, reminding me of the pyramids. Everything is connected together, stone and mortar flowing from one structure to another, giving a feeling of great strength and continuity. They've obviously withstood many hurricanes.

Inside the buildings, there is very little space. It's hard to tell where Father Jerome had room to do anything.

*The hermitage of Father Jerome at Mt Alvernia, Cat Island, was a highlight of the journey, offering interesting architecture, a great view, and unmatched serenity. Father Jerome, both a priest and an architect, was sent to The Bahamas by the Anglican Bishop after a hurricane in 1908 destroyed many of the islands' churches. He built or rebuilt seven Anglican churches on Long Island, Nassau, and Cat Island, all stone and hurricane proof.*

Bromeliads and small purple flowers decorate the stone landscape around the buildings, and little bits of fern climb the walls. The sounds up here are the sounds of small creatures, the buzzing of bees and the gentle songs of birds hidden in the trees. If I stop and let my mind clear, these sounds of nature fill my entire consciousness.

A sundial sits in the backyard, rising out of the rocky soil, slowly keeping time, years after the man who built it passed. I imagine Father Jerome sitting quietly, meditating while the shadow of the gnomon slowly moves across the dial.

The tower, which is about twelve feet tall, looking much bigger from the road below, is hollow, and has a bell inside, along with two windows, one high and one low. A rudimentary ladder of narrow boards set into the stone leads up to the bell, and a blue rope hangs down. I briefly consider ringing the ancient bell, but its apparent age prevents me from trying. Looking through the lower window I can see my little sailboat out in the bay, and the water around *Sobrius* is practically invisible; the water and sky are nearly indistinguishable, one becoming the other along an elusive horizon.

Buttresses and arches support this little structure, domes, pillars, it's amazing he built this, and I can't help but wonder where he found all the rocks, and from where he had to carry them. I'm impressed that his faith was so strong that he devoted himself to building the hermitage, and I wonder what it is in a man that makes him so confident in his religion that he is driven to do something like this.

I stare at *Sobrius* out in the bay floating on the clear blue water that reflects the sky, sitting peacefully with, but much further out than, one other sailboat. I feel like my little ship that was born in France in 1972 could take me anywhere, now that we've sailed all the way here. She seems at home on the water moving from place to place, crossing the ocean, weathering storms, relaxing in calms. I suppose we could go just about anywhere we want, and I suppose we will.

It seems what I enjoy most about this trip so far is moving from place to place. I really have no urge to stay in any one place more than a night or two. I think it's the actual sailing that I enjoy the most, being nomadic, not really caring too much about where we go, just that we move from one place to another, each day.

Solitude and peace flow in abundance as I stand on the rock precipice looking out over the bay and New Bight. I can't imagine what could be better in life than travelling and seeing new places, experiencing nature in all of its forms, finding complete solitude on *Sobrius*, in the water, and at places like this little hermitage. With solitude comes deep thought, with deep thought comes growth, and with growth comes the bettering of ourselves. Perhaps all the things I do are simply a search for a meditative state of mind, a search for solitude, a search for deep thought, meaning, for the meaning of life, an attempt to achieve my destiny.

I believe at least part of the purpose of life is to learn all that we can while we are here. One of the most important things to learn is what it is that makes us happy. Once we have learned what this is, we must do it, but all the while leaving the world a better place, reducing human suffering, as well as reducing or preventing the suffering of all the sentient beings with which we come into contact.

Through solitude we can think, yet it's very difficult to think when constantly surrounded by distractions. Unfortunately, our society encourages constant distraction, a lot of which makes people feel entertained and engaged while their minds are turned off. This might be benign in small doses, but I see that most people do it way too much, filling their minds with garbage, and therefore never spending any time thinking deeply, which is what we should be spending the majority of our free time doing.

Of course while sailing there is ample time to think. On *Sobrius* I only steer, trim the sails, navigate, do chores, and experience nature, all the while giving plenty of time to let my mind wander and do as it pleases, or as I please. Oddly enough, a lot of the time my mind is simply running down little stories in my head, remembering things that I've seen, having made-up conversations with people I know, yet, what I need to practice is turning all that off and letting nature fill my mind, bringing about the meditative state where I can ponder everything I've learned and experienced in my life, make sense of it, and organize my thoughts.

UNUM EST NECESSARIUM O BEATA SOLITUDO QUAESIVI QUEM DILIGI reads an inscription on a wall at the hermitage. I don't know what it means, but I like it.

I paddle back to *Sobrius* with a clear mind, and in the evening I move us to another little anchorage away from town, next to Bonefish Point. It's a bit more exposed to swell than where we were this morning, but it's more secluded. A pristine sandy beach lies ahead, and a rocky shore extends to the left and right. I like it here.

Location: 24° 17.25'N, 75° 27.13'W

Coffee, watercolors, and the weather report make up another fine morning in the islands as the yellow sun climbs over the green hills to starboard. My father sent me the tiny painting kit before I left

Florida; both of my parents are artists, and have always encouraged my creativity.

As I try to capture the rugged beauty of Bonefish Point on paper, I can see the Fernandez Cays in the distance – two small islands just around the point. I locate them on the chart in the cruising guide and determine that I could anchor safely in their lee, and perhaps find some good snorkeling. It is settled then, the Fernandez Cays shall be our next destination, but first I feel the need to explore the beach.

The wind is supposed to be calm today, but I can feel a light breeze as I lounge in the cockpit after hunting for pirate treasure in the rocks ashore. The water reflects the sky like a sheet of glass in some areas, where there is no wind, but the surface is rippled in others, showing that the wind is variable and patchy. There just might be enough breeze to move my little ship.

I hoist the mainsail and the big genoa and pull the heavy Vulcan anchor, which I now think of as Dr. Spock, from the sand. We slowly drift away from land and I put us on course to go out and around the shallow Bonefish Point.

We sail on a beam reach (with the gentle breeze coming from 90 degrees to our direction of travel) at four knots. Sailboats are magical, in the way they can do this, silently propelled by the wind coming from the side.

I see a big patch of glassy-smooth water ahead of us and I tack right before we get to it. I spend the next hour trying to navigate around these windless areas, staying in the rippled water and crossing the glassy areas, when I have to, at their narrowest places.

We are now approaching the shallow waters of the point, and when the depth gauge reads six feet, I tack again, back towards the deep water. But now we have to cross a short windless area. The sails hang limp and I let our little momentum carry us across.

We catch some wind on the other side and keep going.

We play this game of chasing the wind and avoiding calms for about an hour, until land is distant enough that a more consistent breeze blows ripples across all the water.

I sail close around the leeward side of the little cays, and take note of two dark patches in the otherwise bright blue water. These are coral reefs, which are also evident on the chartplotter and the paper charts, but they don't appear to be too shallow.

After surveying the depth, which is around 10-12 feet with sand on the bottom, I sail away from the islands, then tack back towards them. I steer *Sobrius* into the wind and move to the mast, where I release the jib halyard and pull the sail down as it luffs over the deck. I move back to the cockpit and steer us towards the place I want to anchor, now powered only by the mainsail. I sail close to the islands and tack, slowly, almost too slowly. If I hadn't made the tack I might have drifted into the rocks. I'll have to better conserve our momentum next time.

I sail around in circles and figure-eights until I feel confident that we are in a good place to anchor and I then put the boat "in irons" – steered directly into the wind with the sail luffing – and move to the bow, open the anchor locker, free Dr. Spock, and let out just enough chain that he sits on the bottom. I hold the chain until *Sobrius* comes to a halt and starts to drift backwards, then slowly let out more chain as we drift downwind. When all 50' of chain and another 30' of line is out, I cleat off the anchor rode and move to the mast, where I release the main halyard. I move to the cockpit, tension the mainsheet to bring the boom to the center, then move back to the mast and pull the sail down. We are here.

Location: 24° 18.90'N, 75° 29.00'W

I've anchored upwind of a patch of coral reef and now we lie close to it so I can snorkel the reef while not too far from the safety of *Sobrius*. The shark encounter has certainly changed the way I view swimming in the ocean. Before I would not care much about anchoring so close to the reef where I want to snorkel, but now it seems like a necessity. Safety first, second and third.

The Fernandez Cays are tiny but beautiful. They are simply two large rocks, or small islands, about 1000 feet across and 50 wide, rising from 12 feet of clear water, which has undercut the cays all the way around, making them appear to hover over the surface of the water. A shallow coral reef connects the two cays, and low green vegetation covers most of the brown jagged rock that makes up the little islands.

*The Fernandez Cays were one of my favorite places that I visited. The coral reef was beautiful and a swim-through cave between the islands allowed passage from one side to the other.*

As soon as *Sobrius* is safely anchored, the calling of the water compels me to snorkel. I paddle the 12-0 to the small reef, the one separated from the island, and dive while still connected to the board with a ten-foot surfboard leash, which makes me feel very safe. I am pleasantly surprised to find a beautiful, healthy reef, with live coral both hard and soft, and populated by a variety of colorful and curious fish.

One little patch in particular is teeming with fish of various species. A school of French grunt congregates here, along with margate, female parrotfish (which are much smaller and drab in color, as compared to the relatively large and garishly colored males). Mangrove snapper, a male bluehead wrasse (the males have a blue head, the females are smaller and have a yellow head and upper body), a yellow goatfish, blue tang, blue angelfish, squirrelfish with big black eyes, and a majestic queen triggerfish all swim about this little patch of live coral while others hide in the dark caves underneath.

Many of the fish come out to see me, probably wondering what I am. They show no fear. I assume the abundance of fish here is directly related to the relatively high amount of live coral. I see comparatively little fish on the dead reefs that are the norm now.

I freeze with excitement when I spy the most beautiful fish yet, one I'm not very familiar with, but also saw back at Meeks Patch. It is a juvenile blue angelfish – yellow body, electric blue and white vertical stripes, seductive eyes – hiding in a crevice between spikey yellow sponges, but looking out at me curiously.

*A juvenile queen angelfish hides in a crevice among the coral and sponges at the Fernandez Cays.*

Live staghorn coral, which I haven't seen in years, lives and grows along with other hard corals and purple sea fans. In the past few years, I've seen entire reefs of dead and crumbling staghorn coral, lying on the bottom in broken pieces like fallen soldiers after a medieval battle. Seeing it alive is a real treat and gives me a little hope for the future of the species, which in reality is likely to go extinct.

As its name suggests, staghorn coral resembles the antlers of a deer, light yellow and rounded at the ends. Other corals I see are bulbous masses covered in little hexagons representing the tiny animals that make up the structure. Fire coral is dark orange, white-tipped, and looks like flames, sometimes branching out in long slender arms. It stings like a jellyfish if touched. Coral are very closely related to these and are like tiny jellyfish that build hard calcium-carbonate structures around themselves and live together as a colony. These colonies are the coral structures that we see, and they provide habitat for fish and countless other marine organisms.

Gorgonians, purple sea fans shaped like a lady's fan from the days before air conditioning, are veined in purple, between which run a lattice of lighter flesh. Black and red or yellow sponges are oddly shaped, sometimes like a barrel, shot through with pores of various sizes. These strange creatures are in the animal kingdom, but seem to straddle the fence between plant and animal. They filter their food out of the water, yet live attached to the sea floor, usually on rocks or dead coral. The larval forms of sponges, conversely, swim about before settling down to a sessile adult life.

An unfamiliar dark orange creature, likely either a sponge or coral, encrusts large portions of the reef. Sea anemones, which I haven't seen in years, are established here, swaying back and forth with the water, like living purple flowers, yet they are animals. Encrusting spikey and hair-like organisms challenge me to guess their identity, and I have no idea, but can only stare in a state of bewilderment. There are so many different creatures represented here that I am overwhelmed in their presence and do not want to go back to the surface, yet I need to breathe, and reluctantly return to the habitat nature intended for me, above, but only long enough to reoxygenate my blood before diving again.

Under the overhangs on the reef are red patches, green leafy algae, orange sheets… all manner of shapes, colors, and life forms seem to be present here, and the scene is breathtaking in its beauty and complexity. This is what reefs are supposed to look like, and I wonder what it is about the conditions here that allow for healthy coral reef in this age where most are dead or dying. Perhaps it is the remoteness and lack of humans.

*The coral reef at the Fernandez Cays was surprisingly healthy, and in this photo can be seen at least three species of hard coral, as well as sponges and soft corals, and four species of fish.*

Before I return to *Sobrius*, I paddle over to the little islands to take a look, and once again am pleasantly surprised to see an abundance of live reef populated with all my fish friends.

A dark cave big enough to enter coaxes me to swim inside. I wonder what might live there. An octopus perhaps? A big mean shark? My flashlight illuminates the smooth rock walls, but no charismatic sea creature shows itself.

Another cave is a swim-through, leading to the other side of the island, where the sun shines bright and lights up the reef. These islands are a wonderland of coral and fish, so I return to *Sobrius* to get my dinghy anchor, wetsuit, fins, spear, and prepare for some underwater exploration of the reef around the islands.

Myriad fish greet me, moving colors surrounded by more colors, odd shapes, tiny creatures, and all the wonders of coral reef, made even more interesting by the two islands overhanging the water which has undercut the bedrock, creating a rock roof hanging out over the water and shading the reef underneath.

I swim through the short cave that connects the two islands, from the shady side to the sunny side. Inside the cave are many small fish: blue-striped grunt, blue tang, cocoa damselfish, and many others. The sun is illuminating the other side and distinct sunrays project down through the clear water. Large rocks and coral spring up from the bottom, and fish are everywhere, busily swimming about, and wondering who and what I am, and whether or not I am a threat. I'm happy that none wonder if I am edible.

A fabulous queen angelfish looks at me from the coral below, bright yellow with a dark blue crown on her forehead, and blue accents on the edges of her body. These stunning fish are big and flat and slip into narrow crevices to hide, but only after they come get a look at the newcomer to the reef. Another queen, the queen triggerfish, swims majestically through the crowd. She is green, with a flat body, blue lips, eyes decorated with yellow stripes, and blue edges on her fins. A drab grey triggerfish swimming along the edges of the reef acts as her foil.

A grey stingray glides along the bottom, then partially buries itself in the sand. Various little and curious damselfish dart about their tiny territories, sometimes rushing out in an attempt to keep me away from their gardens of algae. Damselfish are territorial, small, and sometimes fearless. They spend a lot of their time running off other fish who would eat their precious algae farms. They try to run me off too, by charging at me, turning broadside and flashing their fins.

Parrotfish, some green with red and yellow accents, others red and mottled with earth tones, lazily drift about the coral, occasionally scraping an audible bite off the rock with their beak-like mouths. Squirrelfish, always present, hide in caves and look out with their big dark eyes, while the stunning royal gramma hover upside down under rock ledges. These fantastic little fish, about the size and shape of a large bullet, are painted brilliant purple on the front half of their body, while the color fades to an equally brilliant yellow in the rear. Purple is a rare color in nature, and these fish display it proudly.

A Nassau grouper hides in a cave. I have my spear, but this shy fish is too big for me to eat in one sitting, so I don't try to shoot it. A strange pipefish, shaped like a long pencil, swims by. These fish are related to seahorses, and are very similar in structure, yet straight in shape. Like seahorses, the males brood the eggs in a pouch.

Schoolmaster snapper are abundant around the two large rocks on the sunny side of the swim-through, just the right size for dinner for a singlehander. I select one, get as close as I can, and take a shot, but my spear only hits rock, dulling the tip that wasn't too sharp to begin with. I keep trying, swimming around the rocks, slowly trying to get in position for a good shot with my pole spear. But all I hit is rock with two more attempts. Today the schoolmaster are safe. I give up on the spearfishing but continue on with the observation.

A lone spotfin butterflyfish, white with yellow fins, disc-shaped body, vertical black stripe through the eye, and a big black spot on the fin near the rear, swims away from me along the bottom. It is thought that these spots, which resemble an eye (and are thus called eyespots) aid in survival by sometimes fooling a predator into attacking the wrong part of the body. Other fish I see include ocean triggerfish, ocean surgeonfish, yellowtail damselfish, beaugregory, bluehead wrasse, yellow-cheek wrasse, stoplight parrotfish, and the curious and tiny sharpnose pufferfish.

Satiated with the fabulous reef and caves and all their inhabitants, I remount the 12-0, pull up the little grappling-hook anchor, and paddle back to *Sobrius*. Sitting at the navigation table and anxious to see what I got on video, I download the files from the camera to my computer. But in watching I realize that I didn't get a video of the swim-through cave, which was the highlight of the snorkel.

There's only one thing to do, and I put my wet wetsuit back on, gear up, and do it all again. However, this time, a bit closer to sunset, the lighting is different and it all seems fresh and new. On the other side of the swim-through, I am greeted by a huge crab, as big as a partially deflated basketball, at the base of the big rocks just past the cave. It takes little notice of me as it sits on the bottom eating something I can't identify. The crab's mouthparts remind me of industrial machines that devour scrap metal. Two horizontal plates move together, then open, and two vertical plates do the same, opening and closing one after the other. Little claws feed the machine with little bits of invisible food. Two enormous claws stand ready to defend the bizarre creature should I get too close, or perhaps to catch a small fish, should it get close enough.

On the other side of the swim-through, I decide to take another look in the cave, thinking maybe this time some strange creature will show itself. I turn on the video camera and approach the cave from the side, turn on the attached flashlight, and swim in. Dark and smooth rock walls taper into a hole in the back of the cave, but no creature comes out to greet my light.

I'm glad I got back in the water, just seeing the crab was worth it, and now I have video of the swim-through (posted on YouTube as Journey to the Ragged Islands, Episode 2).

As I sit in the cockpit eating dinner, the sun moves slowly to the horizon while the sky goes through a series of color changes which reflect off the water and captivate my conscious mind. I feel the blessing of the adventure, the odyssey, and the communion with nature. All is exactly as it should be.

March 20

My plans each day are dictated by the weather, and the forecast this morning predicts that the wind will pick up out of the southeast tonight, bringing with it a possibility of squalls. I need to move somewhere that will provide shelter from southeast winds. The southern tip of Cat Island seems logical, possibly the Hawks Nest area on the southwest corner. I free Dr. Spock from the sand and we sail off anchor. The wind is coming from 190 degrees (south-southeast) and we sail at 5 knots in 10 knots of breeze.

I study the chart as we sail south; Whale Creek looks interesting and should provide the protection we need. There appears to be no civilization in the area, and a creek that leads inland looks intriguing. We sail for the rest of the morning across clear blue water, occasionally passing over dark coral structures, with Cat Island and its low green hills a few miles to port.

When we reach the south end of the island, I direct my little ship to the east side of Whale Creek and survey the depth, which has gradually dropped to six feet. When I feel safe, I drop Dr. Spock, then drift some more and drop the Fortress anchor – two anchors in a V pattern, since there may be squalls tonight.

I put on my mask and get in the water to investigate.

Although the bottom looks like sand from the surface, a layer of hard rock lies underneath only a thin covering of sand – not ideal for the anchors. In addition, little bits of coral that I could not see from above dot the bottom. I don't like anchoring over any coral, as the chain will destroy it, raking the bottom as we drift side-to-side.

I pick up the anchors and move them both by hand while holding my breath, which is a lot of work. It probably would have been easier to do all this from the boat, I think as I walk on the bottom with the heavy Vulcan anchor in hand. One way or another, it must be done. I don't want to harm any coral, and I like being underwater anyway.

Location: 24° 11.69'N, 75° 26.81'W

With the anchors moved away from the coral nursery and set in deeper sand, I get out the 12-0, put on a big straw hat to protect me from the burning sun, and paddle towards the creek to see where it leads and what wonders it has to show me.

A current flows out of Whale Creek at its broad and shallow mouth. Brown rocks cover the bottom and line the shore. Inside the creek, the bottom, visible in the clear water, becomes sandy and the creek narrows to about 20 yards. Mangroves with their thick tangled roots take up residence and dominate the banks further upstream.

I paddle against the current and the wind for about a mile, see a few tall wading birds, and step off onto the bank for a little exploration. I walk around in the bush, like I did on the north point of Cat Island and also at Bonefish Point. I feel attracted to places where few humans have been. I imagine that I might find treasure, pirate treasure perhaps, or other valuables washed ashore. If it be there, and nobody else looks, then I'm sure to find it.

Still treasureless, I start back downstream and a small nurse shark swims by. Little fish swim in the shelter and shade of the twisted mangrove roots as I casually drift and paddle back towards the mouth of the creek. Mangroves not only provide habitat for adult fish, but they are also nurseries for many pelagic species.

At the mouth of the creek, I beach the 12-0 and walk along the rocky shore of the bay. The water looks to be about four-feet deep and the bank is composed of big rocks with caves and chasms between. This looks like a place I should spearfish, and I might even see an octopus in one of the caves.

Later I return with my snorkeling gear, video camera, and pole spear. The fish are abundant, swimming among the rocks and hiding in the caves. Schoolmaster snapper tempt my spear, but none fall prey to its three-pronged tip. The fish are too quick, and my skill is lacking. Finally my spear strikes one, but the force of the spear is not great enough to penetrate the hard scales of the little snapper, and it manages to escape.

A big porcupine pufferfish stares at me from within a cave. These fish always look happy, similar to the way dolphin always look like they're smiling. Sea anemones are a welcome sight, rare these days. I see all of my usual fish friends, as well as some less-common fish, like four nurse sharks lying in caves, and a green moray eel which pokes its head and a foot of its body out of a cave, then quickly retreats. A speckled hind makes an appearance – a member of the grouper family but too pretty to shoot. A crustacean that looks like a lobster without a head hides in a crevice, or maybe it is a lobster, hiding its head. I don't shoot it, because I'm not sure what it is, and I'd be shooting it in the back, which just doesn't seem right.

*The caves along the bank at Whale Creek, Cat Island, provide habitat for a wide variety of sea creatures, like this nurse shark, one of many that I saw here.*

*This green moray eel bit my camera when I stuck it in its cave!*

I look over my shoulder often, worried that a shark might be creeping up behind me. The 12-0 is leashed to my ankle as I swim in and out of the rocks, poking my head in caves, illuminating dark places with my flashlight, while the surfboard bumps into the sharp rocks without complaining.

Finding places like this, where natural beauty abounds and the scar of man is absent, fills me with a sense of wonder. How can a place so spectacular be unoccupied by all others? I only saw two boats today, one large trawler that anchored a couple miles east, and one sailboat that passed by on the horizon, and I have this rocky shoreline all to myself. I slowly swim about, gazing in wide wonder at the creatures around me as they gaze back at me. I am one with nature, and nature is one with me.

I wondered before I left if I would ever get bored and run out of things to do, but so far my days are filled. If not sailing, snorkeling, or walking on the islands, I'm organizing things on the boat, planning where to go next, studying the charts, listening to the weather report, writing, playing the mandolin, or painting with the watercolor set that my father gave me. Cut off from society, options are limited, and this limitation seems to allow me to more easily accept simplicity. Just as the lack of people brings about solitude instead of loneliness, the lack of options brings about simplicity instead of boredom.

Although it's been difficult to decide where to go, I'm considering Calabash Bay, Long Island, for tomorrow's destination. A cold front should pass through tomorrow; the wind is south now, but will shift to the west tomorrow, then north tomorrow night. It's tough to find shelter from all these directions.

It is important for a sailboat to be anchored somewhere where the wind comes from the direction of land, that way the wind doesn't have any fetch and thus waves don't build before reaching the vessel. Also, if the anchor fails, the boat will drift away from land. If the wind blows from the big open water, then waves will pummel the boat, and the wind and waves will be trying to push it onshore. Where to anchor safely is something the island-hopping sailor must think about every day.

For now, *Sobrius* and I are protected by Cat Island from south and SSW winds, but if the wind shifts any more west than this, then we will be in the wrong place. The two anchors will surely hold us well tonight, and I'll wake up early and sail away tomorrow.

Before sunset, I hank the small #4 jib to the forestay, and discover that the uppermost hank (the spring-loaded clip that attaches the sail to the forestay) is broken. It must have broken during the passage from Florida. I replace it with a carabiner. These things certainly come in handy. I also bring the 12-0 inside and lash it to the mast-compression post.

*Sobrius* is packed and ready for an early departure tomorrow. I'm setting the alarm and getting up well before sunrise so we can get moving in the dark, and arrive before sunset. It might take a while, as we will be going slightly upwind for about 40 nautical miles.

I wake up at 2:40 am, well before the alarm is scheduled to go off. I think I can make it all the way to Thompson Bay if I leave early, where the protection will be very good. A few blue holes are shown on the chart around the Thompson Bay area. Three are right behind Eva's Cay, on the south end of the bay, one is offshore a few miles, and another is right by the beach a couple miles south, near Pratt's Hill. I feel drawn to explore this place.

*"Look deep into nature, and you will understand everything better."*
Albert Einstein

## LONG ISLAND

After predawn coffee and oatmeal, I pull up the anchors and set sail in the dark and serene Bahamian night. The stars are beyond magnificent and I stare transfixed at the brilliant sky map as I hand steer on a port tack making 5 knots beating into the wind and small waves. On a night like this, all is good in the world, and the beauty and magic of the setting fill me with a sense of fantasy that blends into and encompasses the world around me. No longer am I on a boat in The Bahamas, rather I am floating on the surface of a planet on the edge of a galaxy populated with innumerable and infinitely fascinating heavenly bodies.

After the lonely white lights of Hawks Nest, on the southern point of Cat Island, are well behind on the dark horizon, I turn to port and put us on a starboard tack (with the wind coming from starboard). Curiously, the speed drops to 4 knots, and I also find trimming the jib requires a different setting of the jib car compared to port tack, which suggests to me that I might need to adjust the mast. I remember that, while docked at Spanish Wells, I noticed a bend in it. I take mental note of this and will deal with it at anchor in the near future.

I try to let my mind relax and focus on the extraordinary surroundings. The sky and the water are both dark, but speckled with light. Confused and choppy waves become more regular and organized as the depth drops from 40' to over 1000' as we pass over the edge of the underwater plateau that makes up the Cat Island Bank. The deep water feels safe and allows me to relax a bit more, knowing that no reef can threaten us here. We are once again sailing across the open ocean, under the stars, and a thousand feet above anything solid.

Solitude I have been finding out on the open water, but it's a lot of work. The body never gets to completely relax out here, as the boat is always moving, and I'm always adjusting my position to keep balance. Solo sailing asks much of the skipper, but the rewards are proportional to the effort, and both are great.

As the sun returns to our side of the Earth, I notice that there is very little traffic here, just one sportfishing boat going back and forth across the same spot a few miles away (setting off my AIS alarm each time), one mega yacht in the distance, and one sailboat also far away. All these boats eventually disappear, and *Sobrius* and I again have our own little piece of the ocean, and the ocean has us.

I consider going to Conception Island instead of Long Island, and turn that way. But then I remember reading that it's necessary to have clear skies in order to see the coral heads when entering the anchorage there, and clear skies are unlikely today. I feel it prudent to keep sailing for Long Island, and I turn us back that way. My plans are so flexible that they can change from minute-to-minute, and since I am alone, I can make spontaneous decisions without debate.

I hand steer for the rest of the day, enjoying the experience, riding up and down the blue waves, making the best of the wind and water, focusing on clouds in the distance to keep course.

Many hours later, Long Island rises over the horizon with cliffs facing the ocean, the Columbus monument pointing skyward above the cliffs, sandy beaches below, and a bright blue bay on the north end of the island. Calabash Bay is the second bay, and it's time for me to find a spot to anchor before it gets dark. I sail past all the reefs around the outside of the bay, opting for the widest, and thus safest, entry. I sail past the anchored mega yacht *Aspen Alternative* and into the clear blue waters of Calabash Bay.

A resort sits at the north end of this bay, the end where I hope to find protection from the wind. But between here and there is shallow water and two reefs I must avoid. A small catamaran zips around, unafraid of the reefs, then comes by for a look at *Sobrius* – I wave to the couple sailing it and they wave back with the enthusiasm of a young couple having a grand time on vacation. My attention quickly returns to the instruments, and when I reach the north end of Calabash Bay, I anchor in 6 feet of water with two anchors, which I hand set in the grassy seafloor.

Location: 23° 39.44'N, 75° 20.28'W

Dinner is 3 small potatoes, half an onion, a can of chili, a can of sardines, a sleeve of crackers, and my soul is satisfied. While washing the dishes in a bucket of seawater, I notice that the wooden spoon I've been using is the one that I carved while canoeing in the Okefenokee, on the trip where the notion of becoming a sailor seized me (as described in my previous book *Becoming a Sailor*). That was December of 2015, 2-and-a-half years ago, and now here I am, sailing solo all through The Bahamas; my dream has become reality, and this realization makes me stop what I'm doing and smile for a moment.

Tomorrow morning I'll catch the weather forecast and if there is no west wind, I'll probably move to the bay north of this one. It looks rugged and interesting, with cliffs, a beach, a rocky shoreline, and possibly access to the north point of Long Island, where there may be surf.

In the morning, I have the urge to keep moving, to sail somewhere new, again, but I try to shake the urge. I remember that I wanted to explore the bay to the north, so I get out the 12-0 and my mask and start paddling out and around the point separating the two bays.

A little house sits on the point, somewhat protected from the sea by a little concrete wall. The windows are all boarded up and the shingles are peeling off in places. A small crescent-shaped sandy beach graces the back yard facing a cove. On both sides of the little beach by the house are tall rocks. A dark coral reef passes beneath me as I casually paddle.

I paddle north across water that seems to be 20-30 feet deep, aiming at the point across the bay. I count my paddle strokes to keep focused as land gets further away to my right. To my left is open water. I pass over two reefs and take mental note that they might be good dive sites. After 600 strokes, I am at the north end of the northernmost bay of Long Island. There are neither boats nor any sign of any civilization here and the bay is strikingly beautiful. I bob in the water next to an undercut rocky wall leading up a hill to scrubby green vegetation. The rocks give way to sand deeper in the bay, and a long beach leads to more rocks further south, then to the point where the house is hidden by vegetation. Beyond the point and out of sight lies *Sobrius* and Calabash Bay.

Swell is wrapping around the north point and into the bay; otherwise this place looks ideal for anchoring. The bottom, quite visible in the clear and nearly invisible water, is white sand with a few patches of coral. A tall hill dotted with caves blocks the north and east winds.

A shallow reef near the shore beckons and I answer the call.

Underwater I seem to hover weightless above the reef with its hypnotizing shapes and colors, like a cloud floating over a city on a different planet. I've entered an alternate universe that's been right below me all along, and I don't want to leave; the fish coax me to stay down with them. *They can breathe water, why can't I?* But soon it becomes clear, as my chest contracts in spasms, that I must return to my world to fill my lungs with air.

I paddle back closer to shore, taking in the scenery and enjoying the exploration of this uninhabited cove. I would move to this bay, but the swell seems more intense here. So I go back to *Sobrius* and gear up for some diving and spearfishing on the nearby reef.

I'm paddling the 12-0 out towards the reef, gazing out over the great expanse of blue water ahead, letting my mind wander and enjoying the view when a wave rocks my little craft unexpectedly. The craft shifts left and I counter to the right, but the speed of my reaction does not make up for my lack of focus, and I spill into the water like a fool, along with the majority of my gear. The fins are floating, so I grab them and put them back on the board. The camera and spear are strapped to the board with a bungee cord, so they are safe, but the mask and the anchor are gone. I quickly swim to the bottom hoping to see them, but my vision is blurred by the saltwater. Two dark shapes on the bottom come into view, and I grab them both. One feels like my mask, and the other is surely the anchor.

With my gear retrieved, I remind myself to stay focused. *What if there was a huge shark next to me when I fell off*, I ask myself, remembering the shark at Cat Island.

I anchor the 12-0 just upwind of the reef and dive. Deep crevices full of fish cover the bottom. Grey snapper, schoolmaster snapper, a graysby that I could shoot – but it's too pretty, and all the usual suspects go about their business. I shoot at a schoolmaster, but he evades my weapon with a flick of his tail.

I see another schoolmaster, a good sized one, and follow him around, trying to get close enough for a shot. He swims into a small cave. I surface and breathe. I dive to the cave, see him, he sees me, and I shoot. I've got him!

But when I pull on the spear, it stays put; I can't get the spear out of the cave. The fish must be wedged between the rocks. I pull hard, then let go and surface, to breathe. I swim down and try again, wary now, as there must be fish blood in the water, and surely a shark somewhere nearby can smell it. I pull on the spear, to no avail. I need to try something different. I turn the spear counterclockwise until the tip unscrews, and the spear is free. I surface and breathe, holding the now-pointless spear.

But I want my kill, and my spear tip. So I go back down and look in the cave, but all I see is an empty plastic bottle with a hole in it, and in the hole is my spear tip. I killed a plastic bottle, and gave my spear tip to the reef. Some hunter I am!

The reef still holds my interest, so I dive a bit more, without the spear, just a spectator now. *I come in peace.* The fish are once again my friends, and I like it this way. They have either forgiven me or are indifferent to the fact that I've been shooting at them.

Back aboard *Sobrius*, we roll with the waves, which come at us from the port beam (directly from the left). We point into the wind, but the swell is wrapping into the bay and hits us broadside, rolling us generously. It's not very comfortable, but I don't really mind. I tell myself it's a lot like sailing at sea in waves – like the whole passage from Florida.

Another sailboat pulls into the bay from the south entrance, like I did. *B Zen* is a Canadian Sailcraft. Claude, the captain, calls me on the VHF, and we chat for a minute. He is a singlehander from Canada. He's going to Rum Cay tomorrow and invites me to join him. I thank him and tell him I might.


March 23

In the morning, *B Zen* is pulling away when I poke my head out of the cabin, which is ok because I don't really want to go to Rum Cay today. I'd like to go there sometime, but a ten-foot swell is coming and I think the waves will likely wrap into the anchorage at Rum Cay and make it quite uncomfortable. Besides, I want to go north to the next bay, the one I explored yesterday.

I pull the anchors and motor out of the bay, over the reef where I lost the spear tip, past the little house on the point, into the clear water of the north bay, past the reefs where I wanted to dive, and all the way to the north end of the bay, as far inside as I can get to try to escape the swell which wraps around the point like the fingers of a closing hand.

I want to try an anchoring technique I've read about – putting a second anchor off the side of the stern to hold the boat facing the waves instead of the wind. I steer us along the upwind edge of the area where I want to anchor, shift into neutral, and drop the Fortress off the stern, letting the line run free. I move to the bow as we slowly drift forward and when we come to a stop I drop Dr. Spock. I hold him just on the bottom until we start to drift backwards, then I let out about 70' of scope. I cleat this off and go to the stern and pull in the line on the lightweight aluminum Fortress. I do this until we face the waves head on, and the motion becomes quite preferable to yesterday's rolling.

Location 23° 40.25'N, 75° 20.51'W

Behind us, to the east, the blue water lightens and terminates at a yellow sandy beach in front of a green hill with a large dark spot that must be a cave. To the north is a brown, grey, and yellow rocky bluff where hill meets water, undercut by waves scouring out its bottom. About forty feet above the water, the jagged rocks of the bluff give way to thick vegetation where short tough-looking trees and green bushes, some dark and some light, spring out of grey crumbled rock. Above it all hangs the bright blue sky scattered with low white cumulus clouds. The scene commands me to stand still and stare, to absorb the beauty surrounding me before I do anything else.

Neither people nor any sign of civilization can be seen, so I swim naked to check the anchors, except for my mask and a dive knife strapped to my right calf. Dr. Spock lays on his side, spiked in, with the end of the shaft, where he is shackled to the chain, buried in the sand; the Fortress is almost completely buried. All around is clear, bright blue water over white sand, a silent, vast, and seemingly empty space through which I glide. The water caresses me and I am once again reunited with my first love. In this moment, all the work

I've done to get here, and all the money I've spent, are justified by the bliss that only raw nature can provide.

A shallow reef lies between *Sobrius* and land. I swim over for a quick look, and am greeted by colorful and curious fish as well as clusters of live coral. It looks like a perfect place for a safe snorkel while leashed to the 12-0.

Back onboard, I look up into the hills surrounding the cove. I'm excited to do some exploring on land; hopefully I can find a trail leading inland to the tall white cliffs and the Columbus monument on the north-facing point that I saw while sailing in two days ago.

The spot where *Sobrius* lies is where I snorkeled yesterday and chose as an ideal anchorage, and ideal it is. We are tucked in just enough to escape most of the swell and the bluff blocks most of the wind, which is about 15 knots out of the north today. This is exactly the sort of place I hoped to find during this trip – uninhabited, peaceful, serene, beautiful, with coral reef and an interesting shore... I could spend some time here, exploring, diving, writing. Perhaps this is the spot that will convince me to sit still for more than a day. So far two nights is the most I've stayed anywhere, and only twice have I done that.

Now the only question is what to so first: dive, explore land, or paint the scene.

Land exploration wins the decision, so I pack up long pants, hiking boots, my camera and a flashlight, then paddle to the beach behind us. On the sand, I change clothes and start making my way through the thick and thorny vegetation in the direction of the big dark cave that I saw from the bay. I pass a shallow pond before coming to the base of a rocky hill, and it's not long before I stand before a large and dark opening in a cliff made of very sharp and jagged rock. Somehow the rocks here have eroded in such a way as to leave them with a rough and pointy surface covered in sharp spikes, holes, bumps, divots, and cracks.

The cave is big enough for a few people to sit in, and while the floor is sand, the walls and ceiling are uneven and spikey, like the rock outside. The view from inside is spectacular, with the entire bay visible, as well as the point of land separating this bay from Calabash Bay. The water is an amazing shade of blue, almost glowing in its brilliance. My little red sailboat sits proudly as the bay's only occupant.

*Sobrius sits peacefully in one of the most beautiful and serene places I've ever been, the northernmost cove on the west side of Long Island, a place I named Serenity Cove.*

I stare out and clear my mind. I'm here, in The Bahamas, doing what I came to do. I think I'll call this place Serenity Cove, since it's not named on the chart.

The treasure hunter in me comes alive and I dig in the dirt behind a rock in the center of the cave. I find some charcoal, then a crab shell, more charcoal, and more bits of crab shell. The image of an Arawak Indian from ages ago, cooking crab over a fire, comes to mind as I dig down through time with my bare hands as treasure hunter becomes archaeologist.

I walk along the base of the cliffs and find many more caves, all different shapes and sizes, each one a new discovery to me. In one cave is a structure built of logs that looks like a crude shelter.

Surely this place was used by the natives of long ago, and perhaps by pirates, castaways, or shipwrecked sailors, to stay out of the driving rain and the fierce winds of tropical storms, eating crabs cooked over an open flame.

On the way down, I find a small cave with four buoys labeled "Sea King" tucked inside, either pushed in by storm surge or stashed by someone for future use, another mystery of the caves of Serenity Cove.

Back aboard *Sobrius*, I do the next obvious thing: gear up to snorkel. The reefs are calling and I intend to participate in whatever they have to offer. I determine to snorkel the shallow reef next to the boat while leashed to the 12-0, a good safe activity. Since the reef is so shallow, I add a second weight to my weight belt, so I can stay down without having to work to do so (we are more buoyant in shallow water since our lungs are not as compressed as they are when in deep water, thus we need more weight to stay down).

I mount the 12-0 and start paddling the short distance to the upwind side of the rocky shore next to the boat. Movement in the clear water to my right catches my eye. It's grey, and it's a shark. The black tips of its fins reveal it to be a blacktip reef shark, and it looks small, but I remember that the big shark didn't look so big the first time I saw it. A moment of fear grips, then releases me.

I get out the camera, turn it on, and stick it in the water. Remembering the problem I had with it last time I saw a shark, I pull the camera out of the water and look at its face to confirm it's on by looking for the red flashing light that indicates it is taking video. But I see no such light and realize that the camera is off. I try to turn it back on, but apparently the battery is dead, and once again I cannot get a shark on video.

I paddle on up the reef, looking back to see if the shark is following me. I'm developing new protocols to increase my safety. One is looking back for sharks following me. Another is not letting the surfboard leash drag behind me (I feel like this might have attracted the big shark, since it hit the water right where my leash was dragging).

When I reach the head of the reef, where I want to get in the water, I stop and look around for a minute – another new protocol – to see if the shark is around. And sure enough, there it is, clearly checking me out, and I feel the fear course through me. I want to run; I don't want to dive anymore, especially without the camera working. But I sit still, pull the leash in (it should have already been in) and sit on it. I can feel my heart beating; I imagine the shark hitting the board and knocking me into the water. But I stop these negative thoughts and slowly paddle back to safety. I return to *Sobrius* dry.

I plug the camera in to charge it, take off my wetsuit, booties, weight belt, and knife, then go up on deck. The water is incredibly clear and I stand at the mast looking around for the shark and wondering if this predator followed me to the boat.

Indeed, something large and brown is moving towards the boat about 100 yards away. Visions of the big shark at Cat Island surface in my mind. A wake forms and a head pokes up out of the water, the head of a sea turtle – a big and harmless animal, my favorite kind! But my heart is racing. Nature is all around here; I don't even have to get in the water. This place is wild!

I love Serenity Cove, but tomorrow might be the time to leave. Monday we should have strong ENE winds, squalls, and the arrival of a 10' swell, which would not be good here, as even small swell wraps into this otherwise peaceful bay. The wind tomorrow should make for a fun broad reach to Thompson Bay, where no ocean swell can penetrate. As a surfer, I've always been drawn towards large swells, but now I'll be running *away from* swell for the first time in my life. After tomorrow I'd have to beat into the wind to get down there. The protection from the wind should be good in Thompson Bay and the blue holes beckon. Diving in blue holes is one of the main goals of this journey and the giant shark scared me away from the only one I've gotten near so far.

On the other hand, the conditions here tomorrow would make for excellent diving. I could also paddle around the point to the north and explore a cove and maybe climb the hill to the white cliffs and the Columbus monument. Decisions…

A big catamaran is pulling into the bay. I peer at it through my binoculars then turn on the AIS to see if it transmits, to get its name and information. The name isn't on the screen, but I see it's from Jamaica. Yosemite

Sam is painted on the hulls, pointing his six-guns and firing away. It looks like a family with two grown children.

I want to dive on the reef in the deeper water and spearfish; company would be nice, so I attempt to hail the catamaran on the VHF.

"Big Jamaican catamaran, big Jamaican Catamaran, sailing vessel *Sobrius*."

No response.

"Big Jamaican catamaran, big Jamaican Catamaran, sailing vessel *Sobrius*."

Again, no response.

I suit up and head out solo, as I have every other time.

First, I snorkel the shallow reef close to the boat, where earlier I saw the shark. This is a casual dive, but I see some live coral and plenty of colorful fish, including for the first time a coney. The coney is a member of the grouper family, smaller than most grouper, dark brown on top of the body, abruptly changing to white below, with iridescent blue spots all over. It is truly a beautiful fish, and seeing one for the first time is like receiving a surprise gift.

After drifting across the shallow reef next to the rocky shore, I mount the 12-0 leashed to my ankle and paddle out to water about 25' deep, where I drop the little grappling anchor in sand next to what looks like a reef from above.

The water is clear, and fish swim about on the bottom, but most of the coral is dead. The skeletons of staghorn coral litter the bottom like a forest after a tornado. Roughly 95% of the coral on this reef is dead, and brown algae covers the crumbled and eroding structures built by the once-colorful coral.

A gag, an uncommon grouper with rectangular spots, swims away from me, watching me as it does. Rising towards the surface, I see a disturbing sight – a familiar black line with a loop in the end is sinking to the bottom while the free end of the surfboard leash fades into the distance. These two things are supposed to be attached to each other. I race for the surfboard, and catch it before it's lost forever, then drag it back close to the anchor, who's line is now on the bottom. I attach my spear to the leash, let it go, and dive to retrieve the anchor line, then catch the board again and tie the anchor line to the leash properly this time, avoiding what would have been a costly mistake.

I dive once more, and right away see what I've been looking for – a lionfish. These are invasive, exotic fish, native to the Pacific Ocean, that do great damage to reef ecosystems in the Atlantic Ocean. They are voracious predators and have no natural enemies in the Atlantic. Their spines carry a poison, and for the most part nothing has learned to eat them – except humans. They don't run away, because their spines, which hide in the rays of their fins, are their defense. When threatened, they sit still and extend their fins like a marine porcupine.

I stretch the surgical tubing on my spear, aim and release. The lionfish remains still, then jolts as the three prongs of the spear tip burst right through its body, and the fish is mine! I swim for the surface with my bleeding kill.

Back on the 12-0, with the bloody fish on deck, I have to retrieve the anchor, which is tied off to the very rear of the board. This is always a difficult task, made more so by the anxiety brought on by the bleeding fish on my board, especially after my recent encounters with sharks.

But soon I've got the anchor line in hand and easily pull up the anchor and paddle back to *Sobrius*. All is well.

A thick pair of gloves and gardening shears that I brought for this purpose allow me to cut off all of the lionfish's fins so as not to get poked with its poisonous spines. Then I clumsily fillet the little fish and make a stew with canned collard greens and spicy Rotel tomatoes, which is a fine meal indeed.

*Lionfish are invasive exotic fish, originally from the Pacific Ocean, that do great damage to reef ecosystems in the Atlantic. While their spines are very poisonous, their meat is quite edible, and they are so easy to shoot even I can hit one!*

March 24

The wind is north today, and tomorrow it will shift to ESE. With the 10' swell coming Monday or Tuesday, it's time to leave this magical place. I'll never forget Serenity Cove, and hope to return someday.

I pull the Fortress from the sand, then raise the main and sail up to Dr. Spock with the tiller tied off. I sit at the bow pulling the anchor rode in as *Sobrius* tacks forward. We are on a starboard tack moving away from the rocks when the anchor releases its grip from the sand and returns to the bow. I hoist the jib, return to the cockpit, and sail out of the bay. The engine is running just for safety, in case I need it to avoid disaster on one of the many reefs on the way out. But the water is deep and the wind powers us right along.

Sailing on this day is perfect – blue water, blue sky, little white cumulus clouds, and a friendly and cooperative wind, north at about 15 knots, while we sail SSE at about 5 knots. We sail all day, passing bluffs and coves that beckon me to come back and visit.

The water color is stunning, absolutely clear and a luminescent shade of blue green. It occasionally darkens as we cross over a reef, but mostly it's like sailing across an endless swimming pool.

*Sailing through the shallow waters of the west side of Long Island was an experience of endless and stunning beauty.*

While studying the chartplotter to make sure I'm not going to run into a reef or a wreck, a little "+" symbol catches my attention, and further investigation reveals it to be a blue hole! I knew there were a few around Thompson Bay, but this one is a surprise. It's a few miles ahead, just past Thompson Bay, and about 2.5 miles offshore. I alter course slightly and aim *Sobrius* towards the hole. Eventually I see a dark circle in the water, sail right over it, and the depth gauge confirms deep water here. My skin tingles with excitement from the anticipation of my first dive in a blue hole.

I maneuver upwind of the hole and heave-to, then move to the bow and release Dr. Spock. The anchor hits the bottom and does its job immediately, but *Sobrius* tacks and the mainsail fills. We accelerate forward, a dangerous situation to be in with the anchor in the water.

I let go of the chain and quickly go to the mast, where I release the main halyard, then the jib halyard. Our forward momentum jams the big shackle that attaches the chain to the anchor line in the bow roller and *Sobrius* lurches to a halt. I have to pull hard to free the shackle, and then I let out enough line to position us right next to the blue hole.

This was not a smooth anchoring and I'll have to modify my anchoring technique after this mishap. I should not have dropped the anchor when hove-to; I should have dropped the jib earlier then slowly sailed directly into the wind and released the main halyard before dropping the anchor. I must have been in a rush, excited to dive in the offshore blue hole.

When the sails are down and the anchor is set, I stand and gaze at dark blue circle in the light blue-green water. It looks to be about 50' across, and what lies beneath is unknown.

Location: 23° 16.49'N, 75° 08.52'W

*Blue holes are doors to another world that lies within the Earth. Entering them is both a privilege and a risk. Diving in this one, known locally as "The Whale Hole," was an experience I will never forget.*

Excited to dive my first blue hole, I am suited up and in the water within minutes of anchoring. I've got on my wetsuit, mask, snorkel, fins, dive knife, dive watch, and my weight belt. I also carry my spear – mainly for protection (or confidence) – and my GoPro video camera.

The sandy sea floor gives way to grey rock at the rim of the dark hole, but I can't see the bottom from the surface. I float motionless, peering down into the misty blue-grey abyss, breathing slowly and deeply, captivated by the otherworldly scene and the mystery within. It's similar to the freshwater sinkholes I dive in Florida, but being in the ocean raises the adventure-level considerably, and I'm anxious to find out what creatures live down there. I remember the legend of the Lusca, the sea monster that lives in blue holes, but push the thought from my mind as I try to meditate and relax.

Movement to my right and below catches my attention; something is coming out of the hole. A school of bar jack, bright silver fish with a curved blue stripe along the length of the body, swims out of the hole and off to my right. As they swim out, I swim in.

Rocky walls, like the inside of a corrugated pipe, lead down, down, down to a sandy bottom, which slopes further down to the right. I become negatively buoyant and sink without effort about halfway down. I check my dive watch, and it tells me the depth is 50', which is deeper than I expected. I note that I became negative around 25 feet, which is shallower than usual, and I remember the second weight in my weight belt, which I added at Serenity Cove to help me stay down in the shallow water. I'm wearing more weight than I need here. But this thought quickly fades as the bizarre scene fills my mind.

All is shades of blue grey at this depth: the curved rock walls, sand and crushed shell on the floor which slopes down to a blackness in the wall. A large and dark cave entrance opens at the bottom of the wall in the deep end like a great mouth leading into the depths of the Earth. In front of the great cave swims a school of fish, perhaps mackerel. All around me other fish add silver movement to the grey surroundings. After only a very brief stay on the bottom, I start for the surface, which seems far away, passing again the curved and bumpy rock walls on the way up. A great breath welcomes air back into my lungs. My dive time was 0:56 (56 seconds) and my maximum depth was 51'.

I float motionless and watch the timer on the dive watch, staying on the surface for three minutes. Then I dive again, this time into the deeper end. I sink the last 30' without effort, arch my back, and set down on the sandy bottom on my knees. I kneel before the dark cave like a pilgrim at a primitive house of worship when when something moves in the darkness of the great and mysterious cave. A big grey snapper, the biggest I've ever seen, comes out for a quick look, then retreats back into the cave, which is too big for my flashlight to illuminate. I shine the little light around anyway, hoping to see an octopus. I look up and the top of the blue hole is lit up by the sun, like a big light at the end of a tunnel. I spend fifteen seconds on the bottom before swimming up, but it feels like too much work, like I'm being sucked down. I wonder if a current might be pulling into the cave, because that's what it feels like. But before too long I'm breathing on the surface again. My dive time is 1:15 and the maximum depth 72'. I stay on the surface breathing deeply and slowly for four minutes before going back down.

My third dive takes me to the shallower end of the hole, and in front of another, smaller cave. I poke my head in for a quick look, then slowly ascend and take in the view of the walls on the way up. I see blue tang, a grey angelfish, grey snapper, and various other small silver fish. My dive time is 1:29 and the maximum depth 49'. My legs are tingling after the dive and I feel light headed. I give myself four minutes to recover on the surface; I know that tingling and light headedness are signs of oxygen deprivation, but I feel drawn to explore the inside of the smaller cave. Just one more dive, I'm not finished here.

I breathe slowly and deeply, then push all the air from my lungs, refill them with new air, and dive, with the top of my head pointing down for better hydrodynamics. I swim into the cave, shining my light around, looking for fish, or sea monsters. The cave is captivating but empty of life. I exit and see a school of small silver fish swimming about in synchronicity, a mesmerizing spectacle at the bottom of a magical place that I don't want to leave.

After one minute and twenty seconds, I look up and see the round light of the sun above, and slowly start to make my way back up. I think to myself, *this will be my last dive here, I'll quit while I'm*

*ahead and call it a day. Four dives in an offshore blue hole is plenty.*
I feel fine on the way up, and at fifteen feet, still feeling normal, I
put the snorkel back in my mouth, as I'm more comfortable
surfacing this way. But my mind starts to wander; I'm thinking about
something else. *Focus Paul, don't lose focus...* The world around me
darkens, changes, and I'm transported into another dimension.

I hear strange music, four quick rising notes, then four quick
descending notes, over and over. A scene starts to play out in my
head like a dream. I'm talking to someone; it's just me and the
person I'm talking to, but I'm looking at myself and the other person
is out of view. Beside me is a staircase leading up and the
background is otherwise white.

Suddenly I'm confused, disoriented, and my whole field of
vision turns white, with a horizontal brown line at the bottom of the
scene. It's very clear, this white and brown, and I see nothing else. I
don't know where I am, just floating in space, blind, between
dimensions. I feel water in my throat and I cough, then I gasp for air.
Still all I see is white with the brown stripe at the bottom. *Why can't
I see? Where am I?*

I realize my left hand is empty, the spear is gone, my right
hand holds the camera, and my vision is returning. I can see that I'm
in the water and *Sobrius* is in front of me about 100 yards away. I
don't know why I'm in the water, but I know I have to get back to
*Sobrius. I've fallen off the boat!*

My mind is confused and I am conscious of this as I swim for
*Sobrius.* It now becomes clear that I passed out while freediving and
the realization is shocking. Water got in my throat and somehow I
woke back up. I was dreaming while I was out. *How am I still alive?
Why am I still alive?*

I climb the boarding ladder and put my head in my hands as I
sit on the coachroof while water drips off my face and lands on deck.
I feel like an idiot whose foolhardy sense of invincibility has led to a
near-death experience. I feel like a child scolded by an angry mother.
I am crushed and defeated. My head feels like it is filled with jello
and thoughts move slowly and become lost in the viscous mass.

I briefly think about going back for the spear, but quickly
dismiss the idea. I remember the two scuba divers in college who
died going back into a cave for a lost fin. I let the spear go, so as not
to end up like them, dying for a lost object, and to show respect for

the blue hole. The lost spear will be a reminder of the mistakes I made today, and perhaps will remind me to never again freedive alone and deep. I think I'll set a limit for myself of 30' while solo.

Other than not diving with a buddy, I made at least four mistakes: 1) I drank coffee this morning, which increases the heartrate and thus lessens one's ability to conserve oxygen; 2) I ate before I dove, and digestion consumes oxygen; 3) I had too much weight in my weight belt which made surfacing more strenuous; 4) I didn't relax and meditate enough before the dive, which prepares the body and mind for the dive, instead I just got right in after anchoring. Any mistake while freediving can quickly lead to death, and I should have taken this dive much more seriously.


I feel compelled to leave this place and anchor somewhere safe. I don't like it here anymore. I hoist the main and sail up to the anchor, but *Sobrius* sails a bit too fast, putting dangerous tension on the anchor rode between tacks.

After getting the anchor up, I realize I'm not on my game. I try to think calmly, but my head isn't right. I tack, and the new leeward jib sheet gets caught on something at the base of the mast. I go forward to free it, but it's tangled in other lines and caught on a cleat. The jib flogs in the wind and the windward sheet wraps around me. *This is about to get ugly* I tell myself as the line caresses my neck. I drop what I'm doing at the mast and return to the cockpit, then steer us downwind so I can fix the sheets while the jib is blanketed by the main.

I use the tiller tamer to tie off the tiller so I can go forward. POP!

A piece of black plastic flies past my face as the tiller tamer explodes, releasing the tiller, which now swings free. I grab the tiller and set the autopilot, untangle the lines at the base of the mast, but then I see a line trailing in the water. It's the jib halyard.

This is all too much. I need to simplify things here before something really bad happens. I take the jib down and decide to go to the nearest safe place to anchor and call it a day.

I head directly east for Pratt's Hill, only another two miles away, and set the anchor in 7.7' of water. But I don't like my spot. It's high tide and shallow water lies to the north. The wind is supposed to shift to the East tonight, and it just doesn't seem like my anchor placement is right. I put on the gloves, start the engine, pull up the anchor, move further south and outside, and drop anchor again.

Location: 23° 16.71'N, 75° 06.83'W

The Bahamas once again have provided more adventure than I anticipated. I'm reminded of the TV show "Fantasy Island." The host would often say to the egotistical man whose fantasy is to be a hero or to have a great adventure, "Be careful what you ask for." My mother used to say the same thing.

I feel like I might have gone to the other side for a moment while passed out. The video I took on the GoPro suggests I was unconscious for about 10 seconds. I feel like I had a brief chat with someone in authority, we agreed on something, then I came back. I must still have an important mission here, and I look forward to finding out what it is and hopefully achieving it. Life is fragile, precious, and unpredictable. We never know what the future holds for us, nor do we know how much time we have left.

I go to sleep after dinner, soon after the sun sets. But my dreams are disturbing. A mermaid visits me. She's got an alluring body and a pretty face, but her skin is green and speckled with black, like a fish, and she displays sharp pointy teeth. The disturbing mermaid tries to seduce me, and I'm interested but cautious. A negotiation follows and we seem to come to an agreement.

The deep water is the mermaid; it calls to me and welcomes me home whenever I visit. It shows me wonderful things – things other people don't get to see. I'm comfortable underwater, but sometimes too comfortable. I stayed down too long yesterday. I didn't feel like it was too long, but clearly it was. My watch tells me that my dive time was one minute and 37 seconds, and my maximum depth was 49'. This is not outside my normal diving parameters, and I felt fine the whole dive. That's the scary part. I had no warning. I just passed right out. I should have dropped my weight belt, but I didn't, because I didn't know what was happening. Even if I were carrying an emergency air source, which I considered buying before this voyage, I wouldn't have used it, because delirium preceded unconsciousness, and it all happened very quickly.

In the evening, I call my parents. I want to talk to my mother and father, but I don't want to tell them what happened at the blue hole, about almost drowning. I don't want them to worry about me. However, talking to them makes me feel better; they always fortify my spirit and I'm still shaken from the near-death experience.

March 25

In the still and quiet morning of Palm Sunday, a loud noise startles me as I sit in the cabin drinking hot peppermint tea. It sounds like an engine revving, or a whale exhaling. I jump up into the cockpit. It *is* a whale! A whale is swimming in front of *Sobrius*, in no more than 8' of water! It spouts again. It has bumps on its back just behind the blowhole, and a small dorsal fin way behind that. The whale spouts once more as it passes by, sending a cloud of mist into the sky.

It must be lost, I think, because it's heading south, from shallow water into more shallow water. Poor whale, I hope it's ok.

There's a blue hole on the chart close to the beach, about a mile away, and it's only 30' deep, or so says the chart. This one is within my new depth limit, and I can't resist diving in it, even though I almost died yesterday.

Part of me says *be more careful, you almost died*, while another part of me says *clearly you will not die before your time, otherwise you would have died yesterday*. Even if the latter is true, and deep down I think it is, I must be more careful. Maybe during our brief meeting yesterday, God (or a representative) was warning me that next time I screw up like this I will die, or maybe he was pulling me aside to give me an important message, perhaps telling me of important work I have to do.

Before leaving I use the chart and the compass to estimate the direction of the blue hole and find a landmark where I think it is. Then I paddle across clear shallow water towards the beach, just to the left and upwind of where I think the hole will be. I paddle up the remote beach and pass the spoils of an old abandoned dock leading to nowhere. Soon after, the hole becomes visible as a big dark patch of blue in the otherwise yellow-green surroundings.

I drop my little grappling-hook anchor upwind of the hole and drift over it.

I swim down into cloudy water to a grey and featureless bottom. A few fish swim in the periphery of my vision and a couple of upside-down jellyfish sit attached to the bottom, doing whatever it is they do. They are the size and shape of hamburgers and look like plants, except for the jellyfish body undulating where the bottom hamburger bun would be.

This is a weird place and I get creeped out on the third dive, overcome by a sudden uncomfortable feeling. I pull up the little anchor and make the long paddle back to *Sobrius*.

The chart shows two more blue holes close to Eva's Cay, in Thompson Bay, only a few short miles north. I pull up Dr. Spock and sail off to the north. We sail around a point on which stands a large two-story house with wrap-around porches that reminds me of Greek architecture, a modern-day fortress with a timeless view. The house sits on a rocky point above the water looking out over the bays to the north and south. Stairs lead down the rocky outcropping to platforms by the water.

I easily find the blue holes behind Eva's Cay and sail right over them. The depth gauge goes from 6 to 28 feet as we pass over, and I anchor in between them.

Location: 23° 19.30'N, 75° 07.64'W

I dive to check on the anchor and find Dr. Spock holds firmly to the bottom, even though it's composed of hard rock with just a thin covering of sand. I'm very impressed with this anchor, the Vulcan 15kg, and its ability to hold well in poor bottom conditions. I swim to both holes to investigate, then return to *Sobrius* and prepare for freediving.

Both of the holes are incredible, and full of fish. A hogfish swims in front of me, making eye contact before disappearing. Mackerel school in one hole, but not the other. Mangrove snapper are abundant in both, as well as schoolmaster snapper with their yellow stripes. A Nassau grouper looks at me, then hides. Blue tang, beautiful and occupying almost every dive site, are here as well, basking in their blueness. Caves in both holes intrigue and invite.

A fishing trap, a square mesh box, lies rusting on the bottom of the hole closer to *Sobrius*, in front of a beckoning cave. I still hope to see an octopus. Inside the cave is a large school of small mangrove snapper, although one is very big. Blue tang lounge near the ceiling, and a lionfish, lucky that I lost my spear, occupies an upper niche in the wall.

I turn around and the cave entrance, curved on top and flat on the bottom, is lit up by the sun, like a glowing blue mouth. The 12-0 waits for me on the surface, 30' above.

In the hole further from the boat, I swim down towards a series of rocky shelves. Spadefish, triangular, flat, and with vertical black stripes, hang suspended in the water, together in a group of six. Blue tang lead me deeper into the darkness yet toward a light within the cave. It must be a pass-through to the other side.

While swimming through the cave within the blue hole, I feel the way an astronaut on a spacewalk must feel, an explorer in a different world, transiting between dimensions in a place where humans were never meant to be. I envy the fish and I want to stay and become like them. It is only prudence and the conscious knowledge that I will soon need air that keeps me moving; I would rather stop and remain here for hours

A school of snapper, at least 20 of them, swim across the light of the exit. I turn around, and take it all in: light behind me, light in front of me, dark walls of rock shelves all around me, and fish everywhere I look. The sunlight makes a bright circle of light on the other side. I swim over the sandy bottom of the exit and into the blue light, then up towards the sun.

*The blue holes by Eva's Cay, Long Island, were spectacular and easy to access. This photo was taken inside a cave about 30' down.*

Later in the day a small fishing boat, *My Athena*, motors over the blue holes while a boy with a hand line fishes while looking expectantly down into the depths. We all exchange a wave and a smile.

In the morning, I move to the lee of Salt Pond Cay. I could have gone into the main anchorage of Thompson Bay, but the spot I'm in is removed from the cluster of boats there, and I certainly didn't come to these islands to be surrounded by people and other boats; I've got plenty of that at home.
Location: 23° 20.62'N, 75° 08.28'W

I paddle to shore, which is about a mile away, with my trash in a black plastic bag in front of me. I pass a large commercial fishing boat, *Southern Comfort*, which is tied up to the government dock, and exchange a wave with the captain, a big man with a big smile.

I find a trash can on shore, but the civilization is sparse to say the least, so I get back on my board and paddle north along the rocky shoreline to the next dock. I find a grocery store and outside I meet a local fisherman, Danny. He's a big friendly man with the unique

Bahamian accent which sounds like a cross between British and Caribbean. We chat for a minute while standing on the front porch overlooking Thompson Bay. He points out his boat, a fishing trawler, in the bay. Danny asks me where I intend to sail next, and he agrees that I should go to the Jumentos Cays.

Inside I buy apples, spinach, cheese, coat hangers for my clothes, cookies, and some canned goods. Then I walk to a grill and order a fish burger from Tyrone. Tyrone surprises me by asking if I am anchored out by Eva's Cay.

"I was yesterday" I answer.

It turns out Tyrone is the skipper of *My Athena*, and he recognizes me from yesterday. I tell him my story of almost drowning in the blue hole, which he knows as "The Whale Hole." He listens intently with one eye squinted shut and his elbows on the bar.

"That's a great story!" he exclaims. I'm glad he didn't call me an idiot.

Back at the dock, I meet Mary and Peter, a cruising couple. She tells me I look like Jesus.

"I've heard that before."

She then goes on to tell me about her daughter, who also has never married, and is a veterinarian in Columbia, South Carolina. At the dock is a well-tanned man in a long white apron efficiently cleaning fish and throwing the scraps in the water, which are then eaten by a large nurse shark. I tell him my story about the encounter with the oceanic whitetip shark, curious about how the locals think of sharks and if they are afraid of them too. I expect him to tell me that sharks aren't dangerous unless you are spearfishing.

"Those things will *eat*-cha" he responds gruffly as he slices into a big grouper with a long knife, countering my expectation.

Peter and Mary invite me to a happy hour on the cruiser's beach at 4:30. It's a long way from my removed anchorage, but I'd like to meet some people and I need some more exercise. At 4:00 I set out for the one-and-a-half-mile paddle.

I meet a handful of friendly sailors at the beach. I bring one of two sleeves of chocolate chip cookies that I bought at the grocery store, which I'm happy to share because I already ate half the cookies in the other sleeve; I have no self-control with chocolate-chip cookies. The big hit of the potluck is curried tuna, and someone else made miniature pizza bites, which were even better with the curried tuna on top.

One of the sailors is talking about his plywood and fiberglass trimaran that circumnavigated before he bought it.

"I asked the seller – when do you reef it?" he says. "The guy tells me at ten knots. 'Ten knots', I say, 'that's not very much wind'. No, 'ten knots *boat speed*!' the seller tells me."

An unoccupied dinghy starts slowly drifting away from the sandy beach and Mary wades in after it, catches the dinghy, then pulls up its anchor to inspect. She holds it up for all to see. The collapsible anchor, which is just like mine, was collapsed, so it could not hook the bottom. We all get a good laugh out of this.

Mary tells me I should move into the main anchorage in the bay before the squall coming tonight. It's calm now, but tonight we are expecting squalls with 25-30 knots of wind, which should remain in the 20's for a few days. I like being out by myself, away from all the other boats, but it's hard to explain this to her. Mainly I'd be worried that other boats might drag anchor and run into me. Out by myself, this won't happen, and I can't drag into anyone else either.

I paddle back to my secluded floating home as the sun sets across the Long Island Bight. I should be protected from the coming wind by the little island in front of me, and I've got two anchors down.

I put all my dirty clothes in the cockpit anticipating the rain, and this is how I plan to "wash" my clothes.

Heavy rain indeed comes in the night drumming loudly on the deck, along with the forecasted wind which howls in the rigging. In the morning the rain has ceased, but the wind is still strong and loud. I run a line through the legs and arms of all my wet clothes and string them up between the mast and the end of the boom. They eventually dry and seem cleaner, and I hang them on my new clothes hangers.

Although the two anchors hold well, *Sobrius* rolls back and forth in the waves that wrap around the little island, and I'm getting tired of being here. I crave some nature, and I want to try sailing under double-reefed main and my storm jib, which I've never used.

Within an hour of getting the idea, I'm sailing out of Thompson Bay and heading north, making 5 knots in 25 knots of wind gusting to 30, in comfort. I like this sail combination, and I should use it in the future in winds over 20 knots.

*Sobrius* and I sail around Indian Hole Point, then in and out of Miller's Bay, which is beautiful, but not very protected from the strong ENE wind.

We sail into the next cove to the north, just south of Whale Head. This looks like it could be a nice place to anchor, and two other sailboats are in here, a monohull and a catamaran. I almost stop, but the sailing is too much fun, and I turn us downwind and back out into the bight.

The next bay, by the town of Morris, is also quite picturesque and inviting. We sail in, tack, and sail back out around some big rocks. Tacking the storm jib is easy because it's so small and the sheets don't snag anything since the clew is well in front of the mast.

We sail around Dilda Rocks, where a couple is walking on the beach, then into the lee of the majestic Bain's Bluff. A white ketch is tied to a mooring; two houses sit high up on a hill. I sail past the ketch and the houses, survey the area, which looks like ten feet of water over sand facing tall cliffs full of caves. The high bluff is blocking the wind almost completely and the scene is one of majestic natural beauty. I let Dr. Spock fall after dropping both sails.

Location: 23° 26.34'N, 75° 13.74'W

The water is much calmer here than where we were this morning, and the scenery is far superior. I dive on the anchor and Spock is buried almost completely in the fine white sand. Then I get on the 12-0 and head to shore, where I snorkel in the shallows at the base of the undercut cliffs, which rise vertically out of the horizontal sand bottom.

The water at the base of the cliffs is only four feet deep and little mounds of coral and rock are spread out in front of underwater caves and ledges. The usual fish are here and all are my friends now, as I no longer have a spear. I feel welcomed by their presence, and somewhat guilty for having wanted to kill them.

The steep and harsh shore looks like the next setting of land exploration and adventure with rocks, cliffs, caves, and tall hills to climb. Since the wind is supposed to stay strong for a few more days, I might stay here for more than one night and check out the caves tomorrow. It's a bizarre landscape full of character and mystery.

I feel much more comfortable here, immediately so, not just because the water is calmer and the wind is less than in Thompson Bay – that makes it physically more comfortable – but I feel emotionally more comfortable too, because I'm away from town, other boats, people, and civilization. But perhaps more so because of the natural beauty here, where I am reunited with my first love – *nature*.

In the morning, I paddle to shore with a backpack containing blue jeans, hiking boots, my camera, and a flashlight. I want to explore the hills, cliffs and caves. I want to find pirate treasure, or at least see something interesting.

A cleft in the hill leads to a rocky beach with a small arch cut in the rock three feet above the water. A black line is wrapped around the arch. I pull the surfboard out of the water and leash it to the black line, then change into the jeans and boots.

The landscape is made up of jagged rock, small trees with thorns, cacti, and vines with thorns. A little way up the hill I find a small cave, big enough to crawl into. I get out my flashlight then smell something familiar and out-of-place. It smells like cow or horse manure, and I notice the ground is covered with small bits of feces the size and shape of rabbit pellets. I crawl in the cave anyway. But this cave quickly pinches off, too small for me to go any further.

I am reminded of the times I spent spelunking in West Virginia. My friends and I used to find caves using antiquated descriptions found in the West Virginia Geological Survey book at the library downtown. We would photocopy a map and description from the book, and then try to find the cave entrance. The caves would go on for miles underground, opening into huge rooms or closing to tiny pinches. We followed underground creeks, found waterfalls, and saw all sorts of magnificent and otherworldly structures built from eons of dripping water precipitating minerals.

After scrambling around the cliffs near the shore, I climb the hill to the top, where I find a loose stone wall, leading to the concrete ruins of a house. Just two walls remain, nearly hidden by thick vegetation. One is a section of a corner and another frames a square window opening. Another wall lies on the ground at the other side of the ruin. This place must have had a spectacular view in its day, looking out across the vast blue water to the south, west and north, and across green land to the east.

The going is slow as I work my way back down the hill, and a cactus manages to insert a half dozen spines into the knuckles of my left hand. I notice a few holes in the rocky ground, leading straight down into blackness. I peer inside, looking for treasure, but find none.

I put my shorts back on and paddle around the bluff, to the cove with the houses. A wooden stairway leads down to a platform over the clear shallow water. A ladder stands ready to help someone down.

Around the corner is a picturesque small cove with a sandy beach and two houses. Hammocks and beach chairs sit under palm trees waiting for someone who wants to relax. The green hills encircle and rise behind the houses, creating an atmosphere of seclusion and privacy.

I paddle around the last bend in the bluff and am exposed to the east wind, the wind that I escaped by anchoring behind the bluff. A big rock ahead of me is severely undercut and looks like a giant mushroom. One day it will fall into the water when its base can no longer support its weight.

*Bain's Bluff, Long Island, offered protection from strong east winds and provided a beautiful anchorage with a fine sand bottom, along with cliffs and caves to explore on land.*

Back onboard while eating lunch, guacamole with cheese and garlic-stuffed olives, I notice the aloe plant that I brought from home is about to fall into the water because the handle on the metal pot is breaking away. I lean over to untie it from the stern pulpit from which it hangs, but I'm too late. As soon as I touch it the handle gives way and the whole thing falls into the water.

I consider going after it, but it's chilly, and I don't feel like getting in the water. I assume it's ruined now anyway, by the salt water.

But after an hour passes I feel foolish for not rescuing my aloe plant. Even if the soil is ruined, the plant can still provide relief from at least one more sunburn. I dive to the bottom to retrieve it, and it's heavier than I expected.

*"Study nature, love nature, stay close to nature, it will never fail you."* Frank Lloyd Wright

## THE JUMENTOS CAYS

March 29

At 4:30 am I wake in the dark, make coffee and oatmeal, and start getting *Sobrius* ready for today's prodigious journey; I intend to sail to Water Cay, in the Jumentos Cays, by way of the shallow Comer Channel.

I've been a bit anxious about this journey for three reasons. First, the Jumentos Cays are remote and uninhabited – there is no help available should I run into trouble. The cruising guide devotes an entire paragraph warning its readers about all the potential dangers of this archipelago, essentially trying to convince us not to go there. Second, the Comer Channel is just barely deep enough at low tide for *Sobrius* to pass through. We will pass near high tide, but that means if we run aground we will really be in trouble, as the tide will only go out and leave us even more stuck. Third, the wind has been blowing east at 20 knots for two days now, which should have produced 4-6' waves. A six-foot wave would make water 3 feet shallower in its trough, and this could make the Comer channel impassable for us. Also, should there be a tidal current in the channel running against the waves, the conditions could be dangerous.

I stayed here at Bain's Bluff for an extra day to let the wind die down a little, and it is forecast to be 15-20 knots today. I hank on jib #4 and take the second reef out of the main, putting the first reef in. I turn on all the necessary electronics, stow everything that needs stowing, and go through all the usual pre-sail chores.

As soon as the sky provides enough light for me to be able to see the ketch on the mooring behind us, I raise the mainsail, but have to push the boom way out because we are not pointing into the wind. I don't know why this is, there must be a current here. With the main up and the tiller bungeed to center (because the tiller tamer broke), *Sobrius* eases forward as I pull up the anchor. In the lee of the big bluff, the wind is light this morning, and I'm able to pull us up to Dr. Spock without too much trouble.

A cargo ship crosses the horizon from right to left, probably going to Thompson Bay. Its dark silhouette stops and sits still, and I assume it's waiting for high tide, which I think will be at 7:30 am, a little before we reach the Comer Channel.

It is now a beautiful morning and I'm glad I left the bluff. We are making 5-6 knots at a bearing of 235°. The sky is cloudy, but the sun is rising behind us; its rays emanate in all directions, penetrating and illuminating the clouds between us.

With these winds, we should easily make it to Water Cay well before dark, and the Comer channel very near high tide.

Long Island is fading into the distance and purple and grey clouds hover over the thin strip of land on the horizon behind us. Above the sky is clear and turning bright blue while the horizon ahead has its own purple and grey clouds. The day is turning into a beautiful one, again.

As the sun rises, I take off my light jacket. I'm wearing a short-sleeve nylon shirt, blue jeans, sandals, and fingerless gloves from Home Depot back in St Petersburg, where I bought *Sobrius*. The gloves are almost worn out, after a year and a half of sailing.

Eventually, the chartplotter tells me we are in the Comer Channel, but all just looks like water in the real-world view. The channel has no buoys to mark its location, and the water is the same color in all directions. I trust the chartplotter, there is no other choice.

I can see three islands in the distance to starboard. I can't think of what they might be, so I zoom the chart out. Of course, it's Hog Cay, Leaf Cay, and White Cay in the Exumas! I'm no longer at Long Island, I'm passing south of the Exumas and into the Jumentos Cays for yet another chapter of my adventure.

A turn is coming in the channel, and I will need to gybe, so I set the tillerpilot and move to the bow to change the preventer from one side of the boat to the other. I really should rig two preventers so I don't have to do this chore in order to gybe.

While at the bow, the jib luffs and sweeps across my head, which is covered by the straw hat that I bought in Daytona Beach before an outdoor gig with my band I-Vibes, in which I'd be playing guitar in the sun. I like the hat because the wide brim slopes downward and provides a lot of sun protection. But the jib sweeps it right off my head and I watch helplessly as it falls into the water and fades into the distance. It disappears very quickly, and I just let it go.

I am reminded of the time I dropped my hat in the water somewhere in The Bahamas when I was a child. My father was at the helm and he mercifully turned the boat around to retrieve it. He didn't suspect it at the time, but I dropped the hat on purpose to see if he would do this, and he got the hat back for me, saying that I would need it. He passed my childish test. However, he treated me better than I treat myself, because I just let this hat go – partially because the channel is narrow and I don't want to risk running aground for a hat, and partially because I have two more hats.

Aside from losing my hat, it's been an easy passage through the Comer Channel so far. We sail almost straight downwind and after trying to sail wing-on-wing, which didn't work, I take the jib down. It was blanketed by the main and not helping our cause.

The preventer is now rigged, and the sailing is smooth. The depth is 9.8' – more than I expected – and we have no problems, making 4.5 knots under just the reefed main. The wind is about 15 knots, and the waves that I worried about yesterday are not here.

I'm really looking forward to making it to Water Cay. It's an island on the map that I've been looking at, reading about, and thinking about for over a year. Water Cay represents an exotic, remote, and far-away place to me, as well as adventure, exploration, and advanced sailing. Water Cay is a goal, and I am a goal-oriented man. If *Sobrius* and I successfully anchor at Water Cay, I'll feel like another dream has been realized, and the thought causes something inside me to expand as if joy is building up, ready to burst forth upon arrival.

We are now through the Comer Channel and I've chicken-gybed to port, put the jib back up, and we make 6.5 knots – hull speed. A chicken-gybe is turning 270°, tacking back through the wind, instead of gybing 90°, because gybing in a breeze over about 10 knots can be dangerous, with the wind trying to blow the sail and boom forward, into the rigging. It's much safer to tack, so instead of turning to port 90°, I turned to starboard 270° – bow to wind instead of stern to wind.

We sail on a beam reach. The water has become clear and the depth has increased to a more comfortable 13'. The Exumas are fading into the past, dipping down close to the horizon. I hope to see them in the future. The wind seems like it has increased to 20 knots, as forecasted, and we fly along as the sandy bottom, punctuated by dark patches of reef, passes below. Life couldn't be better!

As I stand in the cockpit, one hand on the tiller, taking in the dramatic scenery of water and sky, movement below catches my attention. Something is heading straight for us like a missile. It's a big fish of some sort – a shark! *These creatures, are they everywhere?* It swims up towards the boat, turns left and disappears, then returns for another look, swimming fast, effortlessly, like a living torpedo. Its body is brown, probably a lemon shark. A second shark comes into view from starboard, then they both disappear aft. I am left in a state of awe, staring into the clear water as reef glides by below.

Two swells, one from aft and another from port, are confusing the seas here. I occasionally have to steer into the waves, to port, so they don't slam into the hull and roll us. I got soaked by one earlier. But the nylon shirt I wear is now completely dry. This is why I don't wear cotton anymore. The shirt I wear is a work shirt. I wear them at work for the same reason; they wick away moisture and don't hold it, so when I work hard and sweat, they don't get wet. Likewise, when a wave soaks me, the shirt dries quickly.

I have to focus on the horizon, the GPS heading on the chartplotter, and watch for large waves coming from port. Mostly I watch a cloud for a target to steer towards, then I check the GPS heading on the chartplotter and the speed while my eye is there, then I look at the waves, back to the clouds… all the while my right arm is pulling and pushing, hard sometimes, on the tiller, constantly reacting to the waves and the heading. Waves coming from aft roll the boat quite a bit, necessitating constant vigilance on the tiller.

When I see a set of large waves coming from port, I turn into them, and the sails luff. I turn back into the wind on the backside of the wave, the sails fill, and we accelerate. But these waves come in sets of two or three, so I do it again, and maybe again. It's challenging, but I'm having fun, the water is beautiful and crystal clear, and I haven't seen another boat since the cargo ship this morning. All the sea is my playground today.

The water color keeps changing – bright blue one minute, then we go over a big reef and it gets really dark. Sand borders the reefs, and the water becomes bright again, but the clouds passing overhead cast their shadows on the water, darkening it again. The clouds move, and their shadows move with them. It's a strange and otherworldly phenomenon, this constantly changing water color, and it's hard to tell if a dark patch is a reef or the shadow of a cloud.

The hue of the water is not the only thing changing, the wind is getting stronger, and the waves are getting both bigger and more confused as swell comes from both aft and port. My hands are full as we speed across the crazy sea at 7 knots, beyond *Sobrius'* theoretical hull-speed.

*Land Ho!* Pear Cay comes into view off to port as a thin green line on the horizon, the first of the Jumentos Cays, the first one I've ever seen, and the island is a welcome sight that fills my heart with joy! Water Cay is now only 5 nm away, the sun is shining bright, and the water is glowing iridescent blue like a giant LED light. I imagine dropping Dr. Spock in the sand at Water Cay, making a pot of chili, and looking out at a new landscape, and the anticipation of arrival brings a smile to my face and goosebumps to my neck.

*There it is* – Water Cay emerges from the haze in the distance, revealing that it is indeed a real place, not just a point on the map – a real island, green and brown and white, rising up out of the blue water. It has its own little spot on the Earth, and I've found it!

But it's become hard to steer. We are now on a beam reach, and the Atlantic Ocean is just past the little rocks to port. The seas are confused, the wind is strong, and currents push through here. With the tide falling, the water of the Grand Bahama Bank is spilling out into the ocean, rushing through the passes between the little cays and emergent rocks to port, and trying to take us out with it. But *Sobrius* and I have other plans.

*Sobrius* swings left and right, the GPS heading jumps from 220° to 230° to 215°. My intended heading is 228°, and I do what I can to steer in that direction. We've got dry reef coming up to starboard, and giant emergent rocks on the left, surrounded by reef. Between the rocks I can see the open ocean. The wind still blows about 20 knots, and we sail between 6-7 knots.

Whitewater is exploding on reefs to port, shooting up into the air like geysers, warning me to stay away. About a quarter mile to starboard are more shallow reefs, ominously labeled "The Driers" on the charts, also warning me to stay away. The island I believe to be Water Cay in the distance looks like two islands, but then they merge into one as the land rises up over the horizon. More bits of land are to port, as is reef. We are in a narrow passage, but the water here is 20-30' and seems safe enough.

The waves still come from port, and whitecaps cover the surface of the water. Sometimes the reefs look green. The depth changes from 30' to the twenties when we cross a reef. This place is full of energy, and I am very grateful to have this opportunity to be here in this wild, wonderful, and dynamic sea. I'm also glad to be on a boat and not in the water with the sharks!

I am reminded of my ancestor Meriwether Lewis, of the Lewis and Clark expedition, as I venture alone into this uninhabited chain of islands. His presence in my head, and our relation, however distant, bring me confidence that I will make it safely to my destination. Like a talisman of good luck, I stand on the shoulders of my ancestors.

I hear a new sound, a rumbling. It could be the waves breaking on the islands in the distance, or it could be coming from my boat. New sounds always catch my attention and cause a bit of worry. I seem to feel a little vibration under my feet that's new. I hope there's nothing wrong with *Sobrius*. Perhaps we've snagged something like fishing gear, or perhaps a critical part of the boat is about to fall off. Perhaps I'm just being paranoid – I hope it's the waves.

*Ah, but now I've figured it out*. The new sound is just the sound of my own bow wake. The reason I can hear it is because the sea state is calming down. It's calming because we are now getting into the lee of a lot of reef and cays. "Barren Rock" lies between us and the ocean, says the paper chart, which lays on the bench beside me (I use both the chartplotter and the paper charts when approaching islands). The rocks and cays to port, between us and the open ocean, block the waves and calm the water around us, which is a nice relief. It was getting crazy for a while there, but the seas are now calm enough that I can hear the water being pushed aside as *Sobrius* moves forward. It's a nice change and my body relaxes a bit at the realization that all is well.

Water Cay grows to a full-size island and I steer closer to get a good look at the barren rocky shore, void of any signs of civilization, an anachronism in the modern world.

When we near the cove where I intend to anchor, I heave-to and drop the jib, then sail in under reefed main alone. I survey the cove, looking at the landscape and the ripples on the water, trying to determine what spot will best block the strong east wind. The next cove down looks better, and I sail in. I check the edges for depth. The gauge reads 7' when *Sobrius* abruptly decelerates, lurches forward, and I hear a grinding sound. We've hit a rock!

Quickly I steer to port as the keel scrapes the bottom; luckily, we don't come to a halt. The keel is cast iron, so I'm not too worried about it, but I am sorry for the "rock" which was probably coral. I shouldn't have hit it.

I see more rocks, and steer around them, out of this cove and back to the first one. I pick a sandy spot in 11' of water, luff the main by steering into the wind, move to the mast, release the halyard, then step to the bow and release Dr. Spock.

We've made it! We are successfully anchored at Water Cay, in the bay labeled "Fisherman's Anchorage" on the chart.

A curved sandy beach lines the shore straight ahead, to the right of the beach are cliffs with evidence of a recent landslide. Crushed trees lie underneath huge fallen rocks, giving an air of warning, as if the island has an attitude. Directly to the right is an undercut shore of jagged rocks warning me to keep away. To the left of the beach is a large mound of grey weathered conch shells followed by a low rocky shore leading to a point.

Palm trees cover the low hills protecting this cove from the wind. About a mile to the south stand two tall white cliffs with a gap between them that goes all the way down to the beach, like a missing tooth. A series of coves lies between here and the white cliffs. Behind us, a fishing boat crosses the horizon in the distance. *Maybe they will be my neighbors tonight. I hope I haven't parked in their spot.*

This is where I wanted to be, and here I am. It's one of the more remote islands of The Bahamas, far from any civilization, and it is an absolute privilege to be here.

Location: 23° 1.65'N, 75° 42.94'W

*Sobrius lies peacefully at anchor in the "Fisherman's Harbor" of Water Cay, a wild, remote, and starkly beautiful place.*

After standing at the bow taking in the exotic view (and looking for sharks) for a long time, I dive on the anchor, and my head is on a swivel while doing so. I've read in the cruising guide that fishermen use this anchorage and clean their catch, attracting sharks. I'm happy not to see any large predators, but the bottom is littered with conch shells, perhaps validating the guide's warning.

I thought I dropped the anchor in sand, but now I see the bottom is covered in grass. While Dr. Spock is not buried, he has bitten in and is holding firm, as the Vulcan always does. I've come to trust this anchor, and that's what I was hoping for when I bought it.

Next, I paddle to shore for a quick look around, and am stunned by the rugged beauty of this remote island. On the windward side of the narrow island, crumbly, jagged, and undercut cliffs look out at the Atlantic Ocean, reaching down to a rocky beach. Waves break on visible reef all along the uneven beach. An osprey holding a fish in its talons glides overhead without flapping its wings.

I stand surrounded by palm trees shorter than myself as another osprey hovers overhead, looking down at me. Or perhaps it's the same one. He just glides in place, slightly moving from left to right, as if monitoring my presence. Vines and short ground-covering plants sprawl across the hard-packed soil, avoiding the ever-present wind with their lack of height. The sparse and low vegetation makes this an easy landscape on which to move about.

A pond in the flat land below reflects the sky, and a wave breaks in the very shallow water between this cay and Little Water Cay to the north, which are almost the same island. It looks like I will have a lot to explore here and I look forward to an extended stay.

March 30

In the predawn morning, I stand naked on the bow, letting the rain wash the salt from my skin. This is the first freshwater I've had on me since leaving Florida. But either the rain evaporates instantly in the dry wind, or my skin soaks it all up. I'm not even wet when I go back inside.

The rolling of the boat in the swell wrapping around the island pestered me all night, and I use the engine to move us to starboard, where I drop the Fortress off the stern; I use this anchor to pull us so that we face the swell instead of the wind and we stop rolling side-to-side.

After sunrise, I paddle to the island and hike all over it – along the shore, taking many jaunts into the interior, just to see what's there. It looks like people have camped in the scrubby vegetation behind the beach.

I find a bird hopping around with a damaged wing. I get close to the brown bird, about the size of a blue jay, to see if I can help. I look to see if fishing line is wrapped around its wing, but I think its wing is just broken. I can't help it. *Sorry little guy*. I walk on, wishing I could have done something.

Cristina, my friend who lives in Miami, asked for a sea fan, and I actually found one in the sand right next to me when I was changing into my hiking clothes. I find more and strap them to the outside of the backpack.

I walk around the cut where Water Cay and Little Water Cay face each other across shallow water connected to the ocean. The shore here is heaped up with bits of broken coral and shells. I search through the overwhelming bits and find some interesting shells and many pieces of brain and staghorn coral, bleached white by the sun. I imagine giving the pieces to my nieces and telling them "This is staghorn coral; it's likely to go extinct in our lifetime."

Staghorn and elkhorn coral are critically endangered. I haven't seen any elkhorn on this trip, but I have seen live staghorn, which I didn't see in St Lucia, Puerto Rico, or the Abacos last year. Overall, I've been impressed with the amount of live coral I've seen on this journey through The Bahamas, but well over half the reef I have seen is dead. Three things are killing coral: disease, pollution, and bleaching from rising sea temperatures. Coral are very sensitive to changes in temperature and water chemistry. They need very clean, clear, low-nutrient water to survive, and only live within a small range of temperature. Coral also needs to be left alone, not touched by humans, or battered by anchors and chains.

The entire ocean side of this island is dominated by eroding cliffs, and I climb to the top and marvel at the view of the Atlantic. In one cove of a cliff lie scattered pieces of sun-bleached wood from something manmade. I also see shoes here, like waves tossed a wooden boat full of shoes into the cliff and smashed it to oblivion.

I feel the cool pricks of water on my skin, and I quickly put my camera away and strip down, trying to take another shower in the rain. But the result is the same, the water hits me and disappears.

I cross the island through the forest of miniature palm trees and emerge on the shore of the west side. I stop walking and take a minute to look out at the scene.

*Water Cay, Looking South – note that the tops of the palm trees are lower than my camera, which I am holding level with my face. The shallow water of the Grand Bahama Bank is to the right, and the Atlantic Ocean is on the left.*

For a moment, I have a feeling of anxiety brought on by the remoteness of this place. It's just me, *Sobrius*, and this island. There's no freshwater here, and without fishing gear, survival would be difficult. I'm totally dependent on being able to sail out of here, and civilization is very far away. This might be the farthest I've ever been from civilization. One moment, this is wonderful, immersed in nature and solitude. The next moment, it's scary, like being at the bottom of a blue hole, fantastic in spectacle, then frightening in the absence of air.

Hiking along the sharp rock by the water's edge, I see something bright blue in the water. It moves. Another appears, and I assume they must be fish – queen triggerfish is my guess. I'll have to return to dive here, and I take a mental note of the location.

A sailboat appears on the horizon. I find myself hoping it comes to anchor here and provide me with some company, contrary to my usual quest for solitude.

I paddle carefully with the backpack full of shells and heavy pieces of coral as we drift across the cove to *Sobrius*. I have to be very careful lifting it onboard, as I don't want to fall in. I remember the words of the cruising guide, that here can be found shells, solitude, and sharks and it recommended using "extreme caution" when swimming here. When I get in the water, I don't want it to be with a splash and cacophony of mishap.

But I have to snorkel, especially where I saw the blue fish, so I gear up and set out for the rocky shore in the cove south of me.

The 12-0 is leashed to my ankle as I descend into the clear water, only about 10 feet deep. As I guessed, two beautiful queen triggerfish swim about, along with blue tang, a school of French grunt, a graysby, and bluehead wrasse. I constantly look around for sharks, and sure enough, I see one swimming along the rocky shoreline. But it's a small shark, and it turns and swims away. I get it on video and continue swimming. But now I'm even more cautious and soon head back to the Fisherman's Harbor.

*I finally got a picture of a shark underwater while at Water Cay. This one was small and not at all threatening (unlike some of the other sharks I saw).*

The charts show a reef in the center of the cove where *Sobrius* lies at anchor, so I paddle that way, planning on drifting back to *Sobrius* across the cove. I snorkel with one hand on the 12-0, occasionally diving to little clusters of reef below, where colorful fish swim about. I see a big hogfish, grey snapper, and the usual other species of friendly reef fish.

My head constantly turns from one side to the other, looking to my left, then to my right, and also behind me, looking for sharks. A barracuda follows me, however these don't worry me. But they do warrant vigilance, so I keep an eye on it. It follows me. The water gets deeper, about 15 feet. Grass covers the bottom. I swim down to something shiny, but it's just a metal can. I look behind me and the barracuda is gone.

I swim back up to the 12-0, put a hand on it, and look around. Something below catches my eye, to the right, and a little ahead. It's big. It's grey. It's looking at me. It's *an enormous shark!* I can see its entire thick body, pointy fins, face, and its mouth. In a flash, I'm sitting on the board and pulling my fins out of the water. I have a moment of terror as I imagine the shark knocking me off the board and attacking me, ripping off my limbs in rapid angry bites.

I press a button on the camera and stick it in the water, then quickly paddle to the boat, which thankfully is close. I look at the camera and realize that once again all I did was take a picture of me turning it on. It was not in video mode – again. Maybe next time, but I hope there is no next time. So much for not showing fear, this time I ran away scared.


Suddenly I feel overwhelmed by all the drama: two sharks today, two sharks yesterday, a near-drowning experience, a shark at Serenity Cove, and an encounter with an obscenely big oceanic whitetip at Cat Island. I crave the comforts and safety of civilization, and I don't want to get back in the water. I make a snap decision to go to the Exumas next, imagining a nice meal at a restaurant and the comradery of other people. Since this means I'll have access to fresh water, I decide to use up some of my supply. I take the open 5-gallon water jug, which has about two gallons left, to the deck with a bottle of shampoo and take a real freshwater shower, the first one I've had since I left Florida. Then I make a lunch of comfort food, as best I can given the circumstances – garlic-stuffed olives, salsa, jalapenos, an apple, and a can of tuna, served in a bowl with tortilla chips on the side.

I spend the rest of the day writing in the safety of my little floating home.

When I step out for a look around, two other boats are anchored in the bay, and their presence both surprises and delights me. I pick up the microphone of my VHF radio to welcome them. I don't know if this is proper sailboat etiquette, but I feel like it's the thing to do in a place like this.

"Sailboat and trawler, sailboat and trawler, this is sailing vessel *Sobrius*. I just wanted to say welcome to Water Cay. My name is Paul."

The sailboat and trawler captains introduce themselves, and the captain of the trawler thanks me for the welcome. The sailboat is *Dot's Way*, and I realize that I met the couple, Dorothy and Glenn, in Thompson Bay, at the cruiser's beach. They encourage me to continue on through the Jumentos and Ragged Islands, to the end of the archipelago.

"The islands just get prettier as you go down the chain" Dorothy tells me.

This is all the encouragement I need; if Dorothy isn't scared then why should I be? Now I'm back on my game and ready for some more adventure and exploration. It is settled, tomorrow I'll set sail for Flamingo Cay, or as the sailor in Spanish Wells said "FLAH-me-EEN-go key" which is how I pronounce it in my head now.

The night is silent and dark, and I wake before the sunrise. The sky is covered in clouds of varying degrees of darkness and oppression and *Sobrius* is rolling more than yesterday, uncomfortably so.

I step out into the cockpit and notice the anchor line of the Fortress, tied to the stern, is pointing straight down, and when I check it I realize that the anchor is on the other side of the boat now. Apparently, the wind changed direction and we drifted across the anchor. I carefully pull the Fortress in and stash it in the stern locker.

I make coffee and hoist the shortwave-radio antenna. *Dot's Way* pulls out. I had thought about following them, but that's not happening now. I listen to the weather as they sail south under reefed main and no jib. The wind is still blowing 15-20 knots and it has shifted more to the north overnight.

After Chris Parker gives me the forecast for my area, I start going through the process of getting *Sobrius* ready to sail.

Pulling up Dr. Spock is very hard work, but *Sobrius* helps by tacking forward as I pull on the line. I've left the main sheet out almost half way so we don't speed into the rocks when I get the anchor up. She sails on one tack while I hold the rode tight on a cleat, then as the anchor rode pulls us into the wind, she slowly goes through a tack, and I pull in as much rode as I can before she starts sailing in the other direction. I go through this process until I've got most of the rode in, then I make sure she is on a starboard tack for the final pull, so we are sailing away from the rocks. But there is a reef in the center of the bay too, so I have to act fast.

When the anchor is up and catted, I hurry back to the cockpit and put us through one final tack and sail out of the bay, back the way we came in. It's overcast and windy and the whole scene looks ominous. *Dot's Way* is long gone and the ocean looks like rippled steel. Without the sunlight all the water is the same color, yet I know the bottom is peppered with reef.

I've studied the charts, more than usual, because my chartplotter has little detail south of Water Cay. I'll have to be more careful than usual. But the same waypoints on the paper charts are also on the chartplotter, and I should be fine if I follow them.

We pass Melita Cay and Lanzadera Cay. Swell is coming in through the pass to the ocean between them and the sun is beginning to peak through the clouds.

Reef shows all around on the chart, and I watch carefully for shallow water. We pass over many dark patches, but the depth stays over 20'. Still, I maneuver around any that either look particularly dark or colorful, or have waves breaking over them.

For the first leg of the journey to Flamingo Cay, we are on a beam reach (with the wind on our side) making 4.5 to 5 knots under just the reefed main. Sailing with just the main seems casual, and the speed is fine. Flamingo Cay is only 12 nm from Water Cay, so we'll be there soon enough.

I see on the chartplotter that we are passing a blue hole into which I wanted to dive. Many times while studying the charts before this journey, back in Florida, I would see this blue hole and imagine anchoring near it and exploring its depths. But I let it go. It's too windy, the seas are too rough, and I'm sure my new fear of sharks plays a role too. Maybe next time.

I have to focus to stay on course. Two swells are rolling us about: one is from the local wind and comes from the same direction as the wind, and the other is an ocean swell wrapping into the cuts between the islands, about 30 degrees different. As the swells pass under the boat, they cause *Sobrius* to turn to port, as the port waterline increases when a wave contacts the port hull. I steer to starboard to correct this. Then as the wave passes and envelops the starboard hull *Sobrius* tries to turn to starboard, and I push the tiller the other way. I do this about every ten seconds, while keeping my bearing by looking forward at a cloud on the horizon.

The color of the water changes with both the bottom composition and the passing of clouds. It can be bright blue, dark blue, dark grey-blue, or yellow green. The yellow green scares me because I think this might be shallow reef, and I try to steer around these areas. But it might just be grass; I still have a lot to learn about reading the water in The Bahamas.

Hours later Flamingo Cay comes into view and I see a long point of rocks coming off the northwest end. I sail around them, but I don't need to give them much space, as the depth should be 20' right up close to the point. But I do have to sail wide around a reef that stretches out north of the point. I can see three masts behind the rocks. Two look like they belong to a ketch, and the third is probably *Dot's Way*.

As we come around the point, the water calms, the wind decreases, as swell and air flow are blocked by the low hills of the island. A white ketch strewn with the accoutrements of a live-aboard sits anchored in the third cove, the one the cruising guide says has the best holding. It's called Two Palms Beach, but the two palms must not have survived last year's hurricanes. *Dot's Way* is anchored in the next cove, by the cave that hangs over the water. The cruising guide calls it a "dinghy drive-through" and says it's not to be missed. I sail past both coves, like a tourist who wants to see the rest of the island. Two more shallow coves pass, then a shallow cut in the island leads to the open ocean. In front of the cut, surrounded by flat water, stand two tall undercut rocks looking stately and exotic. The rocks are about 30' tall with vertical sides and rounded tops and rise out of water six feet deep. Where the rocks meet the sea, the vertical walls recede inward, eroded from the water. The rock on the left has a mound of sticks on top, perhaps an osprey's nest. These monoliths seem out of place, like two sentinels guarding something unseen for all eternity.

But it starts to rain, so I push the tiller over and leave the exotic scene for another time, heading for the area in between the ketch and *Dot's Way*. Dorothy calls on the VHF to welcome me, and she informs me that I have a line trailing on the starboard side. It's the jib sheet that I untied earlier, but of no danger since the engine is not running. I pull it in, then point *Sobrius* into the wind, release the main halyard at the mast, and let Dr. Spock enter his natural environment.

Location: 22° 52.84'N, 75° 53.18'W

Before relaxing, I go through all the steps necessary for staying here. I put the mainsail cover on, remove the jib, put the jib sheets away, take all the lines from the mast and move them forward so they don't noisily bang against the hollow aluminum pole in the wind all night, and I get out the 12-0.

I dive on the anchor. It's a tradition now, and I don't want to let my new fear of sharks keep me out of the water. The bottom is hard flat rock, but Dr. Spock doesn't mind. He's holding firm to a little projection on the bottom, and shows no sign of having slipped at all. The water is clear and beautiful and feels like home. I love the underwater world, and I wish I could come to terms with the sharks. *Can't we all just get along and coexist peacefully?*

Today's sail has worked up an appetite within me, and I get out a can of New England clam chowder. But the pop-top lid fails and the pull handle comes right off. No problem, I think, I'll just use the can opener. But the lid is incompatible with the can opener. No problem, I'll spike it with a screwdriver and pry the lid off. I set the can on the black rubber non-skid floor that I installed just two months ago in Jacksonville and stab the lid with a long flat-head screwdriver, but this only results in a dent. I raise up the tool and bring it down harder this time. But again, the can resists my assault. I raise the blunt tool a third time and drive it down with *great force*.

The lid gives completely this time and pushes straight down into the can ejecting thick creamy clam chowder all over me and everything else in the vicinity. But at least now the can is open and I can eat, after I clean up.

While the soup is heating, Dorothy and Glenn stop by in their dinghy on the way to the beach and we exchange pleasantries and chat for a bit. They are a friendly couple, and I'm glad they come by; it's a welcome change to have someone to talk to once in a while.

After eating what remained of the soup, I gear up for a snorkel. I want to see the cave, and I passed over some reef while sailing in that looked inviting.

A big lobster walks across the bottom, unaware of my presence and lucky that I lost my spear. It's rare to see them outside of their holes in the daytime and I marvel at how long and skinny its legs are. I get some video before he swims backwards to a crevice under a little reef, where lots of other fish are swimming about.

The cave is unique in that the ceiling is above water and the floor is below water, and thus cruisers can drive their dinghies right in. I look around for octopus with my flashlight, but see none. However, the little isolated patches of reef outside the cave are beautiful, home to many species of fish and live coral. I keep a wary eye out for sharks and one hand on the 12-0.

After I've seen my fill, I paddle around the next cove and into the last one, with the two big undercut rocks. I hear the forlorn call of an osprey, like a hawk but in descending tones, like a child calling for its mother. The osprey is flying overhead, and lands on the pile of sticks, now confirmed as its nest, on the top of the big undercut rock on the left. He continues to call, as if warning all his animal friends that a human is in their midst.

The rocks are both surrounded by water and have vertical walls that sweep back horizontally before reaching the water. The tops are inaccessible to man. The osprey's nest is thus safe, yet completely exposed to wind and weather. The only land between here and the ocean is lower than the rock, so the birds have no protection from the wind. But then it occurs to me that these birds probably like the wind, as it is from the wind that they get propulsion to fly, just like *Sobrius*, sort of.

The nest is big and made of wood, but has green rope sticking out in places. This is the color of the line that was hung up on my keel in the Northwest Providence Channel, and the color of the net I found on the beach at Cat Island, and the color of line I see on all the beaches facing the ocean. The birds have found it useful.

*A lone Osprey sits proudly on its nest atop the rock on the left, at Flamingo Cay.*

April 1

I get no reception on my shortwave radio this morning, and thus cannot pick up the weather forecast. According to yesterday's report, the wind is supposed to continue coming from the east or northeast at 15-20 for two more days, then ease to 10-15. These are good conditions for being in the Jumentos Cays, as the only protection these islands provide is from east winds.

I pack a backpack with hiking boots, jeans, camera, water and my smaller survival knife, and paddle to shore. On the beach, I change into my hiking outfit and start scrambling up the rock that encloses the dinghy-drive-through cave. I wave to a group of sailors staring up at me from a dinghy from one of the catamarans that pulled in after me. One of them asks if I'm Johnny Depp. I wish I were quicker with clever answers, but all I come up with is "Yes, I am." I should have said "He's just an actor, I'm the real thing!"

I hike all over the island, looking for pirate treasure, and trying to think like a pirate with treasure to hide. On rocky soil like this, digging would be too much work. A cave would make a much more convenient hiding place. But it would have to be a hidden cave, not one that could be seen from the water or the shore. I look all around, finding a few small caves and sinkholes, but no treasure.

I come upon a promontory overlooking the osprey's nest on the rock over the bright blue water. The majestic bird flies above me, calling out, swooping one way, then the other, as I follow the bird with my camera.

*This osprey, at Flamingo Cay, followed me around as if it were tasked with monitoring the movements of any humans on the island.*

From here I can see south far into the distance. The two big undercut rocks are in the foreground, standing tall in clear blue-green water. To the left (east), waves in the Atlantic break on the shallow reef between this cove and the ocean. Further south are more islands, and the first one is very close. Green hills rise from the blue water, leading up to the blue and cloudy sky.

A lizard is standing on the rocks at my feet, showing no fear. I stoop down and return his gaze. I assume he has never seen a human. We remain there, observing each other, just two curious animals checking each other out.

I start making my way towards the ocean side, but I have to step very carefully. I'm on top of cliffs made of very jagged, sharp rocks that are slowly tearing my boots to bits. If I were barefoot, I don't think I could walk here at all. The rocks are also loose, so I stay away from the edge of the cliff.

Tiny but gnarled and geriatric trees cover the ground, growing out but staying low and flat, like bonsai trees. Vines cover the rocks in some places. Cacti and very short palms live further inside. Life is hard for plants here, and so the plants are hard.

*The conditions at Flamingo Cay seem to produce natural "bonsai" trees. This photo was taken looking straight down from chest level.*

It takes a long time to get through the thick and thorny vegetation to the open and rocky Atlantic side, the windward side of the cay. As I cross close to the water in the cove, the osprey is there, standing on the ground, still watching me, wondering why I am there and if I pose any threat to its way of life. The bird doesn't move as I make my way east.

The Atlantic side of the island has no vegetation within 50 yards of the shore. All the ground is big loose rock giving way to pools of water and waves crashing into rock covered in algae. I can smell the algae. Plastic trash is also prevalent, as it is on the windward side of all the islands. Shoes, flip flops especially, are strewn all about. The ocean wants your shoes. It wants to take them from you and send them to a remote beach. Hold on to your shoes, should you be on a boat or near the water.

In some places, the rocks are piled into structures that look like walls. But the walls are so loose it's hard to imagine that man built them. Perhaps they are pushed uphill by big swells and naturally form these walls. Maybe pirates built them to hide their cannons behind. I go take a look, but find no sign of man amongst the rock walls.

Finally, I make my way back to the scrubby forest and start up the hill to my ultimate destination, the abandoned light tower at the top.

I start on what might be a path through the woods, but it quickly ends and I must crouch and twist and push my way through the thick palms, shrubs and vines. I use my knife to cut through the vines, and I get into a rhythm, almost like a dance, twisting and dipping through the vegetation.

At the light, I climb the short tower for a few last photos. The cruising guide calls it "ancient," but from here it looks quite modern, built like any other steel tower, with an electric bulb on top. I descend an actual trail back to the beach where I started, where the 12-0 waits for me on the sand.

In the afternoon, when the sun is shining bright, I gear up and paddle to the wreck of the *John T Davis*, a cargo ship that lies on the bottom in shallow water in one of the coves to the north. Before I reach the cove, I can see part of the boat protruding from the water, and a piece of it rusting on the beach. The rusting hulk has stained the rocks around it a dark orange.

I approach with caution, looking all around for sharks, and get up close to the rock wall where I can slip into the water with my back covered. Fish swim all around, in, and under, the steel mass of the *John T Davis*. They run from my flashlight as I illuminate the space between the rudders and the sandy bottom. Brain and staghorn coral grow in small patches on the hull sides. On deck, just two feet below the water's surface, is a large opening. I swim down into the dark belly of the ship, which is full of mechanical apparatus – the engine, cables, pulleys, levers, all rusting steel encrusted with odd sea creatures. Fish are startled by my light, and swim away.

*The Wreck of the John T Davis lies in shallow water on the west side of Flamingo Cay and provides habitat for many fish and encrusting organisms.*

With one hand on the 12-0, I work my way back towards the cove where my little ship waits for me, occasionally diving to the bottom to inspect intriguing clusters of coral and fish. It's amazing how the little isolated patches of coral harbor so many fish of so many different species. Snapper, barjack, and the occasional barracuda sometimes are seen in open water, but all the other fish are always concentrated around coral. The healthier the reef, the more fish I see.

I feel lucky to be alive while the coral is still here. I fear it will all be gone within my lifetime. The decline I have seen in my life has been dramatic. In the 1990's, all the reefs I saw were 100% alive. Elkhorn and staghorn coral made virtual forests of reef on which I snorkeled in The Bahamas, the Virgin Islands, and the Florida Keys. I've yet to see elkhorn on this journey. I saw some in the Abacos last year, but up there I saw no staghorn, with the exception of long-dead skeletal remains on the seafloor. I've seen the same dead staghorn here too, but am thankful to also see some of it still alive. When the coral goes, so do the fish, and the biodiversity of the oceans greatly declines, as does our quality of life. I offer as credentials to back up this statement a master's degree in biology and a lifetime of exploring the natural world.

In the early afternoon, I sit at the navigation table writing these very words, and in the late afternoon, I sit in the cockpit reading the words of Christian Beamish, "The Voyage of the *Cormorant*," describing his sailing adventure along the coast of Baja in his little wooden boat. His writing reveals that we have a common friend, Aruelio, a fisherman in North Baja, a fascinating coincidence. I met Aruelio while on a surf trip exploring Baja in a pickup truck. I went to Aruelio's village to try to buy fresh fish and he invited me into his little one-room house, which looked out over the ocean, and made us lunch. While there he told me that the Chinese had been to his bay around the year 1000, enslaving the locals and mining for gold. As evidence, he showed me a "remache," which looked like a nail with a head on both ends. Apparently, they were used to hold planks to the boats, and were hammered in hot, then hammered on both ends, to form opposing heads.

I prepare *Sobrius* for tomorrow's 40 nm journey to Raccoon Cay, in the Ragged Islands. These islands are a continuation of the archipelago I've been exploring since Water Cay. Of all these islands, only the final one, Ragged Island itself, is inhabited. I look forward to the sail. I'm not sure what I'm looking for anymore, but moving from place to place still seems to be the thing to do.

Late at night the drumming of the rain on the deck wakes me from my peaceful sleep. I put a towel outside to "wash" while keeping another inside, to make sure at least one remains dry. Although I want to lay back down, I feel like I should take the opportunity to shower in the rain, so I step outside into the dark and starlit night. But the rain is sparse and the air is chilly, and I quickly return to the shelter of the cabin and dry off with the one dry towel.

In the morning, I boil water for coffee and pour it into the French press. But I immediately notice hot water dripping onto my feet, followed by hot coffee pouring out of the bottom of the utensil. I hold the doomed French press over my tiny sink and quickly press the plunger, hoping to get some coffee before it all spills out of the bottom. I get a cup, instead of my usual two. From now on tea will have to suffice, unless I can come up with another way of making coffee, and I'm sure the motivation to drink coffee will help me find a solution.

Today Chris Parker is coming in loud and clear, and I eat my oatmeal while taking notes. The wind should be east at 10-15 for the next two days, then decreasing in strength, with Thursday being a possible calm day. I'll have to figure out where I want to be on Thursday, somewhere with good snorkeling would be ideal.

*Dot's Way* pulls out while I put away the radio and start getting ready to leave. I turn on the VHF, anticipating a call from my new friends, and indeed they do call.

"We're going to Buenavista Cay" Dorothy tells me.

"I was thinking about going to Raccoon Cay, assuming the swell would be bad at Buenavista."

"The good news is that there's no swell south of Nurse Cay."

"That *is* good news, perhaps you'll see me at Buenavista."

A moment later, Glenn calls.

"I don't know if your chart mentions it, but Nurse Channel can develop a rage when the tide is going out, which I think it will be when you go by. We swing wide of it by staying at 180 degrees after we pass Seal Cay. I used to wonder why other boats were so far off course until I got caught in it once."

"Thanks, that sounds like good advice. South at 180 degrees after Seal Cay, correct?"

"That's correct. Have a great sail. Over and out, monitoring 16."

"Monitoring 16."

A "rage" is a wild sea caused by the wind blowing opposite a current. Today the wind is east, so when the tide is going out through Nurse Channel, the wind will be opposing the tidal current. The communication brings about a good feeling, like I have friends in this remote place, like we all watch each other's backs in the wilderness of the Ragged Islands.

*"Whosoever is delighted in solitude is either a wild beast or a god."*
Aristotle

## THE RAGGED ISLANDS

When all is ready, I take the reef out, as the wind is less today than it was two days ago, when the reef was necessary, and hoist the mainsail. *Sobrius* sails forward while I sit at the bow, straddling the anchor locker, and pulling up the anchor rode by hand.

I pause while we sail off to port with the anchor line cleated. We tack when the line becomes taught, and I pull in about 20', pausing again as we sail, then tack, then pull in more. Making sure we are on the tack I want at the end, I pull up Dr. Spock and quickly cleat off the chain, shut the anchor locker, and move to the cockpit as quickly as I safely can.

I steer us well clear of the big power cat, which looks like a comfortable apartment in a NYC building, with its windows all around, big sun-deck, and outdoor lounge chairs.

As we are outside of the range of detail on the chartplotter, I have the paper chart book in the cockpit and today I will refer to it as we sail. This archipelago is full of reefs and sandbars to avoid, and so I am vigilant right from the start as we sail NW out of the anchorage.

Once around the reef nearest the anchorage, I set the tillerpilot and go to the mast to raise jib #4. We immediately heel and accelerate while I cleat off the jib halyard.

*Dot's Way* is near the horizon, but I can make out her green bimini and white sails. I hope to be able to either catch them or at least keep them in sight, both from a sense of competitiveness and one of comradery.

We make 4.5 knots on a beam reach and the sun shines just above the eastern horizon while low white cumulus clouds – fair-weather clouds – decorate the otherwise bright blue sky. The air is clean and delicious. My sinuses have been completely clear for the duration of this Bahamas voyage, which is a delight. I'm not allergic to anything on the ocean, and the plants of The Bahamas either don't bother me or are not in sufficient density to do so. I've suffered from allergies for my entire life, and to be free of them is quite noticeable and welcome. It makes me feel like I belong out here. It makes me want to stay. *Is the ocean my new home?*

I'm not satisfied with our speed, so I set the tillerpilot, go below, and bring out jib #3 in its blue bag. I don't want to tack or heave-to to change the sail, as we need to stay on course to avoid the reefs. But I see no obstacles to starboard, and I alter our course downwind a little to blanket the jib with the main, then pull the lazy sheet tight to bring the sail over the deck.

At the mast, clipped in to the jackline, I drop the little jib #4, then roll it up, unhank it from the forestay, and bag it. The larger jib #3 takes its place and I raise it, all the while looking forward to make sure we stay on course. But the tillerpilot is true and steers like an old pro.

With jib #3 up, we now make 5 knots, and I'm happy with that. Today's sail should be about 35 nautical miles, or 7 hours at 5 knots.

A plethora of Cays and rocks pass to port, between us and the ocean, and when we pass
Seal Cay, I put us on a course of 180 degrees, as Glenn suggested, but taking us off the recommended route on the chartplotter. This brings the adventure level up a notch and I feel like I have to be more alert, more vigilant. But looking at the chart and the wind, I see that we will have to tack upwind to get to Buenavista Cay after passing Nurse Channel. The competitor in me would also like to gain some ground on *Dot's Way*, so I change course to 175 degrees. I may be naïve, but I don't anticipate a rage in the channel today.

A long green patch on the bottom runs across my path ahead. I'm not sure if these are areas of grass or shallow reef, but I err on the side of caution and steer around it to port.

The water is beautiful today, with the sun lighting it up and the breeze gentle enough to leave it in a state of relative peace; I can clearly see the coral reefs below as we pass over them. The depth changes from 35' to 22' when we pass over a patch, and I think to myself that this would surely be a good reef on which to dive.

I see Loaf of Bread rock and Sisters Cays to port, and a very dark patch in the water straight ahead. I turn to port to skirt around the reef. But this looks different from the other reefs I've passed today. It's very dark, surrounded by a ring of yellow sand and round. I check the chartplotter and find that it's not a reef, it's a blue hole.

I'd like to come back to this one someday, with a dive buddy. Its location is 22° 34.49'N, 75°54.68'W.

Reefs to steer around, a blue hole, almost no swell, and a 15-knot breeze to take us to another remote island. *This is surely what I came for.*

A patch of reef is marked on the charts just west of Nurse Channel, and is my last obstacle on the way to Buenavista Cay. I watch our course closely and wait until we are past the reefs before turning towards the island. I harden the sheets, bringing the sails in as far as they'll go and put us on a course of 146 degrees, towards the north cove of Buenavista Cay. *Dot's Way* is also beating into the wind further south.

The water takes on an even brighter hue as we get closer to Nurse Cay, then Little Nurse Cay, and finally Buenavista Cay. As Dorothy said, there is no swell here. I'm not sure why this would be, perhaps it's because the water is shallower further out from shore than at Water or Flamingo Cays. But no matter, a settled anchorage is a welcome anchorage.

The long sandy beach of Buenavista Cay occupies the south ¾ of the island. Just behind the beach sits a single house, with the roof blown mostly off and resting one end on a wall and the other in the sand. The north end of the island has a rocky shore with a little cove, and I can see dark patches representing coral in the cove.

I tack, to get the jib on the starboard side of the deck, opposite the anchor, then heave-to. I take the jib down, then sail in to the rocky cove under the main, at 3 knots, half speed.

After tacking around, looking at the bottom and the patches of reef, I point us into the wind, tie off the tiller, and drop anchor. But I don't like where we are, so I pull Dr. Spock back up, move further in, and repeat the process.

Location: 22° 26.26'N, 75° 50.07'W

After pulling down the main, I change into swimming trunks, put on my mask and snorkel, and dive on the anchor. Somehow this place seems friendly, so I'm not worried about sharks, but I keep a lookout anyway.

Spock is dug into the grassy bottom, much better than at Flamingo or Water Cays.

After arranging everything for a night at anchor, I get out the 12-0 and the rest of my snorkeling gear and go for a look at the patches of coral that attracted me to this spot. All my fish friends are here to greet me and I even see a sea turtle, but unfortunately my presence scares it and it swims away, swooping its long fins up and down like the wings of a great bird. It moves impressively fast, blowing up a trail of sand in its wake.

I'm relieved to see no sharks, but a curious barracuda follows me wherever I go.

April 3

In the early morning, I improvise a cup of coffee using various tools in the galley and enjoy it with oatmeal, accompanied by the weather forecast. Afterwards the creative urge overcomes me, and I wish to paint a watercolor. However, the surroundings are less than inspiring, and so I determine to sail around the corner to Rick's Cay, where the cruising guide says one can experience and "unexcelled sense of solitude." This sounds good to me, so I raise the main, pull up Dr. Spock, and sail south, past the other sailboats, and around the corner. I keep a wary eye out for coral heads, and check the depth very often.

A cluster of small islands occupies the space between Raccoon and Buenavista Cays, and the depth is mostly between 10' and 15'. Since the wind is coming from the east, I short-tack up to Ricks Cay and drop anchor in sand with sparse grass.

Location: 22° 24.63'N, 75° 49.74'W

The bow points at a small rocky island in varying shades of grey and devoid of vegetation, the Atlantic Ocean is on the other side, and to the right is an even smaller island, just a quarter-mile long at most. Raccoon Cay is just beyond that. The Ocean is visible between the two little islands, and to the left is Low Water Harbor Cay and Buenavista Cay. The mast of *Dot's Way* pokes up over the latter.

Besides the one man who lives alone on Buenavista Cay, none of these islands are inhabited. The other sailboats have sailed, and I can see two of them leaving right now, heading back up the island chain.

The sun is obscured by clouds, some which stretch out in lines as if pulled by the wind, but it shines through occasionally and changes the color of the water from dark blue to bright blue. As clouds pass, the ocean looks like a giant pulsing blue light.

I get out my paints and sit still for a while, focused on the little islands to the south. I certainly am experiencing a sense of solitude, but I'm not sure if it is unexcelled. However, the natural beauty and serenity of the scene – little grey rocky islands poking up out of the clear blue water – delight the senses and inspire my creative nature. I paint and drink in the beauty of the surroundings.

After painting I almost set sail, but decide the opportunity to paddle around and snorkel a bit should not be passed up, so I get out my mask, the GoPro, my black leather hat, sunglasses, and take off on the 12-0 in search of a mini-adventure.

I pass over a cluster of coral close to *Sobrius* and take note to check it out on the way back. I casually paddle around Rick's Cay, with the ocean in view to both the left and right. The swell picks up a little, and I pass over a dark line which looks like a ledge, and I seem to sense the presence of large predators in the area. I go a little further to the cut leading out to the ocean, just to take a look; I'm curious to see if there are any rideable waves out here. But I see none. I turn back and steel my nerve to swim, then put on the mask and carefully slip into the water.

I'm startled as my foot hits rock on the bottom, which is closer than I anticipated. But the rock is covered in algae and mercifully does not cut my skin. We drift with the incoming tide across the ledge, and a school of yellow French grunt swims about. A grey snapper quickly swims into the cave under the ledge while beautiful blue tang take little notice of me.

I keep a close lookout for sharks and a hand on the 12-0; we are essentially in a channel, and sharks like to hunt in channels, bottlenecks in the highways of the ocean. But I see no sharks, and am thankful. I've seen enough on this journey already.

I paddle back around the east side of Rick's Cay and back into the little bay between the cays. Glenn and Dorothy are in their dinghy fishing, so I paddle over to say hello. We exchange a few stories and they offer me a fish, but since it's still alive, and I have nothing in which to carry it, they offer to bring it over later, which seems extraordinarily generous.

I snorkel two more times on the way back to *Sobirus*, then pull Dr. Spock from the sand and hoist the mainsail. We slowly and casually make way towards Raccoon Cay. I'm in no hurry, so I leave the jib down, which means I won't have to drop it before sailing onto anchor, and the slow movement allows me more time to take in the extraordinary scenery.

The water around Raccoon Cay is bright blue in the morning sunlight, and I sail standing up absorbing the natural beauty all around me, and looking out for reef. There's a blue hole on this island marked on the charts, and I hope to find it. I select an unoccupied cove near the blue hole's alleged location and send Dr. Spock to the sand, where he quickly buries himself like a flounder.

Location: 22° 22.68'N, 75° 49.49'W

I get the 12-0 and my freediving gear ready, and start out for the blue hole, which is somewhere on the island. But first I slip into the water to inspect a patch of coral close by. Immediately a sea turtle swims slowly away. I try to get the camera out, but it's stuck in the backpack and the turtle is gone by the time I've got it. *Always have the camera in hand when you enter the water*, I tell myself. I check Dr. Spock next, and he is happily underground, holding firm in the sand.

I try to find the blue hole, but just end up walking around the bush – in shorts and sandals, so I can't penetrate the thick vegetation. The blue hole eludes me.

I head back to *Sobrius*, where I eat a delicious lunch of salsa, a can of tuna, olives, pepperoncini, and roasted red peppers before retiring to my bunk to read; this is the coolest place in the boat, away from the sun. I've finished *Voyage of the Cormorant* by Christian Beamish, and started *Nine Years Among the Indians*, by Herman Lehman. I'm fascinated with this book, and can't stop reading it. When the author was a child, he was captured by Apache Indians and raised as one of them. But even the gripping tales of adventure cannot prevent me from falling asleep.

I wake to the VHF.

"*Sobrius, Sobrius, Dot's Way.*"

"*Sobrius here*, let's go to 17."

"Up one."

"Did you find the blue hole?"

"No, I couldn't find it."

"Oh well, there's always tomorrow. We've got some fish for you. Do you have a refrigerator?"

"Wow, that sounds great! But I don't have refrigeration, so don't give me more than I can eat for dinner."

"OK, well if you come by, or are cruising this way, we'll give you some."

"Thanks, I'll paddle over."

"OK, I tell you what, we'll meet you half way in the dinghy."

"That'll be great, thanks."

I paddle around the corner and get a view of Spanish Well Harbor, in which sit half-a-dozen boats. Glenn and Dorothy meet me in their dinghy and hand over some fillets in a plastic bag. We chat and swap a few more stories, then I paddle back. I realize now that I've gotten sunburned today, and that's why I am so tired and why I fell asleep earlier.

Needing some sort of protection from the powerful tropical sun, I suspend the 12-0 over the cockpit by setting one end in the lazyjacks and the other on a line tied between the two backstays. I then drape a tent fly over the 12-0, and a towel over the line that holds up the 12-0 over the stern. I now have a makeshift bimini, and the shade is a godsend. This journey that started off cold is now hot.

I cut off some of the little of what's left of the aloe plant and rub its healing juice on my burned skin, which provides some relief. Then I cook up the fish in a can of diced tomatoes, and it's the best meal I've had in a long time. I feel torn between wanting to fish so I can eat like this and maintaining my friendly relationship with the creatures of the sea.

As I eat, I think about my childhood and how I often avoided other people, and how I still do this. I'm anchored where I can't see the other boats, except for a few masts poking up over the spit of land between our coves. I'm much more comfortable in anchorages where there are no other boats.

I remember when, as a child, I used to run home as soon as I got off the school bus, to avoid having to meet a neighbor kid. I literally ran. He later told me how, daily, he wanted to meet me, but I always ran off. I also spent most of my free time as a child in the woods alone. I had plenty of friends that I made at school, but I chose to go into the forest alone nearly every day, both in West Virginia, and earlier in Louisiana.

In Louisiana, when I was very young, I used to roam a dark bayou and catch young alligator snapping turtles by reaching into the black mud and pulling the little turtles out by their tails. I don't know how I learned to do this. I could only see three small dots in the water to find them – their eyes and pointy nose – then I'd reach down into the muck until I found their stubby and rough tail, pull them out, and take them home. I think Sydney, our landscaper, would let them go. I think he also freed a rabbit I once caught.

As I got older, I continued my solo adventures. I always liked mountain biking alone. The solitude of the deep forest is one of the best things I've experienced. I rode in the days before cell phones, so I was truly alone in the woods, relying solely upon myself to get out safely. These are times I cherish and regularly visit in memory.

I still surf alone, although there are usually other surfers out. But I feel no need to have someone else there. The experience I crave has nothing to do with other people. It's just me and my first love – nature – communing.

And now I have another solo sport to explore: singlehand sailing, anchoring in remote places, painting the scenery, writing about the journey, deciding where to go next each morning (although I will leave open the possibility of a female companion to sail with in the future). These are good times; I am in my element, drinking from the cup of salvation, basking in solitude, communing with nature, at one with the universe and at peace with myself.

April 4

I get up this morning determined to dive the blue hole on the island. I skip breakfast, so I'll have an empty stomach, and drink peppermint tea instead of coffee, to avoid the caffeine. I want to let the sun rise to provide good lighting in the hole, so I paint a watercolor and write in the cabin until about 10:00. When I can wait no longer I gear up and paddle to shore, looking for the rock cairn and the white bucket on the stump that Dorothy described to me.

I soon find the signs that mark the trail, and the blue hole, which is really more of a green hole. The water is the color of algae.

I walk around the hole, letting the sun get higher in the sky, hoping the vertical cave will look more inviting with the increased light.

*The blue hole at Raccoon Cay was worth seeing, but did not invite me in.*

The hole is not only dark and ominous, but it also might be a trap as getting back out looks difficult. The rocks along its edge are sharp and jagged and drop off vertically into the dark green water. I can't even sit down to put on my fins, and the rocks beneath the surface are covered in thick green algae.

*You've come all this way to dive in blue holes, don't wimp out now,* I tell myself. *It's no darker than holes you've dove in Florida, and there aren't even any alligators here.* Eventually the self-talk gets the best of me and I decide I have to get in.

I put my foot in the water to test the rocks below the surface, to see if I could stand on them to get out. But the submerged surface is slippery, pointy, and a large plume of silt drifts off the rock as soon as I put my foot on it, further clouding the water. I put my face in the water, and see the visibility is only about five feet.

*No thanks.*

I walk away from the hole, dry. This journey has made me much more cautious and safety conscious. But the bottom line is that I was just *creeped out* by the hole.

Back onboard *Sobrius* I get her ready to sail to Nairn Cay, on the south end of Raccoon cay. The cruising guide says this area has some of the best snorkeling in The Bahamas. I hoist the main, sail off anchor, and casually sail south, past House Bay, where all the other sailboats are. We round the corner of Raccoon Cay and I start the motor to go straight upwind. I could tack upwind, but I haven't run the motor since leaving Water Cay, and then I only let it idle. It needs to work a little to keep it in good shape, and the entrance to Nairn Cay is narrow and dangerous looking on the chart. Using the engine will make it safer to anchor there.

Through Johnson Cut and between grey rocky islands on either side the dark blue ocean shows itself. As we head into the wind, I think about where we will go after Ragged Island tomorrow. I long for another open-water passage. I'm tiring of little day sails and island hopping. There are so many places to go from here: Crooked/Acklins Islands, Castle Island, Long Island, Rum Cay, Samana Cay, the Plana Cays…

Coral appears to be all around the entrance to the little cove between Nairn Cay and Raccoon Cay, but the depth stays between 12' and 20'. I stay close to Nairn Cay to avoid the coral in the middle of the entrance, and select a spot in the back to drop anchor.

Location: 22° 21.01'N, 75° 47.87'W

I'm excited to snorkel on some nice reef, and from the cockpit I can see what look like two patches close by. But first I dive to check the anchor, which I find to be lying on a hard rock bottom. I move it to a little depression where its point can find something to grab onto. But I'm not worried, because *Sobrius* was sitting still before I left her; there seems to be neither current nor wind here.

I paddle to the reef behind *Sobrius* and get in the cool clear water. The days have been getting hotter and the water feels nice. I wear a neoprene shirt instead of the wetsuit that I've worn every other day.

This reef is not at all what I hoped to see. Most of the coral is dead and only a few fish swim about – certainly not what the cruising guide described.

I move on to the next patch, and see a sprig of live elkhorn coral among a forest of its dead brethren. What a majestic reef this must have been before it died, what a disappointment it is now, and how sad to see such stark evidence of the worldwide coral Armageddon.

*This little bit of live elkhorn coral is surrounded by dead coral and was all that was left of a reef the cruising guide called some of the best snorkeling in all of The Bahamas.*

I paddle out to the reef near the entrance of the cove, but find it in even worse shape – flat and dead, with very few fish. Brown rock is all I see, the eroded skeleton of once-beautiful coral covered in algae. The feeling of death is all around and somehow this place makes me paranoid of sharks. I decide I've seen enough dead coral anyway, so I paddle back to *Sobrius* and make lunch.

I feel like sailing now, so I get out jib #3, hank it to the forestay, and tie on the sheets. I start the engine, pull up Dr. Spock, and then motor out of the cove. In the channel outside, I see *Dot's Way* heading south. They call on the VHF and tell me they are going to Double Breasted Cay for the night. I'm not sure where I'm going.

I hoist the sails while the tiller is tied off. We accelerate and *Sobrius* heels. She feels alive again. No more casual sailing, now it's full throttle. With one hand on the tiller and one on the mainsheet, we pass Ben's Cay and I make a snap decision to turn south towards James Cay, releasing one sheet and pulling in on another. Little cays and emergent rocks are all around this area and it's more beautiful than anywhere I can remember right now. I'm reminded of pictures I've seen of the Greek Islands – white rocks in blue water. I dodge dark coral heads, steer around sandbars, tack and gybe my way almost into the anchorage at Double Breasted Cay, where *Dot's Way* and two other sailboats lie at anchor. But I'm not ready to stop so I pull the tiller to me, turn downwind and sail wing-on-wing, with the main to starboard and the jib to port, focusing all my attention on my vessel and her surroundings.

I sail back to the rock labeled on the chart as "elkhorn reef" and drop Dr. Spock in the sand. The water is so clear that I can see the anchor without even trying as it lies on the bottom. Some trick of the current makes us sit still over the anchor, without drifting downwind.

I go ahead and let out the 50' of chain and ten more feet of line, like I normally do in water of this depth. But the chain just falls into a pile on the bottom.

I gear up to snorkel and dive on the anchor. I move it a bit further from the rock and dig its point into the sand.

I paddle the 12-0 across shallow reef in between the two rocks, then out to the reef on the other side – the "elkhorn reef." But as I expected, all the elkhorn is dead; not even a sprig of it lives. However some brain coral remains alive, and some soft corals – sea fans and the like – are alive. I see some interesting fish, and take a bit of video, but overall, it's depressing.

At least I'm anchored in an exceptionally beautiful place, a flat world of blue water punctuated with multiple small grey rocky islands. The scenery makes me want to gaze about all afternoon, and the boat is not stern-to-the-sun, as has been the case lately, so the cabin is cooler than in previous days. So, sunburned still from two days ago, I retire to the cabin and get out the computer to write. This is a writing voyage – an adventure, and a working vacation.

*Anchoring among the small islands south of Raccoon Cay was a beautiful experience and a highlight of the journey.*

April 5

I wake up on this sunny morning determined to be social today. I'll anchor with other boats at Hog Cay and maybe catch a ride with Glenn and Dorothy from *Dot's Way* in their dinghy to Duncantown, Ragged Island (otherwise it would be a 3-mile paddle). I'll stroll through town, talk to people, do a bit of shopping, and take in the local culture.

But as I approach Hog Cay, I see no other boats. However, I do see a structure on the beach, which looks like it has a thatch roof.

I get out my binoculars. I didn't expect there to be a house on the beach here, or any civilization.

The binoculars reveal an open hut with picnic tables and chairs. It looks like a cruiser's social structure of some sort. I remember Dorothy mentioned a "yacht club" at Hog Cay; maybe this is it. I anchor right in front – *I will be social today*.

The days have been getting monotonous, breakfast, weather report, sail somewhere, snorkel, walk on the island, dinner… the trip is about halfway through, and I want to mix it up and make the second half a bit different from the first.

I dive on the anchor, which is dug into a sand bottom with sparse grass, then snorkel some reef patches nearby as a barracuda follows. Unfortunately the reefs are almost completely dead. One is covered in the broken pieces of what was once a staghorn reef. However, inside a cave, illuminated by my flashlight, is a white eel covered in black spots. The eel's mouth is open and I can see its teeth as it pumps water in and out of its mouth. It's a spotted moray eel, always a thrill to see.

*I love sticking my camera into caves, because sometimes I get shots like this – a spotted moray eel illuminated by a ray of sunshine!*

The beach is framed with a white concave cliff that forms a sort of natural amphitheater in one spot. Under the cliff is the hut I saw, and sure enough, a sign in front reads "Hog Cay Yacht Club." Sailors have decorated the beach around the "clubhouse" with crude art made from things that wash up on the sand – floats, driftwood, rope, shells. All over the inside of the hut are hung various objects denoting the names of boats and the dates they were here. I pick up a blank piece of wood and return to *Sobrius*, where I spend the next four hours carving her name and the year 2018.

A Barracuda sits still in the water next to us while I carve.

I've got my Makita cordless drill and impact driver aboard, so I drill two holes in the wood, then take the driver to the beach and screw my creation, that will let future visitors know I was here in 2018, to a rafter.

By the afternoon I am surprised that there are still no other boats in the anchorage. I've no real need to go to town, so I stay onboard and rig a makeshift bimini with a rain fly from a tent and the boom topping-lift. I free the topping lift and attach it to the stern pulpit, then stretch the fly across it. Now I have some much-needed shade.

Today my brother Sam and my sister Elizabeth are at my parents' house in Louisiana. I call my father after dark, when all the stars are out, and stand on the cabin roof to get better reception. He puts me on speakerphone and I get to talk to all of them at once. While I talk, I can see an incredible number of stars, I can even see the Milky Way, our galaxy seen from our position in the outer band of its spiral of stars, stars so dense in number that the light blends together and creates a "milky" band across the sky.

I love being alone, but after a month, it's nice to talk to family. I especially like to be able to share this wonderful adventure with my loved ones.

While I'm talking, I am surprised to see glowing lights, ranging from the size of a baseball to that of a basketball, flashing in the water all around the boat. I've never seen anything quite like this, but I assume the flashing lights are produced by bioluminescent jellyfish. They seem to be communicating with each other in a language of light. It's eerie but fascinating. I'm reminded of a Stephen King short story where an aquatic amoeba-shaped monster would lure people to their deaths with its mesmerizing and hypnotic lights. But this is no threatening monster, and coupled with the innumerable stars above, the light show in the water makes for a magical evening that I will keep with me forever as a priceless memory.

April 6

Today is the first day of the second month of this journey, and it's the day I will start working my way back across The Bahamas towards Florida.

I make coffee and oatmeal and listen to the weather report on the little shortwave radio with the antenna hiked up the backstay with the spinnaker halyard. It's a tricky forecast for me, making it hard to decide where to go. If I go north, to Rum Cay or anywhere else, I will be exposing us to a cold front Tuesday and Wednesday, with 15-knot winds from the south, southwest, west then northwest, along with squalls. If I stay south, I'll be clear of this. However, if I stay south, I'll have a couple of days of weak, variable winds that will take me nowhere.

I remember Dorothy telling me that I should go visit Edward, an old man who lives alone at Buenavista Cay. I could go try to meet and interview him today, then maybe dive the blue hole that I passed on the way to Raccoon Cay from Flamingo Cay the next day, when the winds are light.

I put on my white linen pants and a white button-up shirt that I bought at a thrift store in Chile while on a surf trip. Clean white clothes for the first day of the second half of the trip; it seems appropriate.

I pull the anchor up while the mainsail pulls us forward, tacking back and forth, then sail downwind, away from Hog Cay, shaded by my new makeshift bimini. I realize I'm in the shade so I take off my big straw hat and immediately my head feels cooler with the breeze passing across my hair.

It's hard for me to make myself meet new people. Somehow, I'm more likely to snorkel in places where sharks frequent than I am to go meet an interesting man who lives by himself on an island. But I'm doing things differently on this second half of the voyage. I'm going to face my fears and overcome them. I'm going to go out of my way to talk to a stranger and ask him for an interview.

The wind is light today, and I've got the genoa flying, which I affectionately think of as the "big genny," and the unreefed mainsail. We make about 4 knots on a beam reach sailing north in the east breeze, which is between 5-10 knots. It's easy cruising, but I occasionally steer around dark patches that look like they may be shallow coral heads.

At Buenavista Cay, I drop the big genny and tack towards the house on the beach where I see a man that must be Edward getting into a dinghy. Maybe he's going to Ducantown and I won't be meeting him after all.

But he motors out to a small reef in the bay and starts fishing with a hand line. I set the anchor and dive on it, then paddle over to meet the man of the island.

"Hello!" I yell as I approach.

"Hello *hello*!" he replies in a friendly Bahamian accent.

He's a light-skinned black man, trim and fit, with white hair under a ball cap and a neat white beard.

I introduce myself and make small talk. He tells me some stories, most notably that he saw a bull shark bigger than the 12-0 on which I sit, only yesterday, right here in this very bay.

"Don't swim too carelessly" is his ominous warning, and the words stick in my head.

He tells me about the lights I saw in the water last night. I was right about them being jellyfish. But he also tells me that they are the source of ciguatera, the debilitating condition that one gets from eating certain tropical fish. I ask which fish carry it, but his answer is hard to follow because only certain kinds of fish carry ciguatera, and they carry it in some places but not in others. "Fast fish" he tells me, carry the disease. Between Bimini and the Berry Islands in a place called the Gingerbread Grounds is one place where it's bad, and here in the Ragged Islands, especially on the Atlantic side, he goes on. He won't eat horseye jack – "deadly" he says, or dog snapper. Barracuda he eats if caught on the bank, but not on the Atlantic side, or maybe it's the other way around. It's all very confusing.

I ask if he's a sailor.

"I'm not saying I'm better than you" he says "but I don't think there's anyone better than me."

He also tells me that he believes a diet rich in shark, with shark oil, and shark cartilage, will cure cancer, that the shark oil will prevent hangovers, and that V8 juice will cure seasickness. Edward has lived here by himself for 20 years.

I tell him I am an author, I'm writing a book, and I am a guest interviewer for *The Ocean Sailing Podcast.* I muster up my courage and ask him (I hate asking people for anything) for an interview. "That's no problem" he says.

Easy. What I feared was, of course, easy.

An hour later, I paddle over to his house. He's still cleaning the fish he caught from the reef, and shows them to me, three species of grunt and a queen triggerfish. He probably has a dozen fish, caught with conch as bait, a hook and a sinker, with a line – no rod, reel, or yoyo, just fishing line and his bare hands.

I give him a bottle of V8 juice as a gift.

"But I'm not seasick" he says with a laugh.

I get out my microphone and he suggests we walk up a little hill to the place where he rode out three hurricanes, to get above the water in case storm surge engulfed his house on the beach.

"This is where I crawled on the ground, too much wind to walk. Felt like pellets from a BB gun, from the rain and the sand" [blowing in the hurricane wind].

We walk up a rocky trail. He shows me a lignum vitae tree, and tells me it's the strongest wood in the world. "One time the government, the white government, they take lignum vitae to Scotland yard to make batons for the police."

At the top of the hill he shows me a stout but very short lignum vitae tree with a rope tied to the trunk and a mattress underneath "The surge come up 25 feet. I don't want to get washed away by the surge. So I tie the rope to the tree and put a loop around my waist, so if a wave come it don't carry me." He tells me his dog stayed by his side the whole time.

*Edward Lockhart rode out three hurricanes while tied to this tree. Note the rope and mattress under the tree.*

He tells me of his father's 65' schooner and another one getting washed high up on land on Flamingo Cay in a hurricane. This is what he worries most about in a hurricane; if a wave big enough to wash two 65' schooners up into the hills of Flamingo Cay were to hit his Island, it would wash right over his house.

He shows me an empty bottle of rum, which he drank while he rode out Hurricane Joaquin.

"Three storms I've been here, Irma, Joaquin, and Matthew."

"So you sat up here with no shelter, just a mattress and a rope?"

"*Yes*, at first, there were leaves all over that" he points to the "tree" over the mattress and the rope. It is now about half bare of leaves.

He points to a hill on the other side of the island. "For next time, I'll prepare a place over there too, for whichever way the wind blows."

"Because the roof blew off your house, right?"

"Yes, on the second day."

"You're lucky you weren't inside."

"Standing right inside!"

"You were inside when the roof fell?"

"Yes, this bastard, she's determined to blow my whole house away" he laughs.


"Were you a sailor?"

"Yes definitely. I never physically sailed boat to go anywhere, except Panama to Cartagena, in a 35-foot yacht. The rig was different, short mast in the front, long mast in the back. Getting into some illegal shit."

"Moving some marijuana?"

"Yes. Spent 7 months in a Cuban prison."

"What was that like?"

"Well, they give me 19 years and I serve 7 months, because my family is known. There was no one in The Bahamas we didn't know. Cuba, at the time, had just killed four of our defense officers. So, their government was gonna appease our government, by appeasing the family who asked for a family member."

"Gave me five years for illegal entry into Cuban waters."

"My older brother, he helped build the *Intrepid* and the *Courageous*, for Ted Turner. My grandfather was one of the best boat builders in his day, my mother's father. My grandfather taught him how to build boats, in 1953 when the regattas started in Georgetown. Then in 1955, he built a boat to represent Ragged Island. They couldn't beat us. You knew your position, I knew my position, when to move, how to move, so you couldn't beat us."

"What was your position?"

"On the bow, I was calling the shots. I was only 16 or 17 years old. My older brother, he built it, so he sails it. My next brother is on the jib sheet, next brother on the main sheet, my next brother he's on the pry."

"Is that the board that sticks out to the side?"

"Right. If you have someone who don't know when to move or how to move, then it's a fumble."

"Sometimes, I climb the jibstay, unhank the jib from the top down, for sailing downwind, we pull it to the side of the mast instead of behind the mast."

"So it ends up flying like a spinnaker?"

"Yes. I was very physical, and strong. Now my two shoulders are shot, I can't lift anything. With age, you know, I feel lucky to be still alive. I feel good for my age you know. Last year, in Georgetown, my little cousin and younger brother, refurbished this boat, rebuilt it, but they didn't have one man to go up on top of that mast. I was the oldest man there. I had to go up there and re-reave the halyard. So I climbed up there."

"When were you born?"

"1939"

"In The Bahamas?"

"In Ragged Island."

"How was it different back then?"

"Well… Ragged Island was the most educated island in the world."

"In the world?"

"These people were speaking three languages: Creole, Spanish and English. Every house in Ragged Island had a piano, an organ, or some musical instrument. Had 5000 people on Ragged Island."

"What was the economy like then?"

"Booming. No unemployment. Another thing about Ragged Island, never a murder on Ragged Island by a Ragged Islander. We had two strangers came and one murdered the other one. But they weren't from Ragged Island. That's something I'm very proud of. Every other island in The Bahamas has had murders."

"So, you said your grandchildren are coming to visit, and you saw a big bull shark in the bay yesterday?"

"I *will* kill that shark. There will be no shark in that bay to kill my grandchildren."

"And how are you going to do that?"

"Put a fish on a hook, on a chain on half inch rope, let him pull the boat till he gets tired, then I pull him to the beach."

While Edward is telling me about his mother, Eugenia Lockhart, and how she was instrumental in achieving women's suffrage for The Bahamas, a sloop and a catamaran anchor in the bay, and soon a dinghy pulls up to Edward's house. Mike and Joyce from the Beneteau 40 *MiJoy* step off onto the sand with big smiles and say hello to Edward, who remembers them from last year. Then Brian and Kim from the catamaran *Freedom* show up, and I've now met 5 people in one day, from my efforts at meeting one. As we talk a small shark swims through the shallow water right in front of us.

Edward keeps chickens and a pair of peacocks on his island, and the male struts about entertaining us with his flamboyant display of colorful tail feathers. He tells me that he has so many eggs that he can't eat them all, and he has to check his bed for eggs before he goes to sleep because the chickens lay eggs in it. His bed is suspended in the rafters so the roof won't fall on him while he sleeps, should it complete its trip to the ground. He fetches a one-gallon plastic water jug, cuts off the top, puts sand in the bottom, then alternates sand with eggs, and gives it to me as a parting gift.

Later I speak to Mike on the VHF and ask if he would be interested in diving the blue hole 10 miles to the north, the one that I passed on the way here from Flamingo Cay, with me tomorrow. He says this would interest him, but unfortunately, they are heading south, and I start thinking of making a passage tomorrow instead of exploring the vertical submarine cave solo.

*Mike, from SV MiJoy, was kind enough to send me this photo of Sobrius, sailing away from Buenavista Cay shaded by the makeshift bimini.*

*"Man sacrifices his health in order to make money. Then he sacrifices money to recuperate his health. And then he is so anxious about the future that he does not enjoy the present; the result being that he does not live in the present or the future; he lives as if he is never going to die, and then dies having never really lived."* Dalai Lama

## COMPLETING A CIRCUMNAVIGATIN OF LONG ISLAND

I almost go to the blue hole, but I know the temptation to break my new 30'-depth rule would be too strong to resist, and Edward's warning rings in my head – *don't swim too carelessly*. So, safe and dry in the cockpit, I sail out of Nurse channel and past the lonely day-beacon obelisk on Channel Rock.

The stone marker is a sharp spike in the middle of a big rock in the north edge of the channel that marks the end of another chapter of my adventure, and the beginning of a new one. The Jumentos Cays and the Ragged Islands have been an incredible foray into the greatest depths of nature, and now the second half of my journey is beginning.

I think I'll sail to Rum Cay. I could probably make it before dark tomorrow.

Alternate methods of self-steering have been occupying my thoughts. I've been wanting to try out a sheet-to-tiller system, with a steering sail, and I think now is the time to finally do it. In this system, a storm jib is set aft of the headsail. The storm jib's sheet is run to the windward side of the tiller and a shock cord or bungee is tied to the leeward side to counteract the force from the sheet. When all is properly set and balanced, the sail should steer the boat, or so I have read.

I attached blocks to either side of the rail in the cockpit across from the tiller back in St Petersburg when I was originally fitting-out *Sobrius*, one and one-half years ago, and before leaving Florida I installed a large padeye near the bow to which I can tack the storm jib. I gather the simple materials needed: storm jib, sheet, shock cord, and carabiner.

I use the carabiner to tack the storm jib to the padeye, run its sheet through a block on the windward gunwale and through the block previously mentioned on the cockpit's windward rail, and tie the sheet to the tiller. I also tie the shock cord to the tiller and lead it through a block on the leeward rail, back to the tiller, and cleat off the end on the rail.

I adjust the tension of the sheet and the shock cord, so that they balance each other, then let go of the tiller. To my utter astonishment, it works! *Sobrius* is steering herself now, I just needed to give her the tools!

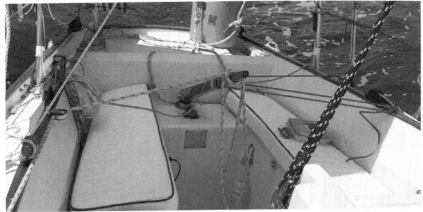

*Sheet-to-tiller is a simple way to achieve self-steering and requires no specialized equipment or electricity. The line tied to the tiller leading to the left goes to the clew of the storm jib via the windward deck, while the shock cord on the right provides resistance to the sheet.*

*This is the sail configuration I used for sailing upwind with sheet-to-tiller self-steering.*

As they often do, my plans are fluctuating, and I'm now thinking about going to Clarence Town, Long Island. I think the wind will be too much out of the south for the Rum Cay anchorage, that is, unless I try to anchor in the northwest bay, which looks risky on account of all the coral shown on the chart. Little Harbor, Long Island, would be a good option, except I would probably get there around 1:00 am – in the dark and therefore not a viable plan. I could go to Crooked/Acklins Islands – Flamingo Bay or Attwood Harbor. I guess we'll see how I feel tonight, and this also depends on the wind. It's supposed to shift to the south, and I would need this to happen in order to make it to Flamingo Bay.

Movement on the water ahead – no – movement just above the water – a flickering of black and white, catches my eye. It's a flock of birds, some sitting on the water, some flying barely above its surface. Sitting and flying, sitting and flying, little black and white creatures of the sea, creatures of the air. It's nice to have some company; seeing life above the surface of the ocean is a pleasant surprise and makes me smile. I know the depths below are alive with all manner of creatures, but seeing these birds gives me communion with nature.

For protection from the harsh tropical sun, I've had the "bimini" up all day, a small rain fly from a tent, supported by the boom topping lift and hooked to the lifelines. It provides very welcome shade on this sunny day. The steering sail has the helm while I read books, write, record voice memos, and take naps. I even record a podcast. Then I sit at the bow and meditate. I used to always sit at the bow when I sailed with my father when I was a child. Now I am an adult and I still like it up here. I am a passenger while *Sobrius* steers herself.

It's very different from all the other sailing I've done – having a self-steering method that doesn't consume power is quiet and peaceful, and I didn't even have to buy it; I already had all the materials, and I just rigged it. Wind vane self-steering rigs are $4000 or more, so if this continues to work, it will represent a huge savings. So far it works, although we've only been sailing on a close reach today, but it steers very well. And I have heard, from a guy with the same boat, that it works downwind as well, with the storm jib poled out opposite the working jib.

I am less fatigued, because I'm not pushing and pulling on the tiller all day, and I can be productive while not steering. This also frees up a good bit of electricity. Maybe I'll install a 12-volt cold plate in the ice box and make it into a refrigerator – what a luxury! Then I could catch fish and store the leftover fillets.

As evening falls and the western horizon climbs to the sun, I am the only observer of a vast light show that covers the sky and mesmerizes with altering hues and shapes. Cirrus clouds occupy the high altitudes above the 360-degree horizon of ocean, as no land is in sight. The horizon around the sun is orange, fading to yellow by the clouds, then from a hint of green to a very bright blue. Above the blue sky drift orange clouds with the same bright blue background. The eastern horizon is dominated by pink cirrus clouds, high enough to be reflecting the colored light of the sunset. Below the cirrus clouds the eastern horizon is purple, and to the south hang dramatic pink, purple and orange clouds. It's absolutely gorgeous and I marvel at the fact that my entire field of view contains no other humans, nor any structure to blemish the natural setting with the clumsy fabrications of man. I am amazed to realize that I am the only person here because I am the only person who wants to be here, yet the reward for being here is to view nature's greatest work of art, its creation and its destruction as the sky darkens and night takes its shift.

I am now drinking from the cup of life, out here deep in nature, sailing on my little ship across this vast wilderness of water and air. Alone. I've seen no other ships today. It's just me and *Sobrius* – and nature. Before I got sober I was drinking from the poison of capitalism, lining the pockets of those in the legal drug business, while I destroyed my health, both physical and mental. Not anymore; from now on the cup of life shall be my only cup.

I stand at the bow holding on to the headstay and gazing out at the endless sea as we sail across its surface. My loose white shirt and pants ripple with the wind as I ponder how different my life has become since I gave up drinking and smoking weed every day. This is infinitely more fun and rewarding; no drug can compare to what I am experiencing right now, and the natural high is delightful in the extreme.

*Sailing across the Crooked Island Passage was as peaceful, beautiful, and serene as anything I've ever experienced. (See note on page 303 about color photos)*

As the faithful storm jib steers my little ship towards our next destination, somewhere ahead yet still undetermined, I sip on a cup of hot coffee while the sky darkens. The only artificial light comes from the masthead tricolor, and the stars soon take over the sky, emerging from the darkness like a vast but slowly approaching army. The silence and the beauty lull me into a state of awe.

The calmness of the sea is a blessing that does not go unappreciated. For most of this trip it's been strong wind and high seas, or at least some waves on the ocean – 4, 5 or 6 feet. But today and this evening the ocean has been placid beneath about 10 knots of breeze. The big genny is flying, and the main is full, while the storm jib acts as a steering sail, and the seas are maybe one foot, hardly even noticeable. Today the ocean is my friend.

I'm actually looking forward to going to Clarence Town and experiencing some civilization. I'd like to meet some people, maybe even interview someone, make some new friends, and do a bit of shopping. The chart shows a blue hole surrounded by shallow water just beyond the harbor, piquing my curiosity. Clarence Town Harbor should provide some of the variety I seek on this second half of the adventure.

The stars are out in full force tonight. Orion rises in the eastern sky, then aims his bow down towards the ocean, as if he intends to shoot a fish, a whale perhaps, or a shark. Countless other constellations fill the sky like graffiti. I even see a shooting star – a meteor, or perhaps a piece of ice from a comet, which has been travelling through space for an amount of time incomprehensible to man, and I am here to witness its final moment of enlightenment.

The wind tangles my hair as I look up into the bright starry sky while the bottomless ocean glides past, making the soft sound only water can. I hear the fluid motions of the elements around me, as well as the metallic ping of the rigging and the pop of the canvass as puffs of wind punch into the old sails, accelerating *Sobrius* onward toward the next island. What creatures swim below I can only imagine. If any exist above, inhabiting unseen planets around the stars, whose light has taken countless years to reach my eyes, I will never know. But I am well aware of my current location – floating on the ocean, between the islands, and nothing else matters.

The dream I've been working towards for nearly three years is now happening, and only time holds me here; with its passing I will no longer be here, in my dream, but back on land, at work, amongst others, surrounded by civilization. For now, time is on my side.

The beauty all around me knows no limits, nor does the ocean, and for now all is well. The wind and the sea state are agreeable, and my little ship finds comfort gliding across the water, as it was designed and built to do. I find supreme peace in the surroundings, far from land, far from other people, rather surrounded and embraced by my first love.

My heart is full, my mind is clear, my lungs are satiated with clean, pure air, and my eyes take in the starlight, the moonlight, and no other.

The night is long and quiet, but the wind is not shifting to the south as I had hoped. The chartplotter informs me that we are sailing towards the southern tip of Long Island, instead of the water to the east of its southern tip. I've been sailing as close to the wind as possible, but unless it veers a little, I will need to tack to get around the island.

A light rises over the horizon ahead, then disappears below. I check the chart to see if it shows a light on the island, but it knows of none. It must be a ship in the distance, and I check the AIS, but just like the rest of the day and night, it shows no vessels. We need to tack anyway, in order to get around Long Island, and the mysterious light ahead is the final impetus to do so.

I tack *Sobrius* to starboard, sail for an hour, then tack to port and sail around the southern tip of the Long Island. The energizing effect of the coffee is starting to wear off, and fatigue is setting in. I'm so tired that I am now thinking of pulling in at Little Harbor, a well-protected anchorage much closer than Clarence Town. We should be there just at sunrise.

As the evening comes to an end, the breeze loses some of its strength, yet we still sail along in the grey pre-dawn light, towards the majestic windward coast of Long Island. Through the light mist hanging above the sea I can just make out cliffs, rocks, and whitewater exploding on the unyielding shore. The entrance to Little Harbor is in there somewhere. The chartplotter tells me I'm pointing at it, but I can't see it yet, and both body and mind are fatigued. I trust the instruments as I steer my ship towards the unforgiving coast.

Little Harbor is described in the cruising guide as pretty, rugged, and remote. There is no civilization here, save for a road leading to a town a few miles away. It looks intriguing on the charts – protected by hills and cliffs on all sides, with one narrow entrance. There could be surf here.

On my phone, I read some reviews of Little Harbor using the app that David, back on the *Kera Vela* in Jacksonville, recommended. I read comments from the skippers of two boats that had trouble in the entrance, getting pushed sideways by the waves that stand up when they hit the shallow water in the narrow channel. I'll have to stay focused. Rocks and reef line both sides and like everywhere in The Bahamas, no aids to navigation will mark the channel.

A cut between the rocky shore becomes visible through the morning haze. Waves break on the left side, and a tall cliff guards the right. The seas are about four feet, rolling into the channel at a slight angle. I might have to time my entrance to avoid larger set waves.

I take down the big genny and start the engine, which hasn't run in a while, so this will be good for it (I feel guilty of sloth whenever I start the engine and feel the need to justify its use). But I think good seamanship dictates having the engine running when entering an unknown inlet like this, with potential for disaster on both sides.

I put her in gear and we speed into the inlet at 4.5 knots, under sail and engine, pushed by the waves, but under our own power, I have enough speed across the water to remain in good control. I take notice of a point break on the left, where I will surely surf later, after some much-needed rest.

Inside Little Harbor, a catamaran sits in the still water in the south end of the circular anchorage. I turn to the north and motor sail around the north end, taking in the scenery – blue water, cliffs and rocks, reef passes to the ocean on the north side, trees and shrubbery on the banks to the west, and no signs of civilization anywhere.

I get a call on the VHF.

"Sailboat in Little Harbor, Sailboat in Little Harbor…" I can't make out the rest.

"This is sailing vessel *Sobrius*, in Little Harbor. Is someone hailing me?"

"Hi, this is the catamaran in the south end. We are leaving in an hour, so don't worry about bothering us. It's nice over here, and less rolly than the north end."

"OK, thanks for the heads-up. I'll come check out the south end."

The cruising guide also recommends the south end of the harbor for anchoring, so I head over there, sail around in a circle looking at the bottom, which looks like it's covered in thick grass – not so good for anchoring. But I trust Dr. Spock entirely now; he doesn't care what the bottom is composed of and holds every time regardless.

Location: 22° 45.60'N, 75° 11.68'W

After setting the anchor, putting on the mainsail cover, and rolling up the jib, I realize that the journey has depleted my energy reserves to the point of total exhaustion, so I lay down and sleep for two hours.

I wake up feeling groggy, worn out from the passage, thirsty, and hot. I'm ready to get in the water, but the water is dark and creepy here, and does not tempt me to swim. The bottom is all grassy and covered in strange shapes that look like braches and logs and I read somewhere recently that sharks are likely to hang out in grassy areas, which seems silly but somehow has stuck in my head. I wish I wasn't afraid of them, rather fearless like I was before Cat Island, but it's different now. *Don't swim too carelessly.*

Regardless, I get out my mask and the 12-0 for an exploratory paddle. I don't dive on the anchor, but I do look at it from above. It's buried in the grassy sand. I trust it.

I paddle over to a reef by the inlet and put on the mask. The coral is almost all dead, but still a few fish swim around. Something large in the sand to my left catches my eye. It's about four-feet long, flat, with a small head and a long thin tail. It looks at me as it digs in the sand with its mouth, stirring up a small cloud. As it swims away I identify it as a spotted eagle ray, something I haven't yet seen on this trip. These are beautiful creatures, and I've not seen many in my life. Their body, dark on top with white spots all over, is shaped like a common stingray, but their head protrudes from the diamond-shaped body, with a face – eyes and a mouth.

I paddle into the inlet and take a look at the waves, which break on the south point of the inlet and wrap inside all the way into the bay. The waves are small, about rib high, but the water is clear and the waves look like they'd be fun on my longboard, and I want to surf!

I paddle back to *Sobrius* and put my mask and the kayak paddle on the deck, then I paddle by hand back to the inlet, wearing a big straw hat. I like surfing with a hat on when in the tropics, but this only works when the waves are small and on a point break. Otherwise I'd lose the hat.

I feel vulnerable paddling with my hands instead of the paddle. This new fear of sharks is really taking hold, but the water calls to me, whether to swim, surf, or dive.

I watch a set of waves break while I paddle out through the inlet and select a spot to wait for a wave. I can see dark masses of coral reef under me, and light silvery things that are probably sea fans. I keep my feet up and a close eye out for sharks – always on my mind now. I can't help but think that I might be the only person to have ever surfed here, which stokes my ego, but then I think it might mean that any sharks in the area, and they are sure to be here, have never seen a surfboard, and thus are likely to come investigate. I'm right on the edge of being spooked – an all-encompassing paranoia where every ripple on the water looks like a shark fin and every movement of the water seems like a shark swimming by me. It is a very uncomfortable mindset, to say the least, and I must work to stay positive.

I line up for a wave that will swing wide of the point and wrap all the way into the inlet, like one I saw while paddling out. Most of the waves break all at once on the shallow reef further up the point, and I let many go by as I patiently wait for a good one. But eventually I reposition further up the point, and a four-foot wave comes right to me.

I paddle hard and drop in, turning to the right to run down the line. I have to push my hat up because it's obscuring my view of the wave. I step forward and crouch to maintain speed through a weak section, then the wave regains force and I speed around the point, almost all the way into the bay. The coral is clearly visible as it passes underneath me, and it gets closer to the surface as the wave rolls on into shallower and shallower water. But I exit the wave before it all breaks in the very shallow water, lay down, and casually paddle back out to the take-off zone.

I catch six waves before returning to *Sobrius*, and while paddling home I see a large animal swimming away from me, which I hope is another spotted eagle ray.

As I stand on deck, taking in the view, relaxing after the surf, I see movement in the water. Something is swimming fast towards the boat. A wake forms on the surface, the water breaks, a big grey creature like a pancake with a silly face drawn by a child, looking at me, flies out of the water, sails through the air with wings extended, tips pointing down, then up, then back down as if it's trying to gain altitude, and finally smacks the water with a loud *crack*! It is yet another appearance of the majestic spotted eagle ray and an amazing wildlife encounter, another example of why I love nature and sailing. *This is surely what I came for.*

In search of coral reef, I paddle across the inlet to the rocks on the other side. I see lots of reef, but it's all dead, and mainly devoid of fish. It's a sad place now. I return to *Sobrius* disappointed and downtrodden by the declining state of coral reefs.

I notice that the water is warm in the bay, warmer than out in the ocean, where I was surfing. Increasing sea temperature has been implicated in the world-wide coral die-off, and I wonder if places like this bay, where the water temperature is a little higher from the lack of depth and circulation and mixing with outside water, would be more quickly affected by global warming. I've also noticed that the further south I've gone on this trip, the more dead coral I've seen.

The oceans have been absorbing more heat than the atmosphere, and thus the oceans' temperatures have been rising faster than that of the air. I believe the declining state of coral reefs worldwide is a "canary in a coal mine" – an early warning of bad things to come. If you have the chance, go see the remaining coral reefs while you still can; they have been in a state of decline for a few decades now, and might be all dead in our lifetimes. And if you can do anything at all to help save them, do it now.

I saw a lot of coral reefs in the 1980's, and the difference from then to now is quite dramatic. What were vibrant bustling "forests" of coral are now ghost towns in the desert.

April 9

I was feeling sick yesterday, so this morning I eat one of the mariposa seeds that Edward gave me, back at Buenavista Cay. "It's a *healing plant*" he told me, and I'm willing to try the remedy. I also think I might have been dehydrated from the passage. All I drank while sailing was a big bottle of fruit juice and two mugs of coffee. I don't think I drank any water. So I drink and then fill my water bottle. I don't think I'll drink coffee on passages anymore. It might have helped me stay awake at first, but I crashed hard afterwards.

I skip breakfast and coffee this morning because I want to dive the blue hole at Clarence Town Harbor. I start the engine, as the wind will be against us going out the inlet, pull up Dr. Spock, and motor back out into the open water.

The sail is nice and relaxing, with a good view of Long Island's rugged east coast. Reddish-brown cliffs and lonely jagged rocks make up the windward shore where waves crash sending whitewater flying into the mist above. The desolate hills are occasionally spotted with widely separated and large houses that look out over the ocean.

We sail on a broad reach on starboard tack most of the way, then gybe to port tack for the final approach into the wide inlet to Clarence Town Harbor.

The harbor is beautiful. The water is clear with sand on the bottom, making the water bright and a very light green. To the east are small cays and rocks topped with palm trees; cuts between them give views of the ocean while shallow reef breaks the waves, preventing swell from reaching us, although I imagine a north swell would roll right in here.

On the largest cay, Strachan, sits a lone blue house, accessible only by boat. To the east is Long Island and Clarence Town. A cluster of houses, large and small, white, pink, blue or yellow, face the water from the low hills. The towers of two churches built by Father Jerome rise above the top of the island, and the inn at the Flying Fish Marina occupies the point on the northwest corner of the harbor, with a few masts denoting sailboats in slips there.

The first thing I do after anchoring is paddle the 12-0 one mile to the big blue hole. The cruising guide calls it spectacular. But all I see is a grassy bottom in 30' of water. It's nice and cool to be swimming, but this blue hole holds little interest for me. I paddle back to *Sobrius* and make ready to go to town. I'd like to inquire about laundry, and also fuel and water.

I paddle to the government dock, walk to the marina, and learn that laundry is for guests only. I could be a guest by renting a slip for the night, but that would cost $2.75 per foot of boat length.

Instead I think I will return later to buy diesel and water and then do my own laundry in a bucket.

While walking out the dock, I stop and stare down at the water. I'm amazed and awed to see three sharks swimming in the shallow and clear water underneath the fish-cleaning table. Two are nurse sharks, one is not, rather it is grey and powerful looking. All three are about five to six feet long. This is yet another amazing display of wildlife; seeing such large predators up close is something one never experiences on land.

I step out to the seawall overlooking the inlet and the ocean. A shallow area with some reef is in front of the wall. I see a large fish swimming down there – surely another shark. I can't seem to stop seeing sharks.

The paddle back to *Sobrius* is long and upwind. But it isn't as hard as my neighbors' paddle, the couple in the trawler next to me. They must have had engine trouble in their inflatable dinghy, because the man rowed it all the way home. Those things are very inefficient to row, so I hear.

I'm thinking about sailing to Rum Cay tomorrow, but I'll listen to the weather first, it might be better to stay here for the coming frontal passage.

April 10

I wake up just in time to hoist the antenna and tune in to the weather report. But reception is bad and I have to stand at the mast with the radio in my hands and the antenna hoisted as high as possible. It seems like the weather will be worse north of here, and Rum Cay is much less protected than Clarence Town Harbor.

I decide to move *Sobrius* to another spot within the harbor with more protection, just a quarter mile away, closer to the ocean and some potentially interesting reefs, and unexposed to the inlet. The wind is supposed to veer all the way around from southeast through west and to northeast, so the inlet might let swell in.

After selecting a spot by driving around in a circle to check the depth, I drop the anchor in what looks like a patch of sand, and I dive on the anchor to see that it is well-dug-in to a bottom composed of crumbled dead coral over sand.

I spend the cool and cloudy morning at the navigation table writing, then I snorkel around noon. The reef out by the ocean holds some live coral and interesting fish. I see a tiger grouper who sees me and hides in a cave before I can get too close. A school of blue chromis swims above a coral head while a school of yellow French grunt swims below. A strange pipefish hides vertically in a soft coral that looks like a menorah. I see a brightly colored stoplight parrotfish, a comparatively drab margate, the ever-present schoolmaster snapper, yellowhead wrasse, an ocean surgeonfish, and the common yet always beautiful blue tang.

On the edge of the reef a large, grey, oddly shaped fish catches my attention. I swim towards it as it slowly swims away. A large block-head with big black eyes fronts a grey body that tapers off towards the tail. It's a smooth puffer, about two feet long, and I've never seen one before. It's a lot like the porcupine puffer in shape, but is grey, larger, and has no spines. It's a silly oddball of a fish and seeing it mellows my mood, which is somewhat tense from my new and unwelcome fear of sharks.

I also see a sand tilefish on the way back, which immediately hides in a hole in the sand, and three barracuda, all of which take interest in me, as they always do. Luckily their interest consists only of watching and following.

Along the bottom of the clear water runs a pair of old and no-longer-used cables, about two inches thick and lying on the bottom, bridging gaps across low spots. Various encrusting organisms cling to the cables, including brain corals. It's nice to see nature accepting a man-made object like this.

*Brain coral grows along an old cable on the bottom of Clarence Town Harbor; tube fan worms can be seen on the right of the coral, and an ocean surgeonfish is swimming away.*

Back onboard, I put the 12-0 up over the cockpit, supported by the boom on one end and a rope tied between the backstays on the other. Over this I drape a small tarp and bungee it to the lifelines. The extra shade makes a big difference in comfort at the navigation table, where I spend the day writing and going over photographs I've taken.

In the evening, clouds nearly cover the sky, but they let through enough light to make for a spectacular sunset, dominated by shades of purple and magenta. I never grow tired of watching the sun set from the cockpit of my little floating home. *This is surely what I came for.*

*Sunset at Clarence Town Harbor on this night delivered an amazing display of light and hues.*

April 11

Back at the marina, I buy five gallons of diesel and this tops off both the tank and one jerry can. I also top off my water supply with 25 gallons. Sharks are swimming around, under the docks, plainly visible in the clear water. I ask Jerome, the man helping me, what kind they are.

"Bull sharks" he says in a thick Caribbean accent. "We have bulls, lemons, and nurse sharks in here. They come to feed on scraps from the sport-fishing boats. Sometimes they follow them in."

I ask him how he feels about sharks, and if he swims. He seems to have little fear of them, telling me that sharks don't bother you if you aren't spear fishing. He also tells me that there has never been a shark attack on Long Island, which is hard to believe.

"It's a good thing" he says "because the nearest hospital is in Nassau."

I motor away and anchor in the middle of the bay, with a clear shot out the inlet. I plan to leave for Conception Island before daybreak.

A dinghy is approaching my boat, coming from a cutter I've been admiring. The man in the dinghy is smiling and pulls right up to *Sobrius*.

"It's a French boat, so we thought there might be French people on board" he says with a French accent.

I give him my best "Bonjour! Je m'apelle Paul, j'habite a Florida. Je parle Francais un peu."

"Ah, well, nobody's perfect" he says, still smiling big. Apparently, my French did not impress him. We continue in English and after a short conversation he looks at the transom of *Sobrius* as he drifts away. "Those are good boats. They were the first of a new generation of sailboats."

I slowly and deeply nod in agreement with him.


April 12, 5:00 am

In the dark and moonless night, we motor, upwind, out of the harbor and into the deep water outside, where I turn *Sobrius* directly into the wind and hoist the mainsail and the #3 jib. Stars cover half the sky, while the other half is black, with clouds obscuring the heavens. I set us on a close reach and we begin our sail to Conception Island, a destination that has been one of the main goals of this journey.

My intended course is NNW, but we sail as close as I can steer to the wind and this is just a bit west of NNW. However, the wind is supposed to veer today, which should allow us to make our intended course to Conception Island.

The wind is light – less than 10 knots. Jib #3 is ideal in 10-15 knots and thus smaller than ideal for today's conditions.

As the sun rises, the wind stays the same, and so I must change the headsail and hoist the big genny. I go below and haul out the big black sailbag and the empty dark blue sailbag. I go through the process of changing sails while the tillerpilot steers. The big genny comes out of the black sailbag and jib #3 goes into the blue sailbag. Working on deck is a real balancing act on the open ocean, as the boat is moving unpredictably in all ways possible, pitching, yawing, and rolling. I look up at the horizon whenever I can, to keep from getting seasick.

Finally, I go to the mast to hoist the new headsail, but there is too much friction in the jib halyard. Something is wrong. I look at the downhaul, which I've been referring to lately as *my least-favorite line*. It serves a purpose, two actually, but it is always getting hung up on things, like one of the four cleats at the bow, or sometimes I'm standing on it, which prevents the halyard from going up. But this time the jib downhaul is innocent, and it is me that made a mistake. I forgot to cleat off the jib halyard after I dropped jib #3, and now the loose halyard has gotten caught on the port spreader. I have to lean out over the leeward rail while holding on to a shroud with one hand and swing the halyard free with the other.

The big genny goes up, and the halyard becomes good and hard. But still something is wrong. The luff of the sail is not tight, but bagged. Aha! My least-favorite line is cleated off and not allowing the sail to be hoisted all the way. I have to release tension on the jib halyard to uncleat the jib downhaul, then harden the halyard, and finally pull the slack out of the downhaul and cleat it off.

At last, I can go back to the cockpit, where I sit and rest for a minute before I turn off the tillerpilot and retake the helm.

Our speed increases from 3.7 to 4.5 knots. This is less than ideal but acceptable. As long as the wind veers, we will be able to reach Conception Island before dark.

Going upwind with the big genny requires the use of a barber haul to achieve good sail-shape. *Sobrius'* jib cars do not slide aft far enough to pull the foot of the sail tight on a close reach. I have a line ready with a small carabiner on the end that I attach to the clew. I run this through a block on the stern pulpit and to the windward winch, pull it tight, and cleat it off. It pulls the foot of the big sail tighter, and I look at our speed to see if we get any acceleration, and at our course to see if we point any closer to the wind. The results are inconclusive, but the sail shape looks better. I experiment with another position of the block, using a snatch block attached to the leeward stern cleat. The results are still inconclusive, but I enjoy the experimentation.

I hand steer all day, wanting to be part of the action. The wind shifts 10 degrees one way, then ten degrees the other, requiring constant adjustment of the tiller and the trim of the sails to keep on course. I spend a lot of time watching the sails, especially the luff of the jib, just above the tack, where I can see it. I also carefully watch the wind vane at the top of the mast. I'm trying to sail as close to the wind as possible. It's a bit of work, but enjoyable. I came here to sail, and that is what I am doing today.

I notice the mainsail is not properly set, with bags along the sailcars. *Is the halyard not tight enough?* No, it is the Cunningham that needs tightening; the boom is not being held down by anything but rather free to rise with each gust. I lash the tiller, creep to the mast, and quickly pull hard on the little black line that secures the boom.

The seas, which kept me up last night, are rolling and heaving irregularly. Multiple swells must be running through the ocean here, created by far-away winds, and the seas are further textured by chop from the local wind.

I enjoy helming, but somehow today I feel slightly ill. I blame it on the peanuts I ate an hour ago. I drank tea instead of coffee this morning to try to avoid any queasiness, and have been trying to drink lots of water. I think peanuts are just a bit too heavy for open-ocean sailing; I've noticed other high-fat foods have the same effect.

Now the uncooperative wind seems to be backing – becoming more north – instead of veering, as I had hoped it would, and we are headed for the north tip of Long Island instead of the open water leading to Conception Island.

I have to tack, which puts us on a course for Rum Cay, and makes me consider going there instead, because all the tacking necessary to reach Conception Island will, once again, put us there after dark.

I take a 22-minute nap in the cockpit, falling asleep quickly as the tillerpilot steers, making its mechanical whirring and whizzing noises like the robot that it is.

In the corner of my eye, I see a boil in the water ahead to starboard, about 200 yards away. The smooth grey backs of two animals break the surface, followed by unmistakable blowholes erupting with misty spray. *Whales!* Small dorsal fins emerge as the animals roll back into the water. They looked like giant dolphin, but with much smaller fins further back on the body. Pilot whales? Minke whales? Seeing whales and not being able to identify them reveals a disappointing lack of knowledge that I feel I must remedy.

The wind freshens and before we get too far heeled, I take down the genoa and hoist jib #3. It takes 20 minutes, which is fairly good time for me, but I feel somewhat nauseous afterwards. I blame it on the peanuts again.

When we get within 10 nm of the island, Rum Cay rises in the distance, grey, almost undifferentiated from the sky, then solidifies into green mounds rising from the horizon, connecting with each other to form the island. At about the same time, Long Island disappears below the horizon behind us.

I sail into Port Nelson, a large anchorage that on the chart resembles a minefield of coral. But I discover that nearly all of the reefs are deep enough to pass over. I am determined to sail in without the engine. I tack, tack again, heave-to, and drop the jib. Then I sail under main alone to the other boats at anchor, select a spot near a shallow coral head where I can snorkel, luff up, and drop anchor.

Location: 23° 38.38'N, 74° 50.46'W

Right away, I put the sail covers on, change into swimming trunks, and get my mask. I need to confront the fear of sharks that has been building in me since Cat Island. I intend to swim out to the coral, around it, and back to the boat, without the 12-0. Lately I've been snorkeling while leashed to the big surfboard, like a child carrying around a "security blanket."

But before I can get in the water someone hails me on the VHF. "New boat in the harbor, new boat in the harbor, *Last Call*."

"This is sailing vessel *Sobrius*."

We chat for a while. It's Mary, the woman I met at the fishing dock at Thompson Bay, the one who told me she has a daughter who is a veterinarian, who also has never married. Mary tells me all about the place, where to eat, who to talk to about surfing… It's a long and one-sided conversation.

Finally, I get in the cool water and swim to the coral. It's a nice little reef, although mostly dead, rising vertically from the sandy bottom to very near the surface – definitely a navigational hazard. I swim down and around the reef, always looking out for sharks, and successfully make it back to *Sobrius* unmolested by the kings of the ocean.

I paddle the 12-0 to shore and find the bar Mary mentioned. Sailors sit outside eating and drinking, and I overhear one of them mention Matt Rutherford and how he used a paintball mask to protect his face while sailing singlehanded through the northwest passage of the arctic ocean, during his solo non-stop circumnavigation of the Americas. The stories I heard about him in podcasts inspired me to become a singlehand sailor.

I step into Kate's Bar, and sit at the bar. The floor is sand and a handwritten menu is taped to the wall in front of me. A few locals sit drinking beer at a table and a few cruisers are also at the bar.

Right away I meet Mike and Dave, two other sailors who also just arrived, on the catamaran *Destiny 3*. Mike lives in Boise Idaho and is visiting his friend Dave, who lives in Port Howe, Cat Island. We get to talking and it turns out Mike has been to the blue hole at the north tip of Cat Island, where the oceanic whitetip shark scared me out of the water.

"I dove there" he says, "we swam over the hole and on the bottom were a bunch of sharks swimming laps in circles." I'm sure I would not have dove in the hole had I found it full of sharks.

He also tells me that Cat Island is one of the few places where oceanic whitetips are known to congregate, that he's seen big bull sharks in Port Howe, and finally that there has never been a shark attack at Cat Island, a familiar and suspicious claim.

I get the attention of the woman behind the bar and ask if she has anything non-alcoholic, which throws her off. She raises one eyebrow and cocks her head as if she's never heard such a request "You can look in the store" she tells me. The store is inside the bar, and is a miniature grocery-store.

I ask her "What's good to eat?"

"What do you want?"

"Whatever you can only get in The Bahamas."

She laughs and suggests a conch burger.

I step over to the store and find a coke, which is really only a little less poisonous than liquor. Before leaving I return and buy 4 apples, 4 cans of tuna, one tomato, one green pepper, and an orange

Fanta. I pack all this is my blue backpack and then paddle my 12-0 home.

In the bay, the mailboat arrives and backs right up to a dock on land. I see *Hornblower*, the Pearson 35 skippered by the French-Canadian couple I met at Thompson Bay. Behind me is a steel Colvin Gazelle, and I wonder if it could be Matt Rutherford's boat, since I heard people talking about him earlier. I peer at it through my binoculars looking for the Ocean Research Project logo, but this is not his boat. Still, I would like to meet the sailors aboard. They must be interesting people; one doesn't buy a steel boat without big intentions.

Tonight, the wind will be southeast at 15-17 knots, and then tomorrow southeast at 17, gusting to 22. This is no good for the anchorage here, which is rolly enough as it is. But this will make for a fast sail to Conception Island, which is protected from the southeast. I might only be able to stay for a couple of days, as a front will pass Monday, bringing wind veering through the south, west, and finally blowing from the north on Tuesday, none of which is good for Conception. No matter, I've been wanting to go to this place since I heard about it two years ago while sailing with Eddie and Liam aboard *Monkey's Uncle* in the Abacos.

Friday, April 13

In the morning, I am sailing around the beautiful southwest corner of Rum Cay, looking at curling waves through my binoculars and wondering if I should stop to surf. I'm just barely offshore, but the depth is over 900', making anchoring far from possible.

But around the corner, on the west side of the island, I see more surf, and the water is around 50' deep. I could possibly anchor and surf here. I can see the backs of waves breaking off a large rock and peeling towards a sandy beach, and it looks good. Multiple coves and beaches make up the shore here, and no civilization is in sight, neither roads nor houses. But I don't want to repeat the mistake I made at Egg reef, so I would need to anchor with the lightweight Fortress, which is in the stern locker, and would thus complicate anchoring, an idea I am already uncomfortable with on account of the powerful waves and the deep water close to shore.

I keep on sailing, on a mission to get to Conception Island, and, possibly, my decision not to surf is influenced by my new fear of sharks. This realization strengthens my desire to overcome this fear.

Regardless, we are now on the way to Conception Island, one of the main goals of this journey to The Bahamas. We make 5 knots at 320 degrees on a broad reach rolling across four-foot seas. The swell is well organized and not a bother, coming at us from ahead and a bit starboard. It should be a fine day of sailing.

Flying fish erupt from the surface to starboard, gliding up the face of waves, then turning downwind at the crests, gliding off into the distance like little paper airplanes.

I've got my still camera and my GoPro video camera ready for action in case we see more whales today.

At 10:00 am we sail out of the lee of Rum Cay and the wind freshens considerably. The swell here is about six feet, but still not causing problems as we move along at over 6 knots. The water is a beautiful dark blue, decorated with more flying fish, little surprises of activity and life above the surface. They are fantastic creatures and I love seeing them every time; flying fish never get old.

I see a sailboat on the horizon, probably coming from Conception Island, and I use it as a target, heading 310-315° at 6.5 knots.

At 11:30 am we are right off Conception Island, and I let the tillerpilot steer so I can gaze at the beauty of this magnificent place. A few white cumulus clouds hang motionless above the island and also northwest, downwind, in the beautiful blue sky. Below the clouds are four different islands: the big main island, and some smaller islands to its right. While *Sobrius* glides across deep dark blue water, the islands are connected by a very thin line of light turquoise blue, the color of shallow water. Waves break in places, and I see long yellow lines depicting sandy beaches. I imagine there's a lot to explore here.

*The approach to Conception Island was one I will never forget. I especially liked the abrupt change in water color making a line around the island.*

We've made it to Conception Island, me and my little red sailboat, and the sea state calms as we enter its lee, as if the island is welcoming us. Yet again the feeling of a dream realized overcomes me, swelling my chest with the joy of life, life lived the way I intend.

As I look at the islands moving from left to right, I see dark blue water, then light turquoise water, a thin line of sandy beach on the big island, followed by rocks, grey rocks topped with green, sandy beach with green hills above, then beach, rock, beach, a long beach at the end, a little green hill above, pointing off into more beach followed by open water, bright green with some breaking waves. The next island is a little green hill with brown rocks on the right and turquoise blue-green water below. To the right is open water followed by a small island, all green, then more turquoise water, two rocks jutting up out of the water by themselves, followed by more rocks, then sandy beach, and finally more brown rocks on the right of the beach, labeled "South Rocks" on the charts.

I sail up the west coast of the island, along a well-defined line of color change, dark blue to the left – very deep water, and turquoise to the right – water 30-40 feet deep. I pass moorings that I assume are for divers. I've heard there is a popular wall dive here that I'd love to freedive, but the moorings are in 75 feet of water, well past my new 30' solo limit.

White birds with absurdly long tail feathers fly above, two of them, gliding in big swooping arcs. I'm not familiar with these birds, and am truly awed by their beauty. [I later identified these as tropicbirds]

We pass the inlet leading to the mangrove creek that I've heard is a must-do. One lone tree stands by the entrance of shallow water, blue green but almost the color of sand.

I approach the anchorage on the northwest side of the island. One other boat, a ketch, sits peacefully. Two people in a dinghy are preparing to snorkel on a reef in the anchorage. Cliffs line the north end with emergent rocks and reef beyond to the left. Low hills, rocks topped with green vegetation make up the rest of the island in view.

Again, I want to sail onto anchor, so I heave-to and drop the jib, then proceed to tack upwind into the anchorage. I pass two orange mooring buoys labelled "Mega Yacht Mooring" on the charts. I tack towards the reef where the couple is snorkeling, then away, then back again. Upwind of the reef I point into the wind, move to the mast, release the main halyard, then creep to the bow and drop Dr. Spock into the fine sand bottom. But I see movement in the water, something large and brownish-grey – a shark!

I let out all fifty feet of chain and let the shackle jam into the bow roller (it doesn't fit through) and go get my camera while we drift downwind. I walk around the deck snapping pictures of this one-shark-welcoming-committee, lost in photographic bliss. But then I realize I've made a mistake – the reef is too close and we have almost drifted onto it.

Quickly I start the engine while staring at the dark coral reef ominously close to the transom. I can clearly see the coral heads, but I get us going before we drift onto them. I pull the anchor up, motor further away, and set it properly this time, undistracted.

When the anchor is set and I stand on the bow, looking at the scenery around me – clear water, 15' deep, sand on the bottom, cliffs, rocks, beach, trees, the wonderful sense of both accomplishment and the presence of a magical place washes through me. Conception Island is indeed a beautiful and serene location, and being here fills me with joy. *This is indeed what I came for.*

It's not long at all before the dinghy with the couple who was snorkeling pulls up to *Sobrius*. After five weeks in The Bahamas, seeking out remote places, I am happy to talk to other sailors.

Mark and Judy from the ketch *Rainbow* pull up alongside, hold onto the gunwale, and introduce themselves. I ask them about the snorkeling, but they are disappointed with the lack of fish on the reef, which surprises all three of us, as this island is a no-fishing zone and therefore fish should be plentiful. Mark wants to spearfish, so he would rather be someplace else, and a large pole spear with a three-pronged tip sits dry in the bottom of the dinghy. But Judy loves it here.

"He doesn't do nature" she explains.

"We eat fish" Mark says "then beef, then chicken, then more fish, and I'm ready to fill the freezer!"

Soon I am alone again and the solitude of this uninhabited island entrances me. I look all around at the scene before me – the green vegetation covering the low island ahead, the rocky shore to the left, the clear water, deeper than my previous anchorages, and the dark blue horizon behind us. Red junk-rigged sails appear on this horizon, and my binoculars reveal the Colivn Gazzelle that I saw at Rum Cay is slowly approaching the anchorage. *Good, I'll have time to interview them after all.*

The clear water calls to me. I am determined not to be afraid of sharks anymore, so I put on my mask and slowly climb down the boarding ladder, putting my face in the water first, to look around and confirm that I am alone. Then I quietly enter the absolutely clear blue water and swim to the anchor, which is buried in the sand, only the end of the fluke and part of the shank are visible. The water looks like an enormous and endless swimming pool, bright blue on all horizons, a featureless bottom of yellow sand below, 15' deep. The enormity of this body of water seems to encompass the whole world. While it feels like home, the familiar and wondrous sensations of the water are coupled with the slight fear that comes with the knowledge of the deep ocean right next to me, and all the creatures within.

I climb out and ready my snorkeling gear, including the little grappling anchor for the 12-0. I'm not going to swim around leashed to a security blanket this time. Immediately upon mounting the board, I see a dark shape swimming below me. I paddle towards it as it slowly swims away, and put my video camera underwater to catch the action, which I hope is a shark. I won't know until I check the video later.

I paddle to the reef next to *Sobrius*, the one that disappointed Mark and Judy, and drop the anchor upwind of the reef letting the board drift over it, then quietly enter the water.

The reef below must have once been magnificent, with coral rising from the sand 20' deep to within 8' of the surface. But while most of the coral is dead, some is still alive, and my fish friends are all here.

I swim to the bottom and illuminate a cave with my flashlight, lighting up royal gramma under the ledge and a large margate hiding below. A gorgeous rock beauty – vertically flat and spade-shaped, yellow face and tail, black body, purple lips – looks at me, unafraid, from the security of the rocks. I pause and hover in the water, taking in her beauty. We have a moment together.

Above the reef blue chromis, small electric blue fish always together in a school, swim over an isolated patch of live coral surrounded by algae growing on its dead brethren. The long sharp spines of a black sea urchin poke up from a dark crevice beneath the coral. These strange creatures eat algae, and are related to starfish and sand dollars. If stepped on or bumped into, their sharp spines will not only puncture a victim but will also break off below the skin. Do not touch! In fact, nothing on a reef should be touched. Coral is very delicate and easily damaged and killed.

Blue tang and various small wrasses swim about while red and white squirrelfish hide in caves. Squirrelfish are nocturnal and have big black eyes. I find a longspine squirrelfish, beautiful with white spots on the blue dorsal fin, which rises in a long spike at its aft end. It poses for a photo.

*The longspine squirrelfish are typically nocturnal and found in caves during the daytime. This individual has a particularly nice shade of blue on its dorsal fin.*

While I am not leashed to the 12-0, I always surface near it and lay an arm across the board while breathing and resting for my next dive. I occasionally pick up the anchor and move it to keep the board near me as I dive on new spots. I always put the anchor in sand and make sure the rode does not contact the reef so it doesn't damage the coral, or vice-versa.

My next dive reveals a brilliant male stoplight parrotfish, bright green with big yellow spots between the body and the tailfin (the caudal peduncle), a red stripe near the gills, and a red dorsal fin. He doesn't want to be filmed and swims into a cave. A female of the same species is here too, smaller, with a brown and grey body, red underneath. This is another species where the male is brilliantly colored and the female is smaller and drab.

A school of unknown fry gather in front of a cave. Coral reefs are nurseries to many species of reef-dwelling and pelagic fish.

Longfin damselfish, dark brown all over, are common here, defending their territories from all comers. One swims to me, threatens a fight, then darts away, repeating the process until I leave the area. This is their game.

*A longfin damselfish tries to run me off while a barracuda watches (upper right).*

*A towering mass of live pillar coral gives shelter to blue chromis and some small yellow and blue fish that I can't identify. Unknown fish always excite me, reminding me that nature is vast and always has surprises to offer the explorer.*

I find more royal gramma under the ledges; they seem to be common here. These fish eat plankton and, curiously, the males brood the eggs of the young in their mouths. I never tire of peering into caves and finding these little living gems swimming about.

A barracuda swims along the edge of the reef; they never tire of watching snorkelers.

Bluehead wrasse swim above a brain coral while live fire coral warns me not to get too close to the reef.

The uncommon peace of the underwater world is shattered by a loud grinding noise, which startles me. It sounds similar to an outboard motor, and continues as I swim up to the 12-0. Sound underwater seems to come from all around, because it's impossible to tell from where a sound comes when underwater. Since the sound is travelling much faster than when in air, our brain cannot detect the difference in arrival time of the sound between our two ears. This makes the noise of a distant boat seems to be coming from directly above, which is always unnerving.

But at the surface, I see another boat has arrived, a red sailboat, and the sound comes from its anchor chain as it pays out, grinding across the bow roller. The sound is gone when I dive again.

On the edge of the reef, over the sand, swims a school of yellow goatfish. These slender fish, about a foot long, with yellow fins and a horizontal yellow stripe on the body are bottom dwellers. They stir up their dinner from the sand with barbels on the corners of their mouths, like moustaches that can work like fingers. A young yellow and blue Spanish hogfish swims with the school.

Further up the reef, a male queen parrotfish completely ignores me and my video camera as he munches on the reef. These fish scrape algae off the reef with their hard beak-like mouths, which produces a very audible sound, commonly heard when diving on reefs. I see a female too, silver with a horizontal white stripe.

I see more schools of unknown fry, swimming together as if they know each other.

While the majority of the coral here, and almost everywhere I dive, is dead and covered with algae, I see a few living species on this dive, including symmetrical brain coral, elliptical star coral, great star coral, smooth star coral, lobed star coral, fire coral, pillar coral, knobby cactus coral, and thin leaf lettuce coral. [I am no expert on coral identification, so there may be errors here, and the names come from *Florent's Guide to Florida, Bahamas, and Caribbean Reefs.*]

Later in the day I paddle to shore and walk on the island. At the beach I meet Pete and his daughter Loie, who are also on a paddleboard, and from the sailboat that made the noise that startled me while diving.

Pete sees me walking toward them and greets me with "From the other red sailboat!" The shared color of our sailboats forms a bond between us. Theirs is a J42, *Merlin*, which, like me, Pete purchased in St Petersburg, Florida.

I chat with them for a while before walking across a narrow section of the island on a trail made of planks of wood, to protect our feet from the ubiquitous sand spines, evil little seeds from a grass, with very sharp spines all over that will ruin your day. One careless step can implant many into the foot, making the victim have to immediately sit down and extract the spiny beasts.

*Conception Island's northwest shore was unique and a pleasure to explore.*

On the way back to *Sobrius*, I stop at the Colvin Gazelle, *Gaia* and meet Jim, a Canadian with a European accent that I can't quite place. He is a friendly man, older than me, and has circumnavigated on *Gaia*, which he and his wife Helen built.

"What kind of boat is this?" I ask.

"A Gazelle."

"A Colvin Gazelle?" I should have guessed this first.

"Yes!" Jim is surprised. "Not many people have heard of the Colvin Gazelle."

"I'm familiar with it because Matt Rutherford, with the Ocean Research Project, sails one."

"I don't know Matt Rutherford."

"He's known for being the first person to circumnavigate the Americas singlehanded and non-stop, via the Northwest Passage and Cape horn." He did this amazing feat in an unlikely 27' Albin Vega.

"Ah yes, I think I have heard of him."

We talk about the weather, the coming frontal passage, and where we will go to ride it out. Frontal passages bring winds from all directions, and this anchorage is not safe when the wind direction has any west in it. We both think Georgetown, in the Exumas and about a day's sail away, would be a good safe choice.

I should ask them for an interview, but I don't. Somehow, I have a hang-up about this.

April 14

The morning is bright and warm, and the sun shines its powerful light down upon us, reminding me that I need to do the laundry, and suggesting that today is the right day to do it. I now have 25 extra gallons of water that I purchased in Clarence Town, so there is no excuse to delay any longer. I clean all my clothes, towels, and wash cloths in the orange bucket that I've been using to rinse the dishes in saltwater. In order to dry the clothes without risk of losing them to the breeze, I string a jib sheet through the arms of the shirts and the legs of the pants, and tie it to a shroud and a backstay.

While the clothes are still drying, which takes all day, I feel slightly embarrassed for the display of domesticity, and while there is almost nobody here to see, Mark and Judy from the ketch *Rainbow* stop by. "Laundry day?" he remarks.

They saw me hoist the antenna up the backstay this morning then sit still next to my little shortwave radio for a half hour while I listened to the Chris Parker weather report and took notes. Mark wants a weather report. I consult my notes and relay to them that the wind is supposed to shift to the south on Monday, veering all the way around to the north, where it will blow 15-20 with possible squalls, continuing NNE on Tuesday at 15-20, with a chance for more squalls. Mark tells me they will go to Rum Cay. He's anxious to spearfish on the deep reefs there.

"It's probably going to be very rolly there. This SE wind we've had will likely kick up a swell, and it seems like the swell wraps into the anchorage there. It was rolly when I was there two days ago."

"That's no problem, I use a bridle" he tells me.

"A bridle?"

"Yeah, I tie a line to my anchor chain and take it through a chock on in the middle of the beam. Then I adjust both until I'm facing the swell. It works great!"

"That's brilliant! I've used a second anchor off the stern, to the side, to pull myself into the swell, but your bridle sounds easier. I've never heard of that."

Judy chimes in "I've been doing this for 17 years and I've never seen anyone else do it."

And now I have picked up a useful technique, just from talking to other sailors. I need to get into the habit of being more social.

I am determined to get over my foolish and childish fear of asking anyone for anything, and have made it today's goal to ask the couple on *Gaia* for an interview. I told David Hows of *The Ocean Sailing Podcast* that I would be interviewing people while in The Bahamas, and now I have to live up to my word.

I sit by the VHF and steel my nerve to call and ask for an interview. I feel like I did as a teenager, phone in hand, wanting to call a girl, but lacking the nerve to dial the numbers. After much unnecessary consternation, I make the call, but they do not answer, and now I need to paddle over and ask them in person.

I get my snorkeling gear ready, step down onto the 12-0, and immediately see a grey shape in the water. I turn on the video camera and slip myself right in the water. It's a big stingray, and I start to follow it, but then I see another one closer, and I swim towards it instead. It stops swimming when it sees me coming and turns to point its barbed tail at me. I don't get close at all. These things can really hurt anyone foolish enough to get within range. I continue to the reef.

I've been wanting to get video of cleaner-fish in action, and finally I get it. On the bottom, in a dark crevice of the reef, a small wrasse is picking parasites off the face and body of a red hind who sits still. This is truly an amazing sight, here we have a piscivore (a predator of fish) letting a little bite-sized fish clean its face. I remember when I was young, on a sailing trip with my family in the 1980's, before the worldwide coral die-off started, swimming across an elkhorn coral reef in the Dry Tortugas. Little wrasses were trying to pick the hairs off my legs. They must have thought I was covered in parasites and did not care that I wasn't even a fish, and that I had no previously-worked-out agreement with them that I would allow this without trying to eat them.

*This red hind was getting cleaned by a cleaner fish; you can see the little yellow and black fish to the right of the big fish's mouth.*

After probing the mysteries of the reef in the clear blue water, I paddle the 12-0 over to *Gaia*, congratulating myself on doing what needs to be done, and feeling a bit odd for having the nerve to sail across the ocean singlehanded and freedive blue holes solo, but still fear asking a sailor for an interview.

When I get close to *Gaia*, Jim sees me from the enclosed cockpit and comes right out.

"I wanted to talk to you" he says, immediately putting me at ease. "There is an all-weather harbor at Cat Island, at Hawks Nest Creek. It's closer than Georgetown."

"I've heard of that, but I thought the bottom wasn't suitable for anchoring." I remember my cruising guide said one could anchor there, but the bottom has poor holding, the current is strong, and it can be "unbearably buggy in a calm."

I talk to him for a few minutes then ask for the interview, and he readily agrees; I will paddle back over at 5:00. *Mission accomplished.*

I dive again in the afternoon, and right away notice the unmistakable outline of a shark on the bottom. It looks like it might be a harmless nurse shark, but then I see its mouth, and its tailfin. No, it is definitely not a nurse shark, but rather the kind with teeth that stick out of the mouth. I think of it like a large dog, or a barracuda – *show no fear*, I tell myself, *swim towards it if it swims towards you, let it know you are not afraid.* It swims around me, not really circling, but certainly checking me out. I stay near my 12-0, and keep the video camera on and pointing at the shark.

It swims away, close to the bottom, then turns and swims slowly towards me, rising, coming right at me. I can see its teeth. I swim slowly right at it. This is how I respond to barracuda, who often swim towards me, and they always retreat when I approach them. But this is the first time I've done this with a shark. Before it gets closer than twenty feet, the shark slowly turns to my left and leaves me be, but it doesn't leave the area, rather it sits still on the bottom at the head of the reef.

*This lemon shark swam around me, checking me out, before sitting still on the bottom. Notice all the dead staghorn coral lying broken on the bottom below the shark.*

*Lemon sharks are identified by the second dorsal fin being nearly as large as the first, which begins just behind the pectoral fins. The shape of the tail and the visible teeth further confirm the identification. My fish identification book ends its description with the ominous phrase "a dangerous shark." Notice how the two bar jack to the shark's left are not afraid.*

I continue snorkeling and diving, always keeping a wary eye on the shark, and am comforted by the fact that none of the fish on the reef seem to care that the shark is here. Parrotfish are abundant during this exploration of the reef, and I get some good video of them scraping their meals from the coral.

I also see humans; Jim and Helen have fearlessly swum over from *Gaia* for a snorkel. I remember he mentioned that their dinghy's motor has been giving them trouble. I can't help but notice that Jim is missing one of his legs.

I see another large shark on the bottom, but this one is just a nurse shark. They also have two dorsal fins of equal size, but the first dorsal fin is positioned well behind the pectoral fins, and they have no lower lobe on the caudal (tail) fin.

*This was a big nurse shark – harmless, but sill commanding attention. Note the shape of the tail fin, which lacks a lower lobe.*

At 5:00, I paddle over to *Gaia* and set up my microphone. Helen makes me a cup of tea while Jim drinks his one beer for the day. We talk for an hour, and they tell me all about building the boat – which took ten years. They built it from scratch, out of steel, with plans from Thomas Colvin, modifying the plans a bit by adding the enclosed pilothouse and the raised rear cabin. *Gaia* is also junk rigged, with two unstayed masts (the masts have no stays (steel cables) to support them). I compliment the pilothouse, which is completely enclosed with a steel roof and low walls, and sliding acrylic windows (*Sobrius*, in contrast, has neither dodger nor bimini, and thus no protection from the weather).

"I've got good foul-weather gear, but I've never put it on" Jim tells me. All the lines are led into the cockpit, so they almost never have to leave the pilothouse. This must be a luxury in the cold or the rain. But I do like the unobstructed visibility from the cockpit of *Sobrius*, and I really love being able to see the entire night sky.

Jim and Helen spent many years in a circumnavigation, and had plenty of stories for the interview, which is now episode 53 of *The Ocean Sailing Podcast* [episode 55 is an interview of myself] https://www.oceansailingpodcast.com/podcast/. Not only did I get a great interview, but I made two new friends, and all three of us enjoyed the conversation.

April 15

At 3:00 am I wake to the sound of Peter Tosh singing "Coming in hot, hot, hot." In the dark cabin, I slowly rise from the inflatable mattress on the starboard settee, turn off the alarm on my phone, switch on an LED light, and put water on the alcohol stove to boil for tea.

I had originally planned on leaving at sunset for Staniel Cay, 40 nm away, but changed my mind last night and opted to get some sleep and then make the shorter crossing to Georgetown. I'd like to see the place and get a bit of civilization, and I need to be in a protected harbor for the frontal passage coming Monday. I thought about staying, but the cruising guide says, about the anchorage here at Conception Island, "Do not plan to ride out a frontal passage here, boats have been washed up on the beach in west winds." I don't need more convincing than that.

I make tea and oatmeal, then start the engine at 4:00 am. As an experiment, I leave the deck lights on as I motor away. They shine down from the spreaders, halfway up the mast, and illuminate not only the foredeck, but also the water around us. I think this might make leaving the anchorage at night safer, helping me avoid obstacles, like the reef and the mooring balls.

The other boats in the anchorage all look closer at night, but I know this is an illusion, yet it still makes me nervous, as does the invisible reef behind me. Motoring out seems like the responsible thing to do, although I prefer sailing off anchor.

I put the engine in gear and we idle forward as I move to the bow and start pulling in the rode. The tiller is tied off in the center. When the anchor is up, I take the extra time to put it in the anchor locker where it will be safe for today's ocean-sailing. But as I do this

*Sobrius* is slowly motoring towards the beach in the dark and my heartrate is increasing at the thought.

I creep like a scared spider back to the cockpit and unlash the tiller, turning us hard to port, away from the dark unseen beach and the shallow reef. The moon is not out, and the only light comes from the stars, and the deck lights shining down from the spreaders, which illuminate two orange balls very close to starboard – I turn hard to port again. The deck lights just prevented me from running over the mooring balls, the same one to which a big German racing boat was moored yesterday.

Outside the harbor, I steer us into the wind, pointing the bow back toward the island and the reefs, and set the tillerpilot. I slow the boat speed as much as I think I can while still maintaining enough speed for the tillerpilot to steer. I move to the mast to raise the mainsail.

Last night I put a reef in the main so it would be ready. But I now discover that I neglected to shackle on the halyard, so I have to move back to the stern pulpit to remove the halyard and take it to the sail, as we slowly motor forward. I start to raise the sail, but something else is wrong. Now I find that I didn't attach the reef tack to the hook on the boom, so I lower the sail and make the steel loop fast, then finally I can raise the main. But I also have to release the boom vang and then go back to the cockpit to loosen the mainsheet in order for the sail to go all the way up. Finally, I raise the mainsail and retighten the vang, as we will be sailing downwind today.

All this happens as quickly, efficiently, and safely as I can, but I know we are slowly motoring back towards the island and its reefs, the same ones on which I snorkeled. They appeared deep enough for me to sail over, but I don't want to test this hypothesis.

When all is finished with the main, I return to the cockpit, turn off the tillerpilot and remove it from the tiller, then look at the chartplotter, which alarmingly tells me that we are over the beginning of the reef. I turn us hard to starboard and we start sailing into the safe, deep water. A minute later the water is thousands of feet deep, beyond the capacity of my depth sounder to measure, and I relax a little at the thought; I no longer need worry about running aground on a reef.

The storm jib is ready to hoist, and I do so once we are underway in the dark. It goes up easy, as it is so small, but the jib downhaul (my "least-favorite line") is cleated too short for it to go up all the way, and I have to reach down and uncleat the line, then raise the sail the rest of the way, then take out the slack in the downhaul and cleat it back. The cleat for this line is conveniently placed right at the base of the mast; at least I did that right.

The wind is blowing at 20 knots, which made me nervous before leaving. A breeze this strong howls ominously in the rigging of sailboats and makes one want to stay put in the safety of an anchorage. But once underway, with the main reefed and the tiny storm Jib flying, we sail comfortably at 5 knots in the dark night with the sea floor invisible a mile below and thousands of stars quite visible millions and billions of miles above. The unique beauty of sailing alone on a clear and warm night is unsurpassed by anything on land and makes one happy to be alive and ever grateful to live in such a glorious world. *This is surely what I came for.*

The seas, as we sail out of the lee of Conception Island, rise to about 6 feet, which makes for a lively ride. But *Sobrius* was designed for this sort of sailing and we move along with no problem. I stay clipped in to the large padeye on the floor of the cockpit, looking ahead across the dark water as my conscious mind wanders off; my subconscious controls my right arm as it moves the tiller back and forth, responding to the water and the rudder without the need for thought.

I wonder for a moment what it would be like to try to swim back to Conception Island in the dark against the wind, and the thought is terrifying. It's good to occasionally remind myself of this reality, but I do not dwell on this for more than a moment, although I reach down and pull on the tether to reassure myself that it is firmly attached to the boat. *Sobrius* and I are one.

The lights from the few boats at Conception Island disappear below the dark horizon, but soon after the black sky lightens to shades of grey, purple, then red. An hour later the sun rises behind us, followed by Long Island rising above the southwestern horizon ahead. Soon I will cross my path from the passage between Cat Island and Long Island, completing a circumnavigation of the latter.

I see a flock of birds behind us, rising above then diving into the water, feeding on something within. I keep looking at the scene, hoping to see whales, but none appear.

As we pass a mile or two off Long Island, the depth decreases from thousands of feet to 60 feet. As we approach the shoal, I worry that the waves might stand up and become dangerous. I consider going further offshore, but a look at the chartplotter shows this would be futile. The shoal extends for miles to the north of Long Island. I let fate take its course, and we sail across the shoal. The waves are no problem, and as we pass Long Island they all but disappear.

Now I can take down the storm jib and put up Jib #4. The storm jib is easy to take down, as it is so small. I just tighten both sheets, bring the little sail over the deck, loosen the halyard, and pull in on the jib downhaul as I let out on the halyard. The sail comes down without any problems. I time myself and the job is over in 11 minutes. My "least-favorite line" (the jib downhaul) did its job flawlessly; the trick was to not let it get all bundled up with the sail, accomplished by keeping the jib halyard in my right hand and letting it out slowly as I pull in on the downhaul with the other hand.

With the much larger jib #4 up, we now make 6.5 knots – fast for *Sobrius*. This is our hull-speed.

I can see the sails of another boat in the distance, moving slightly from left to right, but also in the same direction as us. I assume it is going to Georgetown from Long Island. I use it as a reference for steering.

The Island of Great Exuma and its related cays rise in the distance, first visible as grey blotches on the horizon, then they connect and grow taller, taking on green and brown hues. I hear on the VHF *Drumbeat* and *Serenity* discussing safe passage. I remember that *Drumbeat* was in the anchorage at Thompson Bay while I was there. I see *Serenity* on the AIS, and it soon passes me – a large and stately power vessel, moving fast.

I study the chart before we get to the channel leading in to Elizabeth Harbor. As we near Channel Rocks, I heave-to and drop the jib; I want to sail in under main alone. We will be going downwind through the narrow channels leading to Georgetown for a few miles and the jib will not be necessary, and sailing through channels and around obstacles is much simpler without it.

I pass what seems awfully close to Channel Rocks, then aim for Middle Rocks. The suggested route on the chartplotter takes me right at these sharp-edged, pointy, brown rocks rising vertically from the churning water, again very close, before turning to starboard and proceeding north into the light blue water of Elizabeth Harbor. To port can be seen Man-O-War Cay and its hill topped with the wooden ruins of a fort. Coral reef lies all around, and I focus to stay on the route, careful not to get too distracted with the binoculars and sightseeing, but I am tempted to look at the fort, the islands, the reefs, and other boats.

Foul Cay and Guana Cay pass to starboard, and before I get to the narrow pass between two reefs and the huge cluster of sailboats anchored beyond, I start the engine, turn into the wind, and drop the main, while a catamaran emerges from the mass of anchored vessels and approaches from the north. I get the sail down quickly, then turn back to the north and pass the catamaran starboard-to-starboard. A shirtless man wearing a ridiculous pirate hat and flanked by two ladies in bikinis waves. I wave back, suspecting I am now somewhere quite different from the previous islands I've visited.

I motor through the anchorage at Elizabeth Island, expecting to find reef to snorkel, but the water is cloudy and the chop is strong here, so I motor on. I pass the anchorage to the east of Georgetown by Stocking Island, then a bunch of catamarans around the Moss Cays, cross the deep channel that leads to the government docks, and anchor near a big steel schooner, close to town between the channel and the submerged cable shown on the chart, wondering why more boats aren't here.

Location: 23° 30.58'N, 75° 46.05'W

After anchoring at noon, I sleep for two hours, worn out from the crossing and a bit dehydrated. I need to remember to drink more water while sailing in the sun.

*"Judge your success by what you have to give up to get it."* Dalai Lama

## THE EXUMAS

April 16

Today is a day of rest and writing.

At 11:00 am I paddle to town, and am surprised to see Pete and Loie from *Merlin*, whom I met at Conception Island, as they ride in their dinghy away from town. I buy AA batteries from the hardware store, and some vegetables and bread at the grocery store. Edward, a man selling peanuts, suggests eating at the restaurant Blue at Exuma Yacht Club. I follow his advice and enjoy a delicious hamburger and an expansive view of the harbor from above.

Tomorrow I plan to sail north. It might be that I should have moved *Sobrius* to the other side of the harbor today, as the winds will veer north tonight, but I didn't, for no good reason. I hope this doesn't turn out to be a mistake.

But as I stand in the cockpit looking at the building waves in the harbor, and the long sheltered anchorage on the other side, I feel foolish for staying, and I prepare to move. Within minutes I'm on the other side, in the lee of Stocking Island, looking for a place to anchor among all the other boats. I motor to the north end of the pack, because I'm heading north tomorrow anyway, and anchor in a nice spot away from the city and on the edge of the crowd.

I dive in and set the anchor in a grassy bottom as the sun sets, feeling good about my decision to move.

In the early morning, while sipping hot black coffee, I listen carefully to the weather report, which calls for north winds today at 15-20 knots veering slightly and decreasing throughout the day. I decide to go ahead and sail up the archipelago to Cave Cay, or if I can't get that far, I can stop at Rat Cay, Black Cay, or Lee Stocking Island. I'll have to beat upwind, but if the wind veers, as the forecast predicts, the sail should get easier throughout the day.

We motor out of the anchorage instead of sailing off anchor, to ensure I don't run into another boat. I'm willing to take the chance of running aground, or into an island, but not another boat.

I set sail in the harbor, and motor sail towards the inlet. Another sailboat comes up behind us and sets sail while motoring. They are close enough that I can almost read the name – *Ocean Diamond* perhaps. I keep a close eye on them and give plenty of leeway. We sail out of the inlet together and both continue on port tack, sailing east, in Exuma Sound. After a few miles, I tack and head up the coast, while they continue on towards either Cat Island or Long Island. I'm on a close reach, and trying to keep on a course that will prevent me from having to tack away from the island, but land keeps getting closer.

Soldier Cay looms nearly straight ahead as I point just to its right; I hope to make it past the island without tacking. I watch the stone beacon on the north end of the island as the depth decreases from thousands of feet to hundreds, then to less than a hundred. The brown jagged rocks to port keep getting bigger and the adrenaline starts to flow as I try to keep *Sobrius* as close as possible to the wind. The depth stops decreasing at 45 feet and now I can make out individual drops of water as waves slam into the rocks to port. I stare ahead, trying to calculate if we will make it past the island without tacking or running aground. It's an unnecessary risk, but somehow I feel compelled to take it, and we pass the rocky island, safely but close. White Cay is next, and I know we have to tack this time. We sail away from land for a half hour before I take the reef out of the main and then tack back up the coast.

It's not long before I see Black Cay on the chart, and we pass it without temptation to go in and anchor; the day is still young. I hear boats on the VHF talking to Emerald Bay Marina, and I wonder what it would be like to stay in the marina – convenient, but boring, too close to normal life, I think. I stay in a marina at home for the rest of the year, and I came here for something different.

Before long I see Lee Stocking Island both on the chart and off to port, in the real world. I stayed here at the Caribbean Marine Research Center when I was in college, as a volunteer research assistant. The memories come back to me, SCUBA diving, catching lobster, seeing sharks while snorkeling, night diving on the stromatolite beds. But I also remember devastating mosquitos. I keep sailing. I'm looking forward to getting "inside" the Exumas, into the protected waters of the bank, and Cave Cay is the first opportunity to do so. If we anchor in the islands before Cave Cay, then we will have to come back out into Exuma Sound to continue north.

The whitecaps on the sea surface have lessened, and our speed has followed suit. It's time for a headsail change. I set the autopilot, go below and pull out jib #3, then clip my tether to the jackline and move to the bow. But when I get to the mast, the jib backwinds. I was planning on changing sails while underway, using a tack to drop the jib, but now I'll just go ahead and drop it while hove-to.

I release the jib halyard and pull on the jib downhaul, holding the lines in both hands, letting the halyard out as I pull on the downhaul, so the sail doesn't get ahead of the downhaul.

With Jib #4 bagged, I hank on jib #3 and haul it up, but something is wrong; the leech is twisted near the top. I let it back down and reverse the fourth hank from the top. For some reason the hanks on this sail are not oriented consistently, and I have to pay attention to keep from attaching one to the forestay backwards.

While on port tack, I notice the starboard rear lower shroud is flopping all around. There is only one time to adjust a loose shroud, and that time is now, while sailing on the tack opposite the shroud. I set the tillerpilot, go below and get an adjustable wrench and a pair of channel-locks from the mahogany tool rack that I built and mounted over the drinking-glass rack above the sink. With tools in hand, I clip to the jackline and creep along the leeward deck as the deep water of Exuma Sound rushes past only inches from my feet, which are pressed firmly to the low gunwale. I loosen the two locknuts and tighten the turnbuckle just a bit, then retighten the locknuts, and the job is done.

The wind today is variable, with gusts coming from 5-10 degrees more east. I have to pay attention and either head up, which I do all morning, or let the main sheet out, which I do in the afternoon, after the wind has shifted more east. It keeps my mind occupied.

I'm having trouble trimming the jibs today – both of them. On a close reach, I can't stop them from luffing. I try moving the jib cars fore and aft, and adjusting the sheets, but I just can't seem to get them trimmed properly. I give up after a while and try to ignore it, blaming the problem on the advanced age of the sail.

I'm telling myself to drink lots of water today. The new protocol is *whenever you think about drinking water, or look at the bottle, drink*. I don't want to get dehydrated today, so the water bottle gets plenty of attention. Developing new protocols based on previous mistakes has been a theme of this journey, and perhaps sailing itself is a new protocol developed as a substitute for past indulgences gone awry.

The weather today started off cloudy, with 20-knot winds and 5' seas, but in the afternoon the sky is clear, the seas have settled to 4' and the wind to 15 knots. The water is a luminous dark blue, like a giant sapphire, with the sun reflecting off its many waves and ripples. An endless stream of rocks and islands passes by to my left, with the ocean horizon on the right. Between the two slowly changing views, my mind is constantly occupied and in a state of peace.

Rat Cay, the last possible anchorage before Cave Cay, passes without me noticing, and we are now committed to going all the way to the latter. We should have just enough time to get there before dark, and I feel a hint of anxiety at the thought of arriving after dark, which would necessitate staying outside until morning.

Approaching Galliot Cut and Cave Cay, I notice, for the first time, that the chart warns of dangerous conditions during an outgoing tide if the wind and seas are against it. Indeed, the wind blows towards the cut, and the seas roll that way as well. I check the tides, a whole day too late (I should have checked this yesterday while at anchor). But luck is with me, and the tide is going in, so the current will be going the same direction as the wind and seas. I heave-to, drop the jib, and start the engine before entering the narrow cut between the islands.

Running the engine while in an inlet is a good safety precaution, in case something unexpected happens, as there is little room for error in a narrow inlet. Also, when the current is with you the boat might lose steerage, going the same speed as the water, and so the rudder will do nothing. In this case the engine provides the necessary speed relative to the water.

I learned this in the St Augustine Inlet (in Florida). Luckily the inlet there is wide enough that I had time to start the engine before I drifted into the breaking shoals on the left or the rock jetty on the right.

As we enter the narrow inlet, with jagged and menacing rocks on both sides, I certainly do need the engine. The current is strong, the mainsail is flogging, and the scene reminds me of canoeing in a river, with waves from the current, eddies, and slicks… Once inside, I turn us to the right and the water calms immediately. Ahead is a small sailboat sitting peacefully in the little anchorage behind Big Galliot Cay, where I intend to anchor. The sight of this boat, anchored in such a quiet and serene setting, immediately makes me self-conscious of my offensively rumbling engine. I reach down and shut it off, and the evening is once again silent. I quietly tack into the little bay, drop Dr. Spock, and we are home for the night.

Location: 25° 55.46'N, 76° 17.41'W

I dive, as tradition, and view Dr. Spock sitting on top of the soft sand. I push his point into the bottom, then swim in the clear water for a bit before returning to the dry safety of my floating home.

April 18

In the silent morning, the other sailboat disappears, and I paddle the 12-0 around the anchorage, just looking about like a tourist. The wind is calm behind the little island, and the water is flat and clear. There are no other boats here, nor any sign of civilization visible. The island is uninhabited. I paddle around the corner to the left, into another cove. Jagged undercut rocks pass to my right. To the left is a small bay with another rocky island topped with low shrubs and green trees. No one is here. I pass over some isolated coral heads, and take note to investigate on the way back.

There is a small shallow cut to the ocean, at the end of the cove, and I slide across the surface to see it. The current is strong here, with the tide coming in. Water rushes over the rocks below, falling towards me as it would if I were facing upstream in a river. Eddies and whirls abound in the blue water creating swirling and shifting patterns that capture my attention and nearly cause me to lose my balance. I turn around and make my way back to the coral, put on my mask, and slip into the still water.

I am greeted by small but healthy coral reef, a few patches separated by flat sand. Fish swim about, eying me nervously, some trying to look brave. I casually swim from one coral head to another through the absolutely clear water in the silent and still morning.

*A healthy brain coral erupts from one of the little reef patches at Big Galliot Cay.*

I paddle to the little beach and step onto the sand for a walk. A hand-painted sign made of a piece of driftwood reads "Kiera's Beach." Under the sign lay rocks subtly decorated with red and yellow paint and carefully arranged conch shells.

I paddle around the other side of Big Galliot Cay, which is not big at all, and into the channel that we entered after yesterday's long sail. The current is fierce, but I manage to make a bit of headway along the edge before turning around. The water is clear and deeper here, maybe 20', brilliant dark blue and enchanting.

After the morning swim, I raise the mainsail, letting the mainsheet out about half way, thinking this will prevent us from speeding into the rocks of the island. I go to the bow and pull up the anchor and realize that I am wrong about the sail; as I cleat off the anchor, *Sobrius* is charging ahead on a beam reach, towards the menacing undercut rock that rims the island about which I was swimming only thirty minutes before.

I hurry back to the cockpit, careful not to fall along the way, release the tiller from its lashings, and put it hard over to starboard, and *Sobrius* responds with a hard turn to port. I check the depth, luckily still 12'. Destruction on the rocks was certainly approaching fast, yet now we sail peacefully in the direction of safety.

We sail away from the cluster of small islands, towards the big bright blue waters of the Exuma Bank. We are *inside* now, and will be sailing in shallow water, protected from the prevailing winds and the swells of the ocean, for about the next week. The wind is lighter today so I take down the #3 jib. Since we are sailing downwind, I simply tighten the lazy sheet, pulling the jib mostly over the deck, then pull the sail down as I slowly let the halyard out. With jib #3 bagged, I hoist the big genny and we gain a bit of speed across the still and glowing water lit by the bright morning sun.

We pass Big Farmers Cay and Little Farmers Cay, and then make our way up Great Guana Cay. This morning's destination is a place I found while studying the charts, looking for a spot to snorkel near which I could anchor. It's group of coral heads shown on the chart by an area on Great Guana Cay labeled "Hetty's Land," and about a half mile offshore. I wonder who Hetty was.

Approaching the coral reef, I heave-to and drop the big genny, then sail upwind, slowly, watching for coral and rock and looking for the best place to anchor.

Another sailboat is anchored closer to shore, and I see three people in a dinghy riding around while one of them leans over and peers into the water through a "looky bucket" – a bucket whose bottom has been replaced with glass. Pushing the looky bucket into the water allows one to see clearly what is below.

I anchor and paddle over to a dark reef. The coral reef looks black from above the surface. I drop my little grappling anchor upwind of the reef and ease myself into the water, looking around in a full circle underwater as I do. I see no sharks, and swim to the reef, which is bustling with fish. The coral is mostly healthy. I am definitely seeing a direct correlation between healthy coral and number of fish. This reef has my attention, and I swim to the bottom and sit still while taking video of the fish. They relax as soon as I quit moving, and swim right in front of my camera.

*This reef off Great Guana Cay, Exumas, was teeming with fish.*

A school of French grunt swims in front of the camera; red and white squirrelfish show themselves then retreat back into dark caves. A yellow and black rock beauty gets my attention and I point the camera at her. Queen angelfish slip in and out of skinny crevices. A graysby comes out of a cave for a quick peek at the interloper before darting back in. Blue tang, schoolmaster snapper, various wrasses, spotfin butterflyfish, stoplight parrotfish all swim in front of my camera.

I stay at the reef for a while, trying to get good shots of the queen angelfish. The three people in the dinghy show up and I push my mask to my forehead to greet them properly.

"Hello! There's some nice reef here."

"Yes, I know" says one of the two women, with a French accent. "From two years ago when I dive here. Lots of fish and lobster."

We all continue snorkeling and diving. The man has a spear, but I don't see him shoot anything. Then we all move to another reef and do it again.

Back onboard, I sail off anchor and proceed north, passing Black Point Settlement. This picturesque little town is nestled in a cove with pastel houses on the hill looking down at the sailboats in the harbor. The town attracts me, but I want to see the iguanas at Bitter Guana Cay. Maybe I'll come back to Black Point after I visit the lizard colony.

To get to Bitter Guana Cay, I need to enter the inlet – Dotham Cut – then turn north (left) right before the narrow cut between the two islands. The water is shallow here, but the inlet is deep. The current is strong, and I have the engine in gear. We have to sail into the wind, and the engine provides all the power now. I need to turn left, and the charts all agree that this is safe, but the water is black, the color of coral, or green, the color of rocks. It looks shallow to me and this makes me nervous.

But I have to pull the trigger eventually and I make the turn slowly, watching the depth which stays above 8' as we exit the cut. The first island on the right is Gaulin Cay South, tall, rocky, boasting white cliffs and a beach with a cave. The water below is absolutely clear and the bottom is sand with clusters of black reef. I've seen all I need, and I drop Dr. Spock to the sand below. But looking down I see the tell-tale spots on the bottom denoting young coral. I pull the anchor back aboard, hoist the mainsail, and maneuver to lighter water just a bit closer to the inlet. Here Spock lays happily in sand where the chain will disturb no young coral.

Location: 24° 7.32'N, 76° 24.6'W

While I ready my snorkeling gear, a familiar red sailboat pulls into the cut. I check the AIS and yes, it is *Merlin*, with Pete,

Loie, and crew. I call on the VHF, young Loie answers, and we say hello to each other. No doubt her father is busy at the helm. They are heading to Black Point Settlement. The J-42 draws 6', so *Merlin* is much more limited on where it can go than *Sobrius*. But I imagine Black Point will be fun for them; It's calling me too.

I dive to confirm that the anchor is set and disturbing no coral, then proceed to the island to try to find the iguanas.

These uninhabited islands are protected habitat for the endangered and indigenous iguanas. I've always had a fascination with lizards, and even had a few green iguanas as pets when I was young.

I think I see movement on the beach as I approach, and before I've pulled the 12-0 out of the water, a big dark iguana walks out of the bushes towards me. It stops when only 20' away. It's dark grey, with a black tail and red blotches around its head. The dewlap, a flap of skin under the jaw and neck, is light grey. A row of short black spines runs along the back, from head to tail. Then another lizard jostles out of the vegetation to join us.

*The iguanas at Gaulin Cay South were as curious of me as I was of them.*

More lizards come out of the bush to see what's going on at the beach, and one even sits in the shade under my 12-0. Today, I am a time traveler standing on a Mesozoic beach among dinosaurs, and I'm glad they are friendly.

Leaving the curious iguanas on the beach, I climb the hill of strangely eroded and spiky rocks, much to the dismay of my sandals, and look out over the windward side of the island and the dark blue and windswept water of Exuma Sound. Vertical cliffs fall to the dark blue water. Bitter Guana Cay lies to the north, bordered by a tall white cliff.

The surface of this island is all dark rock, sharp and spiked to the point that I could not stand here barefoot. While shrubs cover much of the leeward side of the island, nothing grows on the top.

Back at the beach, I say goodbye to the iguanas and paddle back out into the clear water, in search of the coral heads I saw on the way in. The black masses in the water are easy to find.

I am amazed at what I see underwater. It's the best coral I've seen in a long time, perhaps since the 1990's. The little clusters of reef are covered in live coral and populated by a plethora of multicolored and happy fish who swim about like the busy residents of a large city.

Lobed star coral makes up most of the reef, with staghorn branching out in places. Plate corals drape over the reef, wrasses swim in and out of the smallest crevices; sponges, like chimneys, reach towards the surface; spiral fan worms that look like Christmas trees emerge from spaces between lobes of star coral, disappearing into their tubes when my shadow passes over. Fire corals decorate the tops of the reef like the antlers of a deer.

Fish I see include red hind, cocoa damselfish, longfin damselfish, honey gregory, and schools of French grunt, bluehead wrasse, sergeant major, blue chromis, blue tang, and spotted goatfish. I even see a lobster.

The reefs are little oases of life surrounded by a desert of sand. Their beauty is unsurpassed by anything on land, and the opportunity to observe wildlife up-close on a coral reef is like nothing else I've seen anywhere. I am very fortunate to be here and the privilege does not go unappreciated.

Before returning home, I paddle over to the inlet, and see on the other side a wrecked sailboat in a small cove. I can't resist and paddle across the swift inlet to investigate. It's a full-keel cutter, perhaps a Southern Cross 31, with a canoe stern on which is painted

*Cimarron*, Marathon Key. *Cimarron* has no rudder, and the inside is a mess, full of things typical of a live-aboard vessel, and water. I leave it alone.

I return to *Sobrius* filled with admiration of the abundant life and stunning colors of the reef below, and happy that my vessel is in better shape than *Cimarron*. Nobody else is here to see this, and the reefs are marked only by little crosses on the chart, along with thousands of other little crosses, which denote, for most boaters, simply things to avoid running into.

*This lobster at Bitter Guana Cay was one of the few I saw on this journey.*

*This lobed star coral at Bitter Guana Cay was the most amazing coral head I saw on this journey, and it was bristling with tube fan worms.*

In the morning, I am faced with a tough decision. Somehow Black Point Settlement is calling to me, and I'd like to be social and see Pete and Loie, and maybe meet some new people, like the two bikini-clad ladies who waved to me as they passed in a water taxi earlier. I could return to the beach and take more photos of the iguanas, dive on more of the reefs that I didn't get to visit yesterday, then go to town for the rest of the day.

But I'd also like to dive at Thunderball Grotto, at Staniel Cay. The cruising guide calls it a "mandatory" place to visit. It also mentions that it should be visited at slack tide, as it's right near an inlet. High tide today is at 11:00, and I can just make it there before then if I leave now. I decide to let the computer decide by looking at the iguana photos I took yesterday. If some are good enough, then I will leave. If none are good, I'll stay.

Indeed, some of the photos are good, and so Thunderball Grotto it is!

I sail off anchor, then along the coast of Bitter Guana Cay, before turning to port and catching the incoming tide in the deep blue water of an unnamed cut. We pick up speed in the slightly turbulent water, and make our way west to go around Harvey Cay. A handful of other sailboats and catamarans are out today, and I sail wing-on-wing, with the genoa to starboard and the main to port.

A sailboat under power (with its sails down, so the engine is running, giving me right-of-way) is coming around the point in the other direction and appears to be heading right at me. I give it a minute, hoping the captain will steer around me, but this doesn't appear to be happening. I pick up the VHF when the potential for collision really starts making me nervous.

"Sailboat under power rounding Harvey Cay, sailboat under power rounding Harvey Cay, sailing vessel *Sobrius*."

"This is the sailboat under power rounding Harvey Cay."

"This is sailing vessel *Sobrius*, the red sailboat in front of you. I just want to make sure you see me and are going to steer around me. Which way do you want to pass?"

"I didn't get all that, please pick a channel."

"One four."

"One four."

The sailboat is getting closer.

"I am the red sailboat in front of you, I want to make sure you see me and are going to steer around me."

"Oh, yeah, you're coming this way, no problem."

Apparently, he didn't realize we were heading towards each other; he probably thought he was following me. It's not always easy to tell such things.

By now we are really getting close, and his boat veers off to his starboard, but this is a mistake and sending him across my bow. *Sobrius* is wing-on-wing, and thus very restricted in movement. I give him a second, as it is up to him to avoid me. I don't want to end up like two people who walk into each other because both change course at the same time, trying to avoid the other.

He corrects his mistake right away and turns to port, and we pass starboard-to-starboard.

I only have a moment to relax, because a catamaran is right behind him, and I almost go through the same process of calling it on the VHF. But they soon make it clear that we will pass port-to-port. This is not at all like the Ragged Islands or the Jumentos Cays, where traffic consisted of only one or two boats encountered in a day, if any at all.

Once around Harvey Cay I can make out in the distance Staniel Cay and Big Majors Spot, with its famous Bay of Pigs, where tourists who wish to swim with the swine can do so. Sailboats of all shapes and sizes, catamarans, and mega yachts cover the surface of the water like duckweed in a pond. I sail into the community of ships, heave-to, drop the jib, and start the engine. I anchor amongst the flock of boats next to a bright red catamaran on the south side of Big Majors Spot.

As efficiently as I can, I get my gear ready and paddle towards the grotto. I pass an aluminum sailboat, *Bilbao*, that has twin rudders and twin dagger-boards, along with an impressive rig. It looks hardy and fast, yet it has painted on the bow the silly face of a smiling whale.

Thunderball Grotto is a small island near the inlet with a cliff facing me as I approach. A dinghy with a radio playing and a jet ski are anchored in front of the cliff, and I anchor here too, then slip into the clear blue water.

I take a deep breath, swim down, see a cave underwater, and I poke my head in; it's big, and I think I see light inside. Right away I notice that I forgot my flashlight, which is usually attached to the stick that holds the video camera, and I remember I left it on its charger on the navigation table. I proceed in the dark, welcomed by schools of fish. I swim further in, towards the light, perhaps foolhardy but enjoying the thrill. I am drawn to the thrill, I can't avoid it. Underwater caves pull me in, and this one is certainly no exception.

But the darkness soon gives way to light, and I see legs above me, human legs, treading water, and light above the legs. There must be air in here, and so I surface. Air there is, lots of it. We are inside a large cavern, roughly the size of a big living room in a house. The ceiling is high, and a small opening at the top lets in sunlight, which sends beams of light penetrating the clear water. Fishing is not allowed here, so the fish are abundant, swimming all about. A small white statue of the Virgin Mary stands among them on the bottom, looking out of place, yet in the real house of God.

I swim through another underwater cave leading out an opening on the other side of the grotto. Here the bottom drops off into deeper water and the entire slope is covered by a huge garden of coral. The amount of coral surpasses anything I've seen since Elbow Cay in 1990, before the worldwide coral die-off began. The fish are as abundant as the coral, and they go about their business without taking notice of me. I am stunned and amazed by the spectacle and hover just outside the cave taking it all in before I begin exploring.

A big queen angelfish – a species that I've found hard to photograph – swims by and I follow her as she swims through many species of coral. There is so much here, it boggles the mind.

*Thunderball Grotto was an amazing place well worth seeing, but don't get caught here by an outgoing tide.*

*At least four species of live coral can be seen below this queen angelfish at Thunderball Grotto, Staniel Cay.*

I continue swimming down-current around the island, thinking I'll casually swim all the way around to the cave on the other side, where I entered. But when I turn the corner, I find the current against me, and I stop to think. *How can this be?* But then it hits me, the tide has started going out, and the current is pulling away from the island, pulling the water out to sea, and trying to pull me with it. I remember the words of the cruising guide: "visit at slack tide." Indeed.

I turn around and swim hard, back towards the cave from where I came, but I make little progress. I put the camera in my trunks, with the long handle against my left leg, so I can use my arms. I swim with everything I've got, kicking with my fins and pulling with my arms. I think about all the mile-long ocean swims that I did before this trip. I told the other swimmers, all of them beach lifeguards, that I was training for a trip to The Bahamas. Now that training is paying off, because I slowly make progress against the strengthening current.

When I get to the cave, I hold on to the sharp rock above, to catch my breath before swimming in, underwater. There's no time to waste; the current will likely get stronger as I wait. I take a deep breath and dive, then swim into the underwater cave which will lead to salvation. The Virgin Mary passes below, and I stop inside the dark cavern, again mesmerized by the beams of sunlight penetrating the water. I can't resist taking a bit of video, then I swim back underwater through the cave that I originally entered. On the outside, still underwater and looking up, I see the legs of a woman treading water and the prop-wash from a jet ski. I surface and see a group of people scrambling to get in their dinghy.

The current is strong, and pulling hard on the dinghy while the man struggles with the anchor line. The current is pulling hard on my 12-0 too, and I have to get back in the water after mounting the board to grab the line and pull in enough slack so that I can hold it while getting back onboard. It's not pretty, but I manage to pull the board to the anchor and finally the little grappling anchor lets go, whereupon we start drifting towards the dinghy and the man still pulling on his anchor line. I start paddling hard and the jet ski zooms off in front of me, with a woman at the helm and a man holding on to her. She apologizes for passing so close, but I just nod in acceptance as now I am paddling with everything I have to get out of the current. Luckily the 12-0 is good at this; it has very little resistance to the water and we make progress away from the inlet. Thankfully the current weakens as we get further from the grotto.

Safely back aboard *Sobrius*, I eat a snack of bread and olives as fast water taxis and tour boats zoom by, leaving prodigious wakes that rock my little vessel. I'm ready to move on. This crowded anchorage, aside from Thunderball Grotto, holds no interest for me.

I motor off the anchor to avoid any potential collisions, then set sail outside, away from the land and other boats, their wakes, and the throngs of tourists.

We sail away from the congestion of other vessels and across the shallow blue waters of the Exuma Bank. I look over the chart, and select a small unnamed cay west of Pipe Cay that looks like it has some coral around it.

The wind is decreasing, and it takes a long time to get to the little cay. Before we are there, I push the tiller to starboard to heave-to, realizing that I forgot to look for traffic behind me when I see a stately and modern sloop motoring up behind us. My genoa is now backwinded, but we make slow progress out of their path. I finish heaving-to and drop the headsail after they pass. Another mistake has been taken note of. I need to look behind me before heaving-to; I'm no longer in the wilderness.

I anchor off the little cay and snorkel, but the coral is no good; it's just rock covered in algae. A lot of exploration leads to dead ends, and this is the case here.

For the third time today I pull the heavy anchor and chain from the bottom and sail away. The wind is really light now and we make only 2.5 – 3 knots downwind, towards Warderick Wells Cay, in the Exuma Land and Sea Park. Eventually I start the engine and boost our speed to 5 knots, so as not to get there after dark. Perhaps exposure to all this civilization has made me impatient.

I anchor off the Malabar Cays, a mile from the big island of Warderick Wells, and next to an interesting sailboat – grey with red trim, a plumb bow, a bowsprit, and a wind vane self-steering rig off the stern. Two mega yachts share this outside anchorage with us.

I make a big dinner of split-pea soup, a can of sardines, and a sleeve of crackers, which I eat while watching the sunset over the water, a scene I never tire of. I've been eating all day, with an insatiable appetite. After dinner, I eat some peanuts, then make a cup of tea as I watch the stars come out for the night.

I check the video I took of the day, and am saddened to realize I made a crucial mistake at Thunderball Grotto. I had the camera off when I thought it was on, and on when I thought it was off. Nearly all my video is from the camera pointing down and swinging about while I breathe on the surface. Cameras will break your heart, or rather, misuse of cameras will break your heart – it's not the cameras' fault.

April 20

I have a clear plan for the day, and it starts with tea, oatmeal, and a weather report. However, radio reception is poor this morning and I sit listening intently to broken sentences and static, but miraculously the reception improves just in time for the forecast for this area. Winds are supposed to shift to the north today, which means I'll have to move to another spot with better protection. Then the wind should be strong out of the east for the next few days, which will be good for going north along the chain of islands.

After breakfast and weather, I spend a few hours writing, and then 2 hours before high tide, I set out on the 12-0 for the stromatolite bed about a mile-and-a-half away. I think this must be the same bed on which I did a night drift-dive when I was in college, as a volunteer at the Caribbean Marine Research Center, on Lee Stocking Island. It seems awfully far to have come here from there to dive, but I distinctly remember them saying that this was the only stromatolite bed known to exist, besides a much smaller one in Australia. So this must be the same one. It's also right near an inlet, so it would have been a drift-dive, as it will be today. I remember a scene from that night, as we SCUBA-dove with flashlights. I turned upside-down and drifted above my schoolmates as they shined their torches on the otherworldly seascape below. They looked like astronauts in a sci-fi movie and I imagined we were drifting through space over a dark and mysterious asteroid.

Stromatolites are similar to coral, in that they are a symbiotic relationship between two organisms that end up building rock-like structures. While coral are made up of cnidarians and algae, stromatolites are algae and cyanobacteria. However, stromatolites are approximately 3.5 billion years old, and the organisms that started the structures have evolved and are different from the ones that live there now. These are ancient and strange things indeed, Earth's oldest fossils, and the stromatolites here are not only fossils, but *living* fossils.

On the way, as I cross some shallow water, a shark swims below me. I try to get it on video but my camera seems not to like filming sharks, and I miss another one. This time it's because of an "SD Card Error."

I find the stromatolites in a cut between Warderick Wells and Hog Cay (there seem to be a lot of Hog Cays in The Bahamas). White mooring balls for dinghies float in the center of the cut. I get in on the up-current side and drift along. It looks just like it did in college. I turn upside-down and drift across the bizarre seascape doing my best to recreate the scene from my youth, and this time I get it on video.

The stromatolites are the size of large rocks or boulders with vertical sides and flat tops. Filamentous growths cover their sides like the fleece of wild sheep. They have no color, besides grey.

Drifting across this cluster of living things from the first period of life on earth, I feel like a visitor from outer space, like I am the outsider viewing something so ancient as to make my world seem insignificant. These simple organisms that build rocks in the water have survived all five of the major extinction events on Earth, and will hopefully survive the sixth, which many scientists say is happening now.

*The Stromatolites of Warderick Wells, Exuma Land and Sea Park, are bizarre living fossils and extremely rare, but they just look like rocks.*

After reliving my youth among the stromatolites, I paddle around the little island of Hog Cay and across shallow water to an area of dark blue water that reminds me of the blue holes. It's a depression in the sea floor that I estimate to be about 30' deep as I pass over it, drifting towards the rock ledges on the other side. A barracuda is following me, and I think I see coral underneath. In a corner of the rock wall over shallower water, where nothing can sneak up behind me, I quietly enter the unknown.

Below me is another garden of paradise, with life blooming in colors and shapes only the ocean can provide. A large green stoplight parrotfish swims by, in front of a spotfin butterflyfish and a blue tang. Coral, both hard and soft, in shades of yellow, green, purple, and red, runs down the slope in clusters of life.

Royal gramma, upside-down because they are not upside down, swim in front of an elliptical star coral. I've never seen them like this, rather always under a ledge and belly-up (not dead – they swim like this).

Purple sea fans, red sponges, brain coral, star corals, queen angelfish, squirrelfish – so many are here, in the shade of Hog Cay and on a slope, both similarities to the abundant reef at Thunderball Grotto, and I wonder if this correlation is a coincidence or if coral survives better in today's warming seas if it is partially shaded.

I fill my senses with the wonders of the hidden coral paradise, but also feel the insecurity of the knowledge that a big shark is probably lurking in the deep water nearby. I mount the 12-0 for the down-current paddle back to the safety and comfort of my little ship.

*Here royal gramma, the purple and yellow fish, can be seen swimming right-side-up, which is upside-down to them.*

*Three species of hard coral can be seen in the center, as well as soft corals that look like plants, and sponges in the upper right. In the foreground on the right appears to be a coral undergoing bleaching.*

On the windward side of the Malabar Cays, I dive, looking for coral marked on the charts. The reefs here are the typical mostly-dead variety. But I do see some large grey snapper, the likes of which I haven't seen yet, and can thank the no-fishing regulations here for that. I also see the strange ocean trigger fish, that swims by sculling with its dorsal and anal fins, and always seems to be swimming in the areas between reefs – bizarre outsiders of the fish world.

After a big lunch, I move *Sobrius* to a mooring at Emerald Bay, just a quarter-mile away and right next to the island. I go for a quick skinny-dip, as most of the boats have left and no one is close enough to notice my nakedness.

Emerald Rock calls to me. I think I see caves. It's a small rock nearby, and I paddle over for yet another underwater exploration for the day.

What appeared to be a cave is rather a long rock overhang, but underneath is plenty of coral and fish. You know the story by now.

Back onboard my pelagic home, I have a message on my Garmin InReach satellite communicator. Cristina asks if I can be in Miami on April 28 for her book club meeting. I assume this means her club is going to read my book *Becoming a Sailor, a Singlehand Sailing Adventure* and I readily agree, but I end with the phrase "weather permitting." A sailor can only do what the weather permits. Going to Miami would mean skipping the Abacos and rather taking the much more difficult route home along Florida's crowded coast and around Cape Canaveral.

April 21

I emerge from the cabin to a cloudy morning and the threat of rain, and I even feel a few drops as I wait for water to boil for coffee. But the clouds go on their way, leaving me dry, and I listen to the weather report while drinking strong coffee and eating oatmeal with honey and dried fruit. This breakfast never gets old, nor does waking up in The Bahamas on a sailboat.

I make careful notes of the weather on a yellow sticky-pad, taking into consideration the detour to Miami. The islands of The Bahamas have been wonderful, but I've been here six weeks now, and am about ready for some contrast, which Miami has in abundance. I'd also like to see Cristina.

I paddle to shore and hike around the island after breakfast, still early in the morning, in shorts and sandals. The sign on the beach shows a trail map and encourages visitors to stay on the trails, so as not to disturb the native flora and fauna, which consists mostly of rocks and thorny vegetation.

I take a trail that, according to the sign, should lead to ruins of old settlements, a wall, and the beach on the windward side of the island, overlooking the deep waters of Exuma Sound. Yellow marks on the rocks underfoot denote the trail and these are the only trail markers I see.

The rocky trail leads up a small hill to a loose stone wall, and some deep holes in the stone ground, like sinkholes, about 8' deep and 12' across. I wonder if these were associated with the ruins, and I'm tempted to climb down and see if they lead to caves, but I don't see an easy way out, and picture myself trapped in the hole, waiting for the next passerby to lend a hand, a passerby which may not come for days.

I stand on a rock gazing at the anchorage below, as well as the park headquarters and the boats moored there. To the east lay the dark blue waters of Exuma Sound, as well as Hog Cay and the stromatolite beds.

I follow the yellow marks on the rocks towards the beach facing Exuma Sound, but the trail is unmaintained and I constantly have to step across fallen branches which grab at my sandals and prick the skin of my feet. I walk carefully. Cuts, even small ones, are a problem when sailing. Saltwater encourages infection, and cuts constantly exposed to saltwater do not heal without treating them with a topical antibiotic, like Neosporin, which I always have aboard. I've heard it said that saltwater helps cuts heal, but this is a myth. Saltwater is full of microorganisms – *really full* – and they want to eat your flesh. Small cuts, scrapes, and abrasions tend to grow instead of heal with daily exposure to saltwater. My surfer buddies and I used to call these growing wounds "sea ulcers."

The trail gets harder to follow and it's difficult to move through the vegetation, but the yellow marks are still there. However, it's not long before I notice random yellow marks all over the rocks underfoot, and I realize that I've been following yellow lichen on the rocks, and not trail markers at all. Defeated, I turn back toward the beach and carefully make my way across the scrubby terrain, ignoring the false trail markings. I stop at a saltwater pond and watch some birds on the way. As I carefully and slowly pick my way through the unforgiving landscape, I see some of the native hutia, which look like little teddy bears, or perhaps large rats with short tails.

*This black-necked stilt made a lot of noise until I walked away from the pond where it was feeding.*

I feel social as I paddle back to *Sobrius*, and I stop to chat with the two couples on *Aventura*, an Island Packet cutter, moored next door. When I mention that I'm headed to Shroud Cay next, they tell me all about how good the kayaking is through the mangroves. One can cross from the anchorage to the windward side of the island and, if the tide is going out, be spit out into the ocean. "It's like a water park" one of them exclaims with great enthusiasm.

I'm wearing white pants, a white shirt, and a straw hat sits on my head as I ready *Sobrius* to sail off the mooring. *Aventura* is on the ball next to me, to port, and a power catamaran is two balls to starboard. I need to be on a port tack as we sail off in order to sail away from *Aventura*.

First I release the port mooring line (I have one on either side of the bow), tie off the tiller, and raise the mainsail. But we go onto starboard tack. I lower the sail and fix my mistake, then change the remaining mooring line from starboard to port, so we face starboard and encourage a port tack.

I pull on the halyard and raise the mainsail again. *Sobrius* responds by getting on port tack and slowly pulling forward. I release the mooring line and let it fly – I'll retrieve it later – one end is still tied to a bow cleat.

After quickly moving to the cockpit, I steer us downwind and we silently sail away, without disturbing the tranquility of this fine morning with the rumblings of a diesel engine.

We sail wing-on-wing, mainsail to port and jib #3 to starboard, leaving Warderick Wells behind, then on a broad reach after passing Warderick Bore, a sand bore which reaches like a long turquoise-blue finger next to Warderick Cut. Long Rock, followed by another bore, the Wide Opening, Lightning Rocks, Danger Cay, Saddle Cay, all pass by on the eastern horizon while I try to focus on the sails instead of the scenery.

A powerboat in the distance has my attention. It seems to have held the same bearing for a long time, and I don't hesitate to call on the VHF. They don't transmit, so I can't get the name off the AIS.

"Powerboat heading south towards Warderick Wells, Powerboat heading south towards Warderick Wells, sailing vessel *Sobrius*."

"This is power vessel *Time Out*."

"Let's go to one four."

"One four"

"This is sailing vessel *Sobrius*, the red sailboat ahead of you. How would you like to pass?"

"Whatever suits you" says the polite captain.

"How about port-to-port?"

"Sounds good, I'll alter course."

"Thank you sir, and you all have a great day."

"*Time Out* back to 16."

Communication makes passing other boats so much nicer; otherwise I worry about collision right up until we pass.

Our destination is Shroud Cay, but I consider going first to a reef at Elbow Cay (yes, there are many Elbow Cays in The Bahamas), but the wind is increasing and should be gusting to 20 knots today, so I decide against it. Instead I sail on past Cistern Cay, Hawksbill Cay, and then between Elbow Cay and Little Pigeon Cay, upon which sits a lone house.

*The anchorage at Shroud Cay was both unique and stunningly beautiful.*

Beyond Pigeon Cay, a well-defined line where the water changes color from dark blue to very bright blue-green denotes the edge of the Shroud Cay anchorage with its shallow water and white sand bottom. We cross this line and enter a different world.

A sailboat sits by itself in the serene environment of water and grey rocks along the edge of the mangrove flats within Shroud Cay, where the water is even brighter. The rocks are a brilliant grey, with hard jagged lines above and concave where they meet the water, shading what lies beneath. The rocks are yellow where they have been undercut by the water. Beyond is the island, grey and white rocks, palm trees, and green bushes. This is stunning scenery, words hardly do it justice, a bright and happy place, where nature rules and man comes to visit and pay respect.

Tropic birds, all white with two very long flowing tail feathers, fly above, swooping, circling, dancing in the sky while *Sobrius* and I sail through the anchorage, passing behind two more sailboats lying peacefully at anchor. One is a classic small sloop from the era of *Sobrius* (the 1970's) and flies a Bahamian flag and a black MIA/POW flag. Another is a modern white sloop. A long and dark blue sailboat lies on a mooring in the distance.

I heave-to, drop the jib, then sail under main alone to my chosen spot, luff-up, tie off the tiller, and slowly drop the 35lb Vulcan known as Dr. Spock into the soft white sand.

Location: 24° 31.67'N, 76° 47.77'W

Traditionally I dive on the anchor before bagging the jib and covering the mainsail, so I can sail away if I decide we need to move – and so I can cool off first and do these chores while wet.

I also need a change today, so I jump in with mask and a knife, no fins, and swim to the anchor, which is safely buried in the soft sand, and then I continue swimming to the majestic rock about 300 yards further. The swimming feels fabulous and I congratulate myself for not being afraid (of sharks). I circle the rock, diving occasionally, then swim to the next rock to the south, before swimming home and finishing my chores.

As soon as the sails are put away, I deploy the 12-0 and, paddle back to the rocks (there are many more than the two I swam around) with hat, sunglasses, mask and snorkel - no fins, no camera, just me swimming and observing. The change is nice and I swim and dive, pulling the 12-0 along via the leash on my right ankle. Shroud Cay seems to be rimmed with big rocks the size of train cars, behind which lies shallow water and mangroves.

I dive down to the coral heads and peer into all the caves and crevices. I swim a long way to the north and eventually come to a small secluded beach with a sign that reads "Exuma Land and Sea Park." I also see, in the bushes slightly up the little hill, a post with a box that resembles the honor-system cash boxes at Florida State Parks. A rocky trail leads to the box, and I wonder what it is – it certainly can't be a cash box. Maybe it's a birdhouse.

Curiosity gets the best of me and I beach the 12-0 and hike up the short trail. The box is exactly what it looks like – a cash box for those on the moorings.

I also see a sign that reads "Trail to Well." This sounds intriguing – and even though I'm barefoot, I begin to follow it, stepping carefully. But the typically jagged and sharp rocks are worn smooth, probably from hundreds of years of foot traffic to the life-giving well.

The well is not far – and is a classic hole-in-the-rock well, with a knee-high mortar and rock wall around the 8' diameter hole.

A thin rope leads to an old plastic bucket, and I give myself an incredibly refreshing and much-needed 4-bucket freshwater shower.

In the late afternoon, with stratus clouds blocking much of the sun and making for pleasant conditions to sit in the cockpit enjoying the cool breeze, swell from the south, having wrapped around the island, is hitting us broadside. The wind is ESE. Everyone in the anchorage is rolling.

I remember the tip from the guy on the ketch *Rainbow* at Conception Island, using a bridle to point into the swell instead of the wind. So I take the line I use for a preventer – a 3/8" line with a large carabiner on one end, and I go to the bow and pull the anchor line in until I have the chain in hand. I attach the carabiner to the chain shackle, then lead the other end of the line to a chock on the stern quarter, and to the port winch. I winch the line tight, then go to the bow and let out rode until we are pointing at the swell. I stand proudly at the bow until I am convinced that we roll no more.

April 22

Early in the morning I paddle to the south mangrove creek, thinking I'll catch the outgoing tide and ride it to the other side of the island – the beach on the windward side. But the wind seems to be overpowering any tidal current, and I struggle to work against it. I paddle hard the whole way through the shallow and clear water, lined with thick mangrove roots like hands with thousands of twisted fingers sticking down through the shallow water and into the sand below.

The water gets very shallow in places and I have to scoot way forward to keep the surfboard's fin from dragging. Eventually, trying to paddle becomes useless and I have to walk and drag the board behind me, determined to get to my destination. Ahead of me lie vast sand flats, with little to no water. But I can see an opening to the beach about a quarter mile away, and now I am committed to the journey and I trudge through the soft wet sand, almost like mud, dragging the board by the leash. I carry the board on my head for the last stretch, up the sand dune to the beach. This was not at all the casual down-current experience I expected.

To the north, a point of rock stretches out into the ocean. I assume that behind this point lies a cove where another creek leading out to the ocean could be hiding. I leave the 12-0 and backpack on the beach and jog north. There's debris strewn along the beach, mostly plastic things: buckets, bags, shoes, a huge boat fender, odd bits of plastic. Something in the dunes catches my eye and I jog up to investigate. A swing and a net hang in the shade of trees surrounded by arrangements of flotsam. It all looks like a post-Armageddon art project. The swing is made from old rope and a piece of driftwood. Plastic bottles hang from the trees, a floating beacon and something that looks like a rocket engine stand in the sand. Shoes and debris are arranged in simple patterns on the ground and in the trees. It's weird. There's nothing around here except the beach and the mangrove flats – no trails lead here. Nobody lives on this island.

I keep jogging. I see something ahead, and I hope it marks a nice deep creek flowing back to the anchorage. It looks like a hut with no roof, or a bunch of poles. Getting closer I see it is some sort of scaffolding structure, but I can't tell yet.

An aluminum tower must have washed off a boat. Perhaps in a previous life it held navigational equipment for some large power-vessel. It stands now in the sand, vertical and proud, with no known use. I keep jogging.

The beach ends at a sharp rocky bluff, and I find no creek – only plastic debris. I jog back, drag the board to a slightly different creek than the one I came here in, then sit way up on the nose to keep the fin out of the water as I navigate back to the original creek. By now the tide has turned, and I am also going downwind, so the paddling is casual. A school of small fish swims by, startled by my presence. A small blacktip shark swims away from me.

The folks on *Aventura* described shooting out onto the windward side of the island in rapids, with a sandbar in the sound preventing one from being drawn out to sea. This was not at all what I experienced, but sand moves and things change; perhaps last year's hurricanes filled the outflow with sand.

I'm thoroughly exhausted when I finally get back to *Sobrius*, but I should probably try to sail to Highbourne Cay today if I am going to get to Miami by the 28th.

It's a fun, fast sail in 15-20 knots of breeze on a broad reach, then a beam reach, with waves pushing us from behind most of the way. I'm expecting a crowded anchorage, and there are perhaps a dozen boats anchored in the lee of the island when we approach. Four hours after departure I anchor in a nice spot at the north end of Highbourne Cay, not too close to any other boats.

Location: 24° 43.14'N, 76° 49.74'W

Soon after anchoring, a modern Dufour sloop pulls in and anchors behind me; the captain and I, fellow Dufour owners, exchange a wave and a smile before he anchors close by. Unfortunately, he is the first of many to do so, and the rest do not receive smiles and waves. Undeterred by my new neighbor, I paddle over to a nearby reef for a snorkel. The reef is nice, but the current is strong, from an incoming tide, which makes me nervous, and I stay close to the security of the 12-0. The most interesting fish I see is a large nurse shark sitting quietly on the bottom.

While I'm snorkeling, I am perturbed to see three large catamarans, all proudly bearing the name of a charter company, pull in and anchor in such a manner as to surround *Sobrius*. From where I am, it looks like one of them is right on top of my little ship, who begs for personal space. Between this and the current, I'm finished snorkeling and head back. The catamaran is not literally right on top of me, but almost. Three young couples bustle about on each of the three new vessels, obviously excited to be here. They swim; they drive around in their motorized dinghies; they wave and yell to each other. While the catamaraners swim, I see the dark shape of a shark slowly swim by, giving them wide berth, but making me nervous enough to point at it and motion for the swimmers to look out. None of them pay me any attention, and the shark moves on, as they typically do.

I've seen enough; I start the engine, pull up the anchor, and move further out, away from shore and all the other boats. Another sailboat near me does the same thing.

More catamarans pull in, more sailboats, and more mega yachts. I knew this was going to be a busy anchorage – it's the closest one to Nassau, so everyone either going to or leaving the Exumas stops here.

A Canadian Jennaeu with a man and two beautiful women in the cockpit pulls in and anchors right in front of the cutter to my left. My eyes gravitate to the women and rest there as they look ahead, unaware of my gaze. I soon hear the skipper of the cutter telling the Jenneau "I'm leaving early in the morning and you are right on top of my anchor!"

The Jenneau moves and anchors in front of me, but I don't think they are right on top of my anchor. I wonder if I will get to meet them, surely one of the two women might be interested in meeting a solo sailor such as myself, but they soon disappear below.

My attention is caught by action from a group of men on the stern deck of a large trawler nearby. One is pulling on a line that leads to the water while the rest look on. All have an air of excitement as the line pulls back, moving through the water. Then the water splashes and the head and tail of a large nurse shark break the surface.

*Why have they caught a nurse shark and what do they intend to do with this peaceful and friendly animal?* I'm disgusted by the egotistical attempt to dominate the natural world at the expense of this sentient animal, and glad I'm leaving this place in the morning.

Another mega yacht is pulling in and I quit looking at the men with the shark. I hope they let it go [I never see them take it out of the water]. It seems very irresponsible to be shark fishing in an anchorage where people are swimming, and really, unless they intend to eat it, isn't this just the torture of a wild animal?

I'm amazed at all the mega yachts in the anchorage, and I check the AIS to see who is transmitting:

*My Book Ends*, Cayman Islands, 47m (meters)
*Kristina*, USA, 33m
*Captain Guilty II*, Germany, 17m

*T/T Remember When*, Cayman Islands
*Remember When*, Cayman Islands, 44m
*Balaju,* Cayman Islands, 45m
*T/T Mary*, 14m
*Mary A*, Cayman Islands, 42m
*Never Enough*, Marshal Islands, 40m
*Freedom*, USA, 34m
*In Your Dreams*, USA, 19m
*Resilience*, Cayman Islands, 20m
*Aqua Cat*, 30m
*The Great White*, USA, 20m
*Sobrius*, USA, 9m

*"If my ship sails from sight, it doesn't mean my journey ends, it simply means the river bends."* Enoch Powell

## EXUMAS TO MIAMI

April 23

The weather today calls for ESE winds at 15-17 knots, good conditions for sailing downwind to New Providence. I motor off anchor, avoiding the unnecessary risk of sailing into another vessel in this crowded anchorage, then hoist the main and jib #3. The boat that was next to me, the one that asked the Jenneau to move, sails out behind me, then passes as I turn into the wind to raise the sails.

I rig the preventer to hold the mainsail in place and prevent dangerous unintentional gybes, and then I rig the whisker pole to hold the jib out on the opposite side as the main. We sail through the morning and into the afternoon wing-on-wing at a little over 6 knots.

Sailing directly downwind with the sails on opposite sides of the mast requires constant monitoring of sail trim. Turning just a little off the wind causes one or the other sail to luff, so I must pay close attention to the sails and steer by the wind and its effect on the sails. I'm enthralled by the interaction of the wind, the waves, and the tiller, and the intense focus keeps me occupied and entertained all day.

Later, I can see something square and white on the horizon. It doesn't seem to be moving, so it must be a building. Soon more appear, followed by the tops of trees, and finally the beach of New Providence Island. I suppose those who believe the Earth is flat have never been sailing offshore.

The wind is picking up, as are the waves, which lift and push us from behind. *Sobrius* is making over 6.5 knots consistently and is getting harder to control. A gust accelerates us past 7 knots and she slips onto her port side, nearly broaching. The lively sailing is enjoyable, but now it's time to reduce sail, and I decide to take the jib down, so I slacken its sheet to take pressure off the pole.

I clip my tether to the jackline and move to the mast. First I have to take the pole down, and this is one of the many things on a sailboat with which I have limited experience. I disconnect it from the mast first (I'm really not sure what the proper procedure is here)

and rest it on the green rope that I strung between the shrouds while in Clarence Town. I like these ropes, and lean against them whenever I stand at the mast.

I grasp the lazy sheet and pull the clew of the jib to me, then unclip the pole from the jib. I'm glad my boat is no bigger than it is, or else I'd probably not be able to do this (although I'm probably not doing it right). I stash the pole on deck, return to the safety of the cockpit, and tighten the sheets to pull the jib over the foredeck. Back at the mast, I release the jib halyard and, holding it in my right hand and the downhaul in my left, I pull the sail down. I have to hold both lines in one hand and use the other to reach out and pull the sail in to keep it from falling overboard, then I pull it down the rest of the way. In times like these, I am grateful that my boat is no bigger than it is.

With the jib down, we still sail at 6.5 knots, a trend I've noticed when reducing sail – when the time is right to do so, little or no speed is lost.

As the wind continues to increase, dark clouds move in and cover the sky. The waves rise up and become more aggressive, and I feel thankful that both wind and waves are coming from astern. Conditions would certainly be far worse going in any other direction. I reef the main, while sailing downwind – something I haven't done yet. While by no means fast, the operation goes smoothly while I stay tethered both to the jackline and the mast, and the fat green rope between the shrouds helps keep me upright while *Sobrius* pitches, yaws, and rolls. I am again reminded that I should take a day and practice reefing, repeating the process on different points of sail.

Although the sky looks angry and the sea reflects its mood, the sailing is now pleasant under reefed main, and our destination is just around the corner.

A boat that looks like a ferry is approaching from ahead, passes to port, just a bit farther out, and stops. I wonder what they are up to and steer by feel as I look abeam at the vessel. A man is at the bow, leaning out and reaching down, trying to pick something from the water with a boathook, but the sea state is making his task difficult. Just beyond the boat are two big tankers. One is docked and the other is being escorted by tugboats. I pass outside of them while the entrance to West Bay, my intended anchorage, comes into view.

A boat is coming out of the bay, conveniently showing me the line in. While all I see is water, the chartplotter shows a narrow entrance flanked by shallow reef on both sides. The boat is just like the one that looked like a ferry, with the same writing on the side. It's a dive-boat, full of SCUBA divers, heading out to sea. The other vessel must have been a dive boat from the same company, trying to pick up a mooring. I find myself glad not to be with them; today does not at all look like an ideal day to be diving.

I sail into West Bay, with the engine idling just to be safe, and the angry sea turns friendly. Two other sloops, a catamaran, and two power vessels sit comfortably in the relatively calm water. Houses line the beach, with a park on the right. I drop the main and motor around in a big figure-8 surveying the depth and bottom composition looking for the best place to anchor. At 4:30 pm *Sobrius* and I are at our home for the night.

Location: 25° 01.24'N, 77° 32.95'W

A south swell wraps into the anchorage through the same entrance that we used, coming at us about 120° to the wind. I rig a bridle and point *Sobrius* into the swell. We now point in a dramatically different direction than all the other boats here, which seems quite odd, but I am happy not to be rolling.

I recognize the sloop nearby, *Brigadoon III*, from Highbourne Cay. I believe this is the boat that, like me, moved away from the three catamarans. Soon another boat that I recognize pulls into the anchorage, the cutter that asked the Jenneau to move. They must have gone somewhere else first, as they were well ahead of me, and on a more eastward track, all day. The three of us sit in the little anchorage like migrating ducks resting for the night.

April 24

No other boats are near me in the morning, so I sail off anchor and silently slip away, towards the north exit, which is also surrounded by reef on both sides, but much wider than where we entered to the south. I have plenty of time, so I raise the #3 jib on the way to the inlet.

*Brigadoon III* is motoring out the inlet at the same time, moving slower than *Sobrius*, which I didn't anticipate. We approach from their port, staying well away, but I assume I have right-of-way, as we are under sail. They maintain course, which puts us a bit close to the reef on the left, but not uncomfortably so. They wave as we pass, I wave back, and I realize that I'm overtaking them, which would give them right-of-way. I don't know who has right-of-way now, and I do my best to stay well away from them, but I want to turn to starboard and sail across their bow.

Soon *Brigadoon III* turns into the wind to raise their sails, and I make my turn to starboard. All is as it should be as we sail downwind towards Chub Cay, on the way to Miami, the book club, and my old friend Cristina.

Eventually I take the jib down, which has been flapping in the wind and blanketed by the main. Our speed stays above 5 knots, which is fine with me. This will put us at Chub Cay around 2:00. There's no need to get there sooner.

I decide to go ahead and put up the storm jib, which is small enough that the main won't blanket it, and it might give us a bit more speed. We don't need more speed, but I'm curious and like to experiment with the sails. I like, and have much, to learn.

The storm jib does not give us a noticeable boost in speed, but now I realize that I could try to set up sheet-to-tiller self-steering with it. I set the tillerpilot, then run a bungee to the tiller from the leeward side of the cockpit, using the cleat that the tiller tamer once used, before it broke early in the journey. Then I run the storm jib's sheet through a block on the leeward cockpit rail (that I installed for this purpose back in St Petersburg when I originally fitted out *Sobrius*) then across the cockpit to a block opposite, on the windward side, and then to the tiller, where I tie it off. I remove the tillerpilot and spend the next ten minutes adjusting the bungee tension, the sheet tension, and the mainsheet, until *Sobrius* is steering herself at 335°.

This setup is so simple, and it steers us for the next two hours while I sit at the bow, remembering how I liked to sit here as a child while sailing in The Bahamas with my father. Sheet-to-tiller is a great backup to the tillerpilot, and since it uses no electricity and doesn't wear out expensive components, I can let it steer indefinitely.

But after two hours of inactivity, I am bored; I retake the helm and steer the rest of the way to a nice anchorage between Frazier's Hog Cay and Bird Cay, in the beautiful Berry Islands.
Location: 25° 23.77'N, 77° 49.96'W

At 11:00 am the next morning I take a break from writing and emerge from the cabin to look around. It's been calm all morning; the surface of the water is flat and motionless, and I've been sitting at the navigation table writing. But as I step outside I feel a south breeze starting to pick up, a perfect wind-direction for going west to Cat Cay, my next destination on the way to Miami.

Excited by the new breeze, I sail off anchor, easy in the light air with no obstacles around, and then out the anchorage, past *Invictus*, a 65-meter mega yacht that pulled in this morning. As the enormous yacht was anchoring, its tender, a fast-looking center-console boat with a T-top and four big outboard engines, was circling slowly around the gigantic pleasure-craft, I assume surveying the depth. My AIS tells me *Invictus* draws 12 feet.

The water turns a dark sapphire blue as the depth increases dramatically from 20 feet to 1500 feet. We sail around Diamond Cay, a series of brown and lifeless rocks, like the peaks of mountains barely emerging from the light blue water. The remote outpost of Chub Cay and its marina pass to starboard, brightly lit in the powerful sun, as we sail on into the wilderness and towards the Northwest Channel, 15 nm away.

But the breeze changes direction, veering more west, and lightens. It comes and goes, variable in strength and direction. I alter course to the north in response while other sailboats motor by with their sails down, directly to the channel, and disappear over the horizon. Meanwhile we zig-zag towards the channel, endlessly tacking as the hours pass. I am determined not to start the engine, at least not until I get to the channel. The wind continues veering, and *Sobrius* and I continue tacking as morning gives way to afternoon.

At 6:00pm we are almost to the channel that leads to the bank. A container ship is passing through, in the opposite direction, and I let it pass before starting the engine to begin motoring west, through the narrow channel, leaving the deep water behind and entering the shallow waters of the Great Bahama Bank.

As we noisily motor across the endless shallow water, I'm thinking about Bernard Moitessier and why I so enjoy his writing. I love his descriptions of sailing, which make me feel as if I'm there with him in the Southern Ocean, circumnavigating, surrounded by the vast expanse of raw nature. His relationship with birds is intriguing; he befriends the birds of the ocean, and gives them cheese and sardines. They are his only companions in this wild and unforgiving place, and he even calls his ship "a bird of the capes."

There is no traffic as we motor along in the bright blue water in calm, soothing conditions. I take a nap in the cockpit as the autopilot steers. The mechanical whirring of this device used to keep me awake, in the beginning of my time on *Sobrius*, but now it puts me right to sleep.

I wake to the alarm on my wristwatch 20 minutes later, shaking off the sleep, and slowly sit up and turn to face ahead. I'm startled by something flying at my head, and I dodge the unknown projectile. It's a bird, a little brown bird. It lands on the stern pulpit. This is not a sea bird, but a little land bird, perhaps a palm warbler and an anomaly out on this vast expanse of water. I assume the little fellow is lost and sees my ship as a safe place to stop and rest; there has been no land in sight since this morning.

The little bird flies off, out in front of *Sobrius*, low, makes a big looping turn, and comes back. It hops around, investigating the boat while I sit still so as not to frighten it. Amazingly, the bird lands on my foot. I'm not sure if this has ever happened at any time in my life. Then it hops up onto my leg, then my life vest. This is wonderful! A little wild animal, totally unafraid of me, is hopping about on me as if I were a shrubbery.

It flies about the cockpit and alights on the aloe plant, poking its small beak in between the leaves. I've set out a bowl of water for it and some crackers, crumbled up. But it shows no interest. Then it lands on my right hand, which is on the tiller. This is one of the greatest moments of my life, a wild bird on my hand, the hand that steers the ship. *What could be better?* This whole journey has been a communion with nature, and this experience solidifies the pact, completing our union.

*My first passenger on this Bahamas cruise was a palm warbler, whom I called Bernard. It's perched on the tiller pilot. The rope is a shock cord that holds the tiller pilot in place when not in use.*

The irony of the situation does not escape me. I was thinking about Bernard Moitessier and his fascination with birds that come to his ship as he sails solo around the world during the Golden Globe race in 1968, a race which he could have won, but instead of returning to England to claim victory, he decided to continue on around the world again, going to Tahiti instead. Robin Knox Johnston, who became Sir Robin Knox Johnston afterwards, was the eventual winner and the only contestant to finish the race. He also became the first person to singlehand nonstop around the world. His book about the race is called "A World of My Own," Moitessier's is called "The Long Way," and "A Voyage for Madmen" by Peter

Nichols tells the tale of the race from a non-competitor's viewpoint. All are fabulous books.

As the bird hops around the boat, I wonder if someone I know has died. I think sometimes the recently deceased come back temporarily as animals to say goodbye to their loved ones. I hope this is not the case, and so I call this bird Bernard.

Bernard flies into the cabin, then comes out and enters a cockpit cubby, where I keep small things like gloves and a winch handle. Bernard is still with me when night falls.

Progress slows as the night progresses. I still have a very long way to go and now we make only one knot in the darkness, into the increasing wind and waves. This is not worth the fuel we burn, and I decide the best thing to do is anchor and wait for the wind to change. I'm approaching the pass through the shallow water of the White Bank. I reason that the narrow pass will cause other ships to stay on the chartplotter-route. I turn to starboard, motor a half mile off the course marked with a dotted line on the chartplotter, to lessen the chances of being run over in the night by a yacht on autopilot, and drop the anchor.

The waves make for a lot of uncomfortable motion, but I've been in worse, barely. I compare the conditions to a night I spent last year anchored in 50 feet of water in the ocean five miles east of Jacksonville, Florida. I wanted to dive on an artificial reef, but a thunderstorm rolled in before I got in the water. I waited it out, but it just got worse and stuck around for the rest of the day and all night. Though tonight's conditions at anchor are far from pleasant, they are much better than my evening with the thunderstorms, and the comparison comforts me.

Much later, after three hours of sleep, the wind and waves ease and I wake up, determined to carry on. The journey continues in the dark night, motoring and motor sailing upwind, towards Cat Cay. Bernard makes another appearance and flies off to the north as the sun rises in the east, continuing his long and mysterious journey after a night of rest on my little ship. I hope he makes it to his destination.

Nearing Cat Cay, the water gets shallow, about 10', and it looks like an endless swimming pool, bright blue-green, calm, reflecting the sky all the way to the horizon. Dark clumps on the bottom look like reef, and I am tempted to stop and dive. I steer towards a long line of dark patches, but closer inspection reveals that they are vegetation and not coral at all. But as we motor along in the flat and clam water, I continue looking at the bottom and am entertained by the occasional passing starfish.

The water depth continues to decrease and hangs around 6' for a while, keeping me in a state of partial anxiety as I visualize the bottom passing just 1' 4" underneath my keel.

My original plan was to anchor at Cat Cay, but Gun Cay looks more interesting. In my yellow binoculars appear a structure that looks like an old fort, a lighthouse, trees, and a beach. A black ketch resembling a pirate ship lies at anchor off Gun Cay near the inlet. Other sailboats are anchored further north. Gun Cay is uninhabited, while Cat Cay is lined with houses and even an airstrip. The anchorage is right by the airstrip and the cruising guide specifies the importance of not anchoring in the path of the airplanes. Gun Cay wins the decision.

The dark pirate ship looks big from a distance, with rat lines running up the shrouds. A dinghy pulls up to its port side and a couple scrambles aboard. The ship shrinks as I approach and as I pass I think it's a Tahiti Ketch. At 30' these tough steel boats are the same length as *Sobrius*, but more than twice the weight. I share a wave with the couple as I pass.

I drop Dr. Spock in the grass (the bottom is all grass near Gun Cay) and right away dive into the cool water, swim to the anchor, and spike it into the soft sand beneath the green vegetation. A sloop, a catamaran, and two powerboats are further out, presumably anchored in sand. Four dinghies line the narrow beach on the island. Through the few palm trees past the beach I can clearly see the ocean beyond.

Exhausted, I eat dinner and go to sleep at 6:00 pm, well before the sunset.

Location: 25° 35.02'N, 79° 17.85'W

At 10:00 pm I wake up and step out into the cool and dark night to check the wind direction, and it appears to be coming from the south, good for crossing the Gulf Stream to Miami. I consider making breakfast first, but I could make something to eat on the way. I feel like if I leave right now I can make it to Biscayne Bay before dark.

I left *Sobrius* in a state of ready-to-go, so preparation for leaving is minimal. I turn on the instruments, don my lifejacket, hoist the main, and sail off anchor. We sail north, out of the way, but towards a safer-looking inlet. The cut between Gun Cay and Cat Island, although close, is narrow and yesterday I could see the shallow reef extending halfway across. The charts agree, and I sail to the next cut north, which is four nm away, but 20' deep, wide and safe.

I hoist jib #3, anticipating a fresh breeze from the south. The moon is out and nearly full, and I can see the cays around me as I pass through the cut and into the Atlantic Ocean and the Gulf Stream. But out here the breeze is less south and more west, and not as strong. It's as if I'm a victim of a "bait and switch"; what appeared to be favorable wind in the anchorage is not at all favorable out here in the ocean.

Distant thunderstorms light up the sky to the south and west. The moon dimly illuminates dark clouds that explode with lightning over the warm waters of the Gulf Stream. *Is it foolish to be crossing tonight?*

The radar app on my phone shows large band of thunderstorms south of us is moving northeast, and another patch lies to the west, with a space in between, essentially confirming what I can clearly see. While the lightning is dramatic, I cannot hear the thunder, which makes me think the storms must be far away, although I'm no meteorologist. I think I might be able to pass between the systems, and I continue slowly sailing WNW in the light breeze, going with the momentum of the already-begun voyage, instead of letting good seamanship turn me back to the safe anchorage. Ignorance begets bravery.

I have to put up more sail in order to make any progress, and I take jib #3 down and raise the big genny while watching the light shows in my peripheral vision. I still feel like I'm making a mistake by not turning back. I could be safely anchored in less than an hour and could reassess in the morning. But now that I am outside, I feel the pressure to continue, like a ball rolling down a hill. Going backwards does not seem to be an option, though logic dictates such. Perhaps my inexperience is showing, but I press on regardless.

With the big genny up, I return to the cockpit in the dark, point us as west as I can, but the big genoa is having trouble staying full. The lights of Cat Cay and Bimini are clearly visible behind us, yet somehow the icon of my boat on the chartplotter is facing these islands, as if we were headed that way, and the effect is very disorienting. Lightning flashes in the west, ahead of the bow. Yet the chartplotter claims we are sailing east, backwards, towards the cays. I don't understand. Lightning continues to flash. *Is a current pulling us towards the islands? How can we be sailing backwards?*

I start the engine, confused but at least with a solution at hand. I had hoped to sail to Miami on a beam reach, but at least for now, we motor. I steer for a visible gap in the local storms, 260 degrees, a convenient course for heading west, a bit into the current of the Gulf Stream. Miami is about 270 degrees, and the 10 degrees south will hopefully combat the northward current of the Gulf Stream.

A menacing line of dark clouds approaches as lightning continues to flash in the distant sky. I prepare for a squall by taking down the genoa, which isn't helping anyway, bagging it, and putting it below. I install the lower sliding hatch board, closing off half of the companionway, and put the upper board within reach. I get out my yellow rain slicker, then make a pot of black tea, pour half into a mug to sip now, and the other half into an insulated and covered cup for later.

The approaching horizontal line of dark cloud looks like a steamroller in the sky, and it connects larger masses of clouds to the right and left, like a cloud bridge. I put on the big yellow raincoat as I feel a few drops, remembering the squall I encountered in the Gulf Stream on the way to The Bahamas.

But the few raindrops that fall are not followed by more, and the sky on the other side of the cloud-bridge is relatively clear. The feared squall does not materialize, but the lightning continues to threaten from the south and west.

Also threatening are big ships to the north, south and west. I watch the AIS carefully, looking at the Danger-List page to constantly monitor who is around me and if I need to take evasive action. I see the lights of a ship to starboard and find it on the AIS, which seems to tell me it will cross my bow 1.5 miles ahead of me in 12 minutes. This doesn't seem to make sense. From what I can see, it looks like the ship is running parallel to me and is not too far away. *Maybe the ship is much bigger than I think, and much further away.*

I check its stats on the AIS. It certainly is bigger than I thought – it's 265 meters long and is moving at 20 knots!

Soon it does cross in front of me and then disappears to the south. This jolts my adrenaline and for the rest of the night I have no trouble staying awake. This is but one of many ships out here tonight. Soon two more pass safely behind us. But another one ahead is not on my AIS. These are the ships that really scare me. There will be no naps tonight as we motor sail west pointing 260 degrees but heading 280, pulled north by the Gulf Stream.

[A man in the industry told me that cargo ships without their AIS turned on are sometimes running drugs and switch off the AIS when no satellites are above to monitor them. They then rendezvous with smaller vessels and offload the contraband.]

I haven't been sailing for very long before I realize that the clouds to the west are lit from below by the lights of South Florida, another display of the curvature of the Earth.

I'm tired in the morning, the clouds are gone, the sun is shining, and I've seen no other boats for hours. I set the countdown timer on my watch to 15 minutes. My naps have always been twenty-two minutes but I think I should try fifteen. I check the AIS, scan the horizon for boats, then lay down in the cockpit, and quickly fall asleep. When I wake up, the timer is still counting down, from seven minutes, so I've only been asleep for eight. I sit up slowly, facing aft, and am shocked to see a small fishing boat right behind, just off our path. Either they just pulled up behind us or I passed way too close to them. I make a new rule: *from now on I will scan the horizon with binoculars before taking a nap.*

I continue steering at 260 degrees according to the magnetic compass but now head 305 degrees according to the GPS heading on the chartplotter. I can see the tops of the buildings of South Florida when we are 26 nm away. *I guess I'll be looking at the buildings of South Florida all day.*

As the day wears on, I hoist the sails, catch a little wind, then put them back down when it's clear they just add drag. Perhaps they add a half knot at best, but then they slow us down when the wind dies or heads us. I wish I was sailing. All this motoring is getting me down, yet *Sobrius* rumbles along, closing in on Florida.

I keep expecting to be out of the Gulf Stream soon, but though the beach is visible now, we still point at 260 degrees magnetic and head at 305 degrees GPS. I watch the water temperature and the depth for clues about when we will be out of the warm current. I keep sailing closer and closer to the beach, hoping the current of the Gulf Stream will let go of my little ship, yet we continue drifting north as we point towards the yellow sandy beach, the condos, and the shallow water.

As we approach the western edge of the Gulf Stream, the depth drops from thousands of feet to less than one hundred, and the water temperature falls only less than a degree. When we are one mile off the beach and I can see people walking, close enough to wave, the magnetic compass and the GPS heading finally agree with each other, indicating that we are out of the current. I point us south, motoring along the coast; the inlet to Biscayne Bay is 12 nm south and I might just make it before dark.

Rain is falling. The wind is increasing, and backing to the south. South wind would have been nice for the passage across the stream, but now it heads me. I turn on the NOAA weather radio and listen as the robot voice warns me of a small-craft advisory and thunderstorms that could produce strong winds, heavy rain, hail, and waterspouts. "Waterspouts can produce very high winds and dangerously large seas very quickly. Small boats can be overturned. Seek safe harbor immediately" the ominous robot voice warns.

I consider my options. My progress south is less than two knots now, into the wind, the waves, and sheets of driving rain. Going back out into the ocean would cause me to travel with the storm and negate any chance of making it to Miami. The next inlet north is about 20 nm away. Government cut, the inlet to Port of Miami, is in front of me, but checking the chart I see no deep water inside this inlet where I might anchor.

I have to press on, but *Sobrius* motors so slowly into the wind and chop that we might never get there. Also, at this speed, I can't safely cross in front of Government Cut if any ships are coming out or going in.

It occurs to me that we are moving awfully slow, and I sense the engine's RPM's are lower than they should be. I throttle down and then throttle up, but the RPM's don't come back, and now we are essentially idling, not making any forward progress at all. I also know I need to refuel. I have more diesel in jerry cans, but I can't refuel in the rain or else rainwater would get in the fuel tank.

The water is only 20 feet deep and the waves are only 2-3 feet. I drop the anchor and pay out 150' of rode, it's all I can do.

I consider my bleak situation: foul weather with a chance of disastrous waterspouts, low fuel, a throttle problem, rain, wind on the nose. I could abandon the trip to Miami and just start sailing north, but then I'd be following the waterspout-producing storm. As I ponder my next move, the rain slows, then ceases. Opportunity has presented itself and I scramble to get a jerry can of diesel out of the stern locker. I also get a blue shop-towel from under the stove, and hold it over the fuel inlet while I pour in the diesel, to block any stray raindrops.

Though the tank is now full, I still have to address the throttle situation. Without it, I can only sail, and I can't sail upwind between the beach and the Gulf Stream for 12 nm unless I want to short-tack for the rest of the day and all night. I have to look at the engine and see if I can figure out what's wrong. I'm no diesel mechanic, but I decide to have a look and see if anything is *obviously wrong*.

I go below, remove the engine cover that makes up the companionway steps, and peer in. The throttle is connected to the engine via a steel cable that terminates at a pinch bolt, just like the brake cable of a bicycle. I can see there is no cable protruding past the pinch bolt, as if it might have slipped. This makes sense, but I'll be lucky if this is all the problem is.

I reach behind me to the mahogany tool-rack that I built and installed right over the sink (blocking the wine-glass rack). I grab a small adjustable wrench and needle-nose pliers. I loosen the pinch bolt with the wrench, then use the pliers to pull the cable through, and finally tighten the bolt back down. Satisfied with my effort, I return to the cockpit and start the engine, and am elated to hear the high-pitched roar of success as I throttle up.

The wind and waves have decreased with the passing of the storm, of which I only caught the edge. The rain has ceased altogether and it occurs to me that bad weather is always followed by good weather.

I back the throttle down to idle speed, put *Sobrius* in forward gear, and put on my red full-finger gloves. At the bow, I pull Dr. Spock from the Miami-Beach sand, then back in the cockpit I throttle all the way up, and *Sobrius*, with her new-found power, makes progress forward at nearly 4 knots, which should put us at the mouth of the Biscayne Bay Channel just before dark. *We are going to Miami after all!* Just fifteen minutes ago I was beginning to doubt this.

Cruise ships are pulling out of Government Cut as I approach, and I hope for a pause in the traffic. My good luck perseveres and we pass without any of these floating behemoths getting in our way, as we motor on towards the inlet through the abandoned stilt-houses of Stiltsville, where I entered Biscayne Bay last year while sailing *Sobrius* home from St. Petersburg.

As the sun sets and we approach the south end of Key Biscayne, I point us more east, away from the shoals that reach way out from land, towards a distant pair of lighted buoys marking the safe channel. It's strange to have to sail away from the land that is my destination. But although the water all looks the same, I can see the shoals on the chartplotter, and I must be patient. There's no logic to cutting corners here.

Now I must choose between the deeper, more familiar, yet slightly further away channel through Stiltsville, well-marked but by unlit channel markers, or the cut along Key Biscayne's south end, which is closer, but unfamiliar, shallower, and has fewer channel markers. I reason that the closer channel might be easier to follow in the dark as I can simply skirt the shore and stay in the deeper water. The Stiltsville channel might be hard to follow at night, unless the markers are reflective enough to see with my spotlight.

As we approach the decision point, I shine my spotlight on the nearest marker to see how visible it is, and its red triangle lights up and reflects red light, clearly visible. I spot the next one, further away, and it shines bright as well, green. Stiltsville it is – safety over shortcuts.

The moon was bright last night, but tonight it is obscured by clouds, and a light rain falls. I protect the spotlight by holding it inside my yellow rain-slicker as I stand at the helm, holding the tiller behind me, peering into the dark night across the stillness at the space between the stilt houses, standing like skeletons over the black water. I do not let my focus lapse for a second as I illuminate the red markers to the right and the green markers to the left, repeating to myself the phrase "red-right-return" and occasionally checking my depth to confirm that we are still in the channel.

Although I am exhausted, the passage is easy, and soon we are in the safe and protected waters of Biscayne Bay. The wind is supposed to be 15 knots out of the west tomorrow morning, so I select a spot close to land directly across the bay, motor there, circle my selected anchorage, surveying the depth, then drop Dr. Spock in to the bottom. We are in Miami at last!

Location: 25° 36.05'N, 80° 17.13'W

I'm tired but hungry; I dig through my stock of canned foods and am thrilled to find a can of Amy's Organic Spicy Chili, and a can of Prince Edward Sardines – my favorites! I add roasted red peppers to the dish and the dinner is *fabulous*. It's a gourmet meal in the best of locations – the cockpit of my little ship, in the place to which I sailed, surrounded by water and nature. There is no finer meal than that enjoyed by a sailor at anchor after a difficult passage. I eat, and all is right in the world of Paul and *Sobrius*.

I sleep the sleep of the exhausted as my inflatable mattress slowly deflates and embraces me throughout the night. At some point the drumming of rain on the deck wakes me, and I get up before the cabin gets wet and close all the hatches, easily falling back asleep on my partially deflated bed.

In the morning, I hoist the main and sail off anchor, then beam reach at 5.5 knots, under main alone – past another sailboat at anchor, towards the Dinner Key Marina Channel. The wind is gusty, so I hold the mainsheet in one hand and let it out when the gusts heel us. It's fun sailing, and I think about a hamburger at the waterfront restaurant near the marina where Cristina and I ate last year when I arrived from the Dry Tortugas.

To the east I can see literally hundreds of tiny sails dancing across the water and reflecting the morning light. [I later discover that this is the USOD Optimist Team Trials.] The boats look like a swarm of insects flying over the water on the horizon. Biscayne Bay is certainly a hub of sailing activity.

I call the Dinner Key Marina on VHF 68 and am assigned mooring ball #35. I pull up the map of the mooring field on my phone – a marvel of modern technology – and am happily surprised to see that #35 is on the edge of the field, outside of all the other boats, which is fortunate, because the mooring field is crowded. I'm grateful that I can pull into the big city of Miami and easily get a mooring without a reservation.

I pass #35, then three other rows of boats, turn into the mass of sailboats tied to their moorings, and slowly approach #35 from downwind. Mooring singlehanded in a crowded field is trying, and ripe with the possibility of error and collision. I'm lucky to be on the outside, next to the channel. Still, boats lie ahead, behind, and to starboard. I must be careful and precise.

The boathook is out, mooring lines are prepared at the bow, and I very slowly approach #35, pointing directly into the wind. As we reach the ball at minimum speed, I shift into neutral, then move to the bow, carefully but quickly. I reach into the water and snag the pennant as *Sobrius* loses her forward momentum. I loop a line through the large thimble at the end of the mooring line, cleat it off, then add another line from port. We are here!

Location: 25° 43.34'N, 80° 13.84'W

The contrast all around me looms. Yesterday and for the previous 7 weeks I have been in The Bahamas, bathed in the silence and beauty of nature, exposed to only minimal civilization. Here, tall buildings dominate the horizon. Hundreds of boats crowd around me in all directions. While nature is my first love, variety and contrast are still appreciated. One extreme accentuates the appeal of the other.

My first task is to clear customs. Last year I registered with the Small Vessel Reporting System at the Customs and Border Patrol office in Tampa. This is supposed to allow me to clear in with a phone call, and I make the call to the number on the card I was given in Tampa. Curiously, the officer on the other end asks what kind of phone I have, then tells me to download the app "CBP Roam" and follow the instructions to clear in. While this process takes a lot of time and patience, involves multiple websites and a small fee, I tell myself that this is still way easier than finding the customs office in

Miami and taking a cab there to clear in. An hour later I have a short facetime chat with a customs officer, and it is done. I'm cleared back in to the good ole USA.

Cristina has organized her book club, the "Page Sailors Club," to meet on *Sobrius*, and aside from visiting my old friend, this is why I am here. Writing about sailing is my nest-egg and future, and this seems like a good opportunity to further the career that shall bring me the freedom to roam and explore.

I am riding in the marina shuttle-boat, returning to my vessel after spending the day on shore with Cristina, when I get a call on my phone. It's the marina, warning me that I need to check on *Sobrius*, as she appears to have become hung-up on the mooring line. He says it looks like the whole system might fail if I don't get out there and free her. As I hang up I can see *Sobrius* is laying 90 degrees to the other boats in the mooring field.

I change into my swimming trunks, deploy the boarding ladder, don my mask, and get right in the dark water hoping to fix the problem quickly. The mooring pennant is covered in growth, and I pull hard on the fouled line, hoping barnacles don't cut my hands or other creatures sting me (hydras often live on these, and sting like jellyfish). Unsuccessful in my first attempt, I return to the surface to breathe, then go back down for another effort. This time I put my feet on the keel and use my legs to push the boat one way while pulling the rope the other. I work it off the keel, return to the surface and board my vessel as she swings to face the wind. All is well, except for a scar in the paint where the mooring ball ground against the hull for who knows how long. If this is the worst damage *Sobrius* bears when we return to Jacksonville after this journey, I'll be pleased.

The book-club meeting does not disappoint. About ten of us sit comfortably in and around the cockpit, talking about sailing, books, art, music – one man plays Spanish guitar and sings beautifully, captivating us as the moon rises over the bay to the east and the lights of the Coconut Grove skyline decorate the view to the north. They ask me to read from my writings and I select some passages from the ship's log, which is the rough draft of this very book. The scene is perfect and makes all the effort to get here worthwhile.

*It was an honor to host the Page Sailors Club on Sobrius.*

Cristina shows interest and I invite her to sail with me to Jacksonville. It takes a unique person to want to do something like this. I've been sailing for the past 7 weeks and the ocean feels like home to me now. I'm adapted to the motion and ready for the trials the ocean may bring. But Cristina has been on land for many months, and has never sailed offshore in such a small boat as mine, with only one other person, but rather is used to a 65' racing yacht with a full and very experienced crew. None-the-less, she is enthusiastic, even though my life raft is but a 12' surfboard. She certainly is brave!

Cristina and I grew up in West Virginia and independently became sailors in our adult lives. When we were young, I told her that I wanted to take her canoeing on the Allagash Wilderness Waterway in Maine. We never got to do this, but now we are going to embark on an adventure of even greater proportions and a childhood dream is coming to fruition.

I spend the last morning in Coconut Grove shopping for provisions so we can eat comfortably. I push the shopping cart all the way to the marina and return the food to *Sobrius*, then take the shuttle boat back to land with two empty diesel jerry cans. I return my shopping cart to the Fresh Market then walk to the fuel dock next to the marina. But the nozzle on their diesel pump is too large for my jerry cans. I can get no fuel here.

Undeterred, I use my phone to find a fuel station a mile away and start walking. I hope to get an Uber (a private taxi) back to the marina, so I am very careful not to spill any diesel on the cans as I fill them with the pungent fuel. The first can is a success – not one drop spilled. But I have to pee, and when filling the second jerry can, I flinch and spray diesel *all over it*. I do my best to clean it up, but it's an impossible task and now I don't feel like I can call an Uber, and besides, I want to see if I can carry the two 5-gallon containers back to the marina.

But the jerry cans are very heavy and I have to stop every two blocks to rest my shoulders. Then my luck changes for the better about two-thirds of the way back when I spot a parked yellow cab and get a ride the rest of the way for only $3, arriving just in time to catch the 12:00 shuttle boat to the mooring field.

It doesn't even take one jerry can to fill *Sobrius'* tank. Finally I lay down for a nap, worn out from the diesel-hike. I sleep until 2:30.

With a guest coming, there seems to be no end to all the little chores I find.
Everything needs to be cleaned and everything else needs to be put in its place. I also ready the starboard quaterberth for Cristina. I switch my berth from starboard to port, as I anticipate sailing all the way home on starboard tack (with *Sobrius* heeling to port).

I move the heavy Vulcan anchor and its rode to underneath the starboard settee. My little ship should sail better without all this weight at the bow. But I want an anchor accessible up front, so I move the ultralight Fortress anchor and its significantly lighter rode to the bow anchor locker.

The oil needs to be checked, and when I do, I see that it's very low. All the motoring of the last few days has burned off a lot of motor oil. I fill it back up, congratulating myself for having a fresh bottle. I also add oil to the transmission. I have to remember to check the oil every time I use the engine; I have read this is the thing to do and I now see why.

All of the rechargeable batteries get recharged – for the spotlight, two flashlights, the little vacuum, and the GoPro video camera. I stock the abandon-ship bag with a VHF radio, food, water, flashlights, hand-held flares, and the flare gun.

I keep finding things to do until the evening, when I relax for about an hour until Cristina shows up. We stay up talking in the cockpit until late, enjoying each other's company, the moonlight, the gentle rocking of the ship, and the beauty of the sailboats around us with the colorful Miami skyline in the background.

*"To get the full value of joy, you must have someone to divide it with"* Mark Twain

## THE FINAL LEG

In the morning, the wind in the marina is east, and we sail south to the inlet and then out through Stiltsville. A catamaran and a sailboat are coming in as we go out. We continue sailing SE for four nm, so we can benefit a bit from the Gulf-Stream current, before turning just east of north on a close reach. The wind is 15-20 from the east and all is as it should be.

As the morning progresses, the wind strengthens and backs, much to my dismay. I expected it to veer. But who can say for certain what the wind will do?

We can no longer point as north as we want to, and very slowly we get closer to land while sailing just west of north on a close reach. The waves have been building, and now we sail into them, occasionally getting hit by a bit of spray. But the sun is out and Cristina and I don't mind. It's warm enough that an occasional bit of cool saltwater feels good.

When we get within a mile of land, we tack and sail ESE back out into the ocean, then after five nm, we tack back to the north, hoping for the wind to veer, so we can sail on a beam reach. But the close-reach sailing continues and the wind strengthens. The robot voice on the NOAA weather radio calls the wind 20-25 gusting to 30 ENE with 5-6' seas, occasionally 8'. These are not the conditions I expected, but neither of us complains. We both understand that once in the ocean, a sailor takes what the ocean delivers; there is no other option. *Sobrius* handles the conditions just fine under reefed main and jib #4. But we heel at 20 degrees, and are right on the edge of what I think would be time to further reduce sail, by switching to the storm jib and/or the second reef in the main.

We see sails on the horizon. One other sailboat is out here, lending us a bit of comradery on the ocean. Occasionally a powerboat passes in the distance, but overall, the traffic is minimal and no cruise ships or container ships get in our way.

As the day progresses, spray flying over the deck and into us becomes much more common, and every time I get sprayed, I think I'll put on foul-weather gear after the sun dries me off, but then I get sprayed again. Finally, my shirt dries and I get my big red jacket on. Cristina has on a borrowed pair of yellow bibs much too big for her and a green jacket with the hood pulled up. We take turns at the helm and it's nice to have company and help steering; I'm not used to having anyone else aboard with me. I nap a few times on deck, then go below for a more serious rest of twenty minutes. I know the night will be long.

I am awakened by Cristina calling my name. The jib has become backwinded and the traveler has her pinned in her seat. The traveler is missing its pulleys and is free to slide from one side of the cockpit to the other, something I had neglected to point out to my crew. I try to remain calm and tell her to push the tiller away, letting *Sobrius* go through a full 360 degrees. The main is sheeted in, so it can't hurt anything in a gybe, and as the boom crosses the cockpit the traveler lets her free. I take the helm, but her knee is hurt. She doubles over in pain. I ask if she is injured, buy she says she can't tell yet; her knee is numb. We just passed Port Everglades and I offer to turn back and go in. She disagrees. Her knee comes back to life, and although it still hurts, it doesn't appear to be injured.

She stays in the cockpit with me as darkness falls. It's rough down below, hard to maneuver, but she needs rest and I can see she's pushing herself to her physical limit to stay awake. I coax her to go below and get some sleep. The 12-0 acts as a leeboard, so a sleeping sailor can't fall out of the bunk, and I convince her that although the short trip to the bunk will be difficult, once laying down with eyes closed, she will be happy and comfortable.

I set the autopilot and help her get settled below, turning on the small light over the bunk so she can see, then I go back to the helm in the dark, reunited with the ocean, steering into the waves and feeling the wind in the sails, close reaching as best I can to minimize our need to tack.

But before too long we need to tack and I shout below "Tacking!" The light is still on, hours later, and I wonder why. *Is she reading a book?* I want to tell her to turn it off and get some sleep, but I don't want to tell her what to do. The light doesn't bother me, and I just keep steering.

Lake Worth Inlet is ahead, and I decided a while back that we should go in, even though I've never been through this inlet. Cristina is hurt, and we are both exhausted. She doesn't seem comfortable with the fact that there's no one aboard but me and her, and if I should get injured, she wouldn't be able to singlehand *Sobrius*. I'm looking forward to anchoring and eating a hot meal, but I also know that an unfamiliar inlet at night, in these conditions, is an un-seamanlike decision. The tide will be coming out, with 20-25 knots of wind and 5-8' seas in opposition. The inlet is sure to have large standing waves, and I can only hope they won't be breaking. Before collapsing from hypothermic exhaustion, Cristina warned me that the inlet was narrow and had a jetty on its south side.

I do my best to look at the chartplotter as *Sobrius* rises and falls while moving across the dark water. I zoom in and out, scroll up the coast, and see Fort Pierce Inlet is only 10 nm further. I've been through this inlet before, two years ago, onboard *Monkey's Uncle* with Liam and Eddie. I consider this as an option, but reject it. I'm tired and ready to go in and this inlet would be about three hours further.

It's 2:00 am when we get to Lake Worth Inlet. I heave-to outside, and the maneuver shows how big the waves really are. I drop the jib, using the downhaul, and am thankful for having it rigged. It's no longer referred to as "my least favorite line." I simply need to pull on it while releasing the halyard at the same time, so one doesn't get ahead of the other, then cleat it and the halyard off. Everything goes smoothly in the dark and rolling night.

The motor is running when I return to the cockpit, and I use all its power, and that provided by the wind in the mainsail, to sail in against the outflowing tidal current in the narrow inlet with, as expected, standing waves. My spotlight cuts through the dark night and reveals the rock jetty on the left, then the whitewater of breaking waves on the right.

The inlet is much narrower than I expected. In the future, I need to study inlets that I will pass in the days before leaving port, in case I need to use them. This one is neither as wide nor as deep as I expected, and the big waves rolling in behind me threaten to push us sideways and into the jetty or the seawall. I'm ready to turn around if the waves start to break. I want to turn and face backwards to keep an eye on them, but I have to look forward to stay in the channel. I can only afford to steal quick glances back. The further into the inlet we get, the more the waves lift the stern and accelerate us forward. I have to point exactly forward or we might slew sideways, broach, and meet our demise on the rocks. I chance a look behind and the stern light illuminates the large waves moving towards us, green and slick, like waves I might surf at the beach.

Adrenaline courses through my veins and wakes me all the way up. I am focused like a laser beam and my mind is clear, or at least a lot more so than in the previous hours. I see the inlet, the lighted channel-markers, I feel the waves on the hull and the wind in the mainsail. There is only one possible outcome, and that is to move forward, in the center of the channel, to the protected waters inside. Nothing else seems possible; success is imminent; I move through the motions that will get us there safely, not allowing any lapse of concentration.

Success comes gradually as the waves settle, the water calms, and we pass into the Intracoastal Waterway, leaving the angry Atlantic Ocean behind. I turn to port and see a mass of boats anchored in here, the location I selected to anchor. There seems to be room on this side of the crowd. I drop the main, then motor around in figure-8's, selecting a spot that seems safe, and then drop the light Fortress anchor in 20' of water, and let out 150' of rode. This is a fine anchor, but with all these other boats around, I wish I had easy access to the heavier Vulcan and its very heavy 50' of chain.

But the Fortress holds firm, we are here, and the contrast between here and outside is intense.

Location: 26° 46.07'N, 80° 2.57'W

I make a pot of chili with sardines and eat it with crackers in the cockpit while taking in the scene: pretty houses to the east, commercial ship docks to the west, still and dark water reflecting the lights of civilization. The calmness of the water brings me peace, and the hot food is an absolute luxury. I am wide awake now, kept so by the adrenaline of the inlet experience. But I fall asleep immediately after washing the dishes. I sleep in the quarterberth behind the navigation table, with only a folded towel for a pillow. I've never slept in this bunk, but no matter, exhaustion lays me to rest.

In the morning, only 3 or 4 hours after falling asleep, I wake to a bump that shakes the boat. We have hit something! I assume it's the bottom. I leap out of my bunk and up the companionway only to find that *Sobrius* is 90 degrees to the bow of our neighbor. As I stand on deck in my boxer shorts, surrounded by some of the most expensive real estate in Florida, surveying the situation, the owner of the other boat, which looks like a Wauquiez, emerges in his boxers. I'm lucky that he is a friendly guy and is not accusing me of damaging his boat. We ask if each other's boats are OK, and I apologize for my mistake. It appears the tide has pushed us against the wind, and this has resulted in *Sobrius'* keel running over the anchor rode, just like it did the mooring line in Miami.

I quickly put on my swimming trunks and mask, deploy the ladder, and climb in. As expected the anchor rode is caught under the keel. I should have deployed the kellet last night. Underwater, I free the rode from the keel with a pull and *Sobrius* turns to lie to the wind while I climb back aboard. As we drift away from the Wauquiez I pull in 50' of rode to avoid another collision with the neighbors and determine to leave as soon as possible.

The weather report today predicts conditions similar to yesterday, and neither of us wants a repeat of yesterday: cold and wet while beating into 20-25 knots of wind and 5-6' seas.

It's an easy decision to motor sail up the Intracoastal Waterway today.

The waterway is surprisingly beautiful, especially Hobe Sound – charming houses, green grass, lots of pretty boats. But it takes constant concentration to stay in the channel all day long, and we encounter a lot of drawbridges, which have to be hailed by name on the VHF radio in order to pass. Neither my paper charts nor my chartplotter knows their names, so I am listening to the radio on channel 9 trying to pick up the names of the bridges from other boats ahead, and using the binoculars to try to see any identifying signs on the bridges. Some have their names on signs, some did not, and some drawbridge operators are more accommodating of my ignorance than others. Cristina pencils in the names of the bridges on the charts as we learn their names.

We pass Jupiter Inlet 10 nm north of Lake Worth Inlet, and I realize that this is the inlet that I thought was Fort Pierce Inlet while looking at the chartplotter last night. This inlet is not navigable and I can see waves breaking on shoals across the narrow channel. Disaster would have struck had I attempted to enter here. This further reinforces the principle that one should not enter unfamiliar inlets at night, and that one should study the charts thoroughly before making a passage, familiarizing oneself with safe harbors and navigable inlets.

We anchor 2.5 nm south of Ft Pierce all by ourselves in some big open water. I want to anchor here because there aren't any other boats around, Cristina thinks maybe other boats will provide us with some safety. A woman from the city avoids open and empty places, she explains, where crimes might have no witnesses. But this morning's collision weighs heavily on my mind, and I think passing this opportunity to anchor safely would be a mistake.

It's a great luxury to be able to pull over, anchor, make dinner and watch the sunset, a lot different than what I'm used to – the usual slogging it out for days at a time in the ocean – and since we are not in an urban area, the remoteness of the anchorage brings a peace that we both appreciate.

Location: 27° 25.74'N, 80° 18.19'W

May 3

In the morning, we motor to the Fort Pierce Municipal Marina and buy fuel. I only need six gallons, but I want to have all my capacity full for the remainder of the journey. I know we will probably need to motor for six hours up the St Johns River (which should only burn two gallons at most) but why pass up the opportunity to buy fuel? I also fill a five-gallon jerry can of water, just to be safe.

We talk with Brad and his wife on *Bobcat*, a power cat docked next to us. Brad enthusiastically tells us about his beloved town of Cocoa Village, to the point that I assume he must be a Chamber of Commerce representative. It's a chat with friendly people on a beautiful and peaceful morning, and I feel the slight euphoria of a plan nearing its conclusion. We listen to the weather report on the VHF radio, which calls for east winds at 15-20, decreasing to 10-15 later in the day, with 4-6' seas. These are good conditions for ocean sailing and we agree to head back outside.

As we motor into the inlet, a big tugboat comes in. I get a call on the VHF, but I can't tell who is calling. I look behind and see a Coast Guard boat coming up towards us – *it must be them*. The caller asks to switch to channel 68, and I do, but can't pick up their signal. We communicate again on 16 and agree to try 17. Again, I can't get them. The Coast Guard boat slowly comes up to starboard and I wave, expecting them to start yelling instructions, but they just wave and keep on going. It's not them trying to call.

At last, I get the other boat, *Bobcat*, on the radio and it's Brad, from the marina and Cocoa Village, calling to give me his number in case we take his advice and stop at his town. I'm relieved it wasn't the Coast Guard calling to tell me I was in violation of something, or heading into disaster.

We proceed towards the ocean.

A dredging barge is in operation on the south side of the inlet, something I recognize from living in St Augustine Beach, where every five years or so a similar operation renourishes our beaches with sand from our inlet. I can see the water is shallow where they are removing sand, and shoaling just past them, stretching out from the jetty into the inlet, maybe halfway across. This is an ominous sign.

I stay in the darker water closer to the north side of the inlet, but the depth keeps decreasing – 12', 10', 9'… When it gets to 6.9' I almost push the tiller over to turn back, but then the depth starts coming back up, and soon we are in 12' of water. I've made another mistake by not studying the inlet first and asking about it at the marina. Just because I was here two years ago in a bigger boat doesn't mean the inlet is safe today. Sand moves, conditions change, another lesson is learned, I hope.

Outside in the ocean, the sky is clear and sunny, the wind is 15-20, mostly east with maybe a bit of north, and we make over 6 knots consistently on a reach between beam and close. The main has one reef in, jib #4 is up, and it's great to be back in the ocean, with no traffic, no channel to stay in, and no drawbridges to hail. We are in the vast wilderness, we have it all to ourselves, and the freedom washes over me like the waves spilling across the bow. This is where *Sobrius* is meant to sail.

While I love the solitude of sailing alone, Cristina's company is quite pleasant. We share a delicious banana bread with chocolate chips from the Fresh Market in Coconut Grove, along with red apples and green garlic-stuffed olives. It's also nice having Cristina helping me at the helm, and I take two naps during the day while she steers. This is vastly more pleasant than our first day on the water.

At 10:00 pm we are officially starting to round Cape Canaveral, and lucky to have caught it in a good mood. The stars are out in full force in the moonless sky and the crisp night air requires a light jacket. The sparse lights of the cape, I assume from the Space X facility, shine upwards and add to the light show. The mast light looks like a big star, the sky behind it is full of stars, and the water is full of stars – light from bioluminescence – stars above, stars below, on earth as it is in heaven.

While we sit on the starboard bench of the cockpit, sharing each other's warmth and both looking towards land across 15 nm of dark water, marveling at the beauty of it all, a dolphin jumps right next to us, perfecting the magnificent scene. Only the appearance a singing mermaid could top this.

Tonight is a magical night, quite the opposite of my experience here last year, alone and beating into a cold north-west wind, pushing my endurance to the limit. No, tonight is fantastic, this is the reward for enduring the harder times at sea. This is why we come back, to experience the vast ocean on a beam reach in a peaceful night with all the stars out and dolphin jumping alongside.

*Cristina at the Helm of Sobrius*

May 4

In the calm and sunny morning, I change the headsail to jib #3, and soon after change that to the big genny. We make 4-5 knots all day in pleasant conditions. There are no other boats around, in fact we saw none last night and still none yet today. *Why is there no one else here?*

Cristina wakes and joins me in the cockpit. The day is starting off beautifully in conditions that could not be improved – sunny, light but adequate breeze, clam sea, fine company.

A wake in the water ahead of us signifies a large animal approaching fast. The grey head and a flash of a fin show it's either a shark or a dolphin. But of course, it's dolphin, not one but a pod of perhaps half a dozen. They leap, they spout, they roll and play in the wake. I suggest to Cristina that she clip her tether to the jackline and go forward to watch this magnificent wildlife display, and go forward she does. We both watch, mesmerized by the marine

288

mammals, swimming and playing; one makes eye contact with Cristina and broadens her already broad smile.

After the dolphin leave, something else catches our eye, floating on the water. Cristina says it looks like an upside-down skateboard. Clearly the base is wood, and two white objects stand on each end, symmetrically. Birds, two white terns perched on a piece of driftwood, standing still, strike identical poses. They remain motionless as we pass. I can't say I've ever seen this!

Dolphin, again, and they never cease to amaze and delight. Then we see a sea turtle floating in the distance, complete with barnacles growing on its shell. What a fine day this is turning out to be!

We pass St Augustine with Cristina at the helm and the warm colors of the setting sun decorating the horizon – it's been a beautiful day, just calm seas and 10 knots of wind, easily cruising along all day under the bright sun. The ocean is our own little private playground. All the hundreds of other sailboats are on the ICW, which is just amazing. It's amazing that we are out here – this is the place to be! *How is it possible that nobody else is here in this huge expanse of wilderness?*

As the completion of the journey nears, and it becomes clear that I will return with *Sobrius* intact, a great emotion of contentment and accomplishment washes over me. It's an incredible feeling to be almost home and successfully completing this voyage, this voyage that I wasn't sure that I was going to be able to complete. I knew I was going to go for it, but I was mentally prepared to return without a ship, if I were to crash and sink on a reef in The Bahamas; I knew this was a possibility. But now it is becoming clear that I will return successfully with my beloved ship intact, and I smile at the thought.

Land is barely visible just past the horizon, with occasional buildings poking up over the curved line of water. Cristina is trying to stay awake and keep me company in the cockpit, but dozes off with her head leaning against the bulkhead. I need some rest too, so I set the countdown timer on my watch for 5 minutes, tie off the tiller, lean back and doze off.

I sleep, then wake to the buzzer on my wrist, sleep again, and pass an unknown amount of time in a state between sleeping and awake. I open my eyes and see Cristina asleep, but in the same moment she and I are talking to each other, and yet she is asleep. My confusion clears as I realize she wasn't really talking to me, she's been asleep the whole time. Five-minute naps are inadequate, I decide, and sent me to a hallucinogenic state not at all appropriate for sailing.

We get to Jacksonville (Fort George Inlet) at 1:00 am, only partially rested but excited to be here. Three enormous container ships wait motionless outside, further out than us, great rectangular anomalies on the black ocean.

I heave-to and roll up the big genny, planning to motor sail straight downwind into the inlet with the main up. I expect the tide to be coming out, but haven't been able to confirm this. I rig the preventer. We haven't suffered an unintentional gybe on the journey back from Miami and I intend to keep it that way.

The water in the inlet is pleasantly calm, and we are able to make 6 knots going in. Luck and the tide seem to be with us tonight.

Bright lights ahead grow, and whitewater appears in front of the lights. What I see is in the middle of the inlet, and I am briefly confused by the apparition. It looks like a seawall, where one should not be. *Am I hallucinating again?* But now I see the bright entangled mass of lights is moving, and I edge closer to the north side of the inlet. A huge shrimp boat is heading out, white, lit up, and with its arms extended, as if ready to catch anything in its path. I stay out of its path, and soon we are alone again in the inlet, then alone in the still and silent St Johns River, passing Mayport Naval Station, then the picturesque town of Mayport. We pass a huge battleship in a dry-dock on the water, getting to see what the underside of one looks like, and it's very impressive.

The dark night gets colder, surprisingly cold for May in Florida, and I realize that I'm very tired. The moon slowly rises over the horizon behind and lights up the black water and the houses on the banks. It is a beautiful and bizarre experience to be on this river with no other boats around and the perfectly still water reflecting the light of the moon. Cristina does not have proper cold weather gear and goes below to get some rest, telling me not to let her sleep the whole way.

My mind starts to wander and a dream state tries to take over as I stand at the helm. I need to stand so I can see over the cabin and keep track of the channel markers. I'm not accustomed to dozing off while standing, but it starts happening none-the-less. I shine the spotlight below and shout Cristina's name to wake her, to no avail. I try again a few minutes later, but still no luck. I go below and wake her while the autopilot steers. Her eyes open and she looks at me from her cozy berth, and I go back up. But she does not follow.

I am standing at the helm, dressed in all my cold-weather gear, moving from foot-to-foot to try to stay awake and warm, when I feel myself falling backwards. I catch myself and realize I am *really* falling asleep at the helm, even while standing. I set the trusty Pelagic tillerpilot for the last time and go below to wake Cristina, and this time I make sure I succeed. The lights of downtown are ahead and the Main St Bridge is lit with beautiful blue lights. I coax her to come up and see.

This time she wakes and joins me in the cockpit. I call the bridge, expecting a long wait. But the friendly female voice says they open on demand and to come on up. What luck! It figures, I'm a lucky man.

We pass through the vertically rising blue-lit bridge, which looks like something from an amusement park, and I thank the bridge operator. She calls back and thanks me for passing through, then laughs. I laugh too. I can scarcely believe my two-month Bahamas adventure is coming to a fine and successful conclusion.

The train bridge just past the Main St Bridge closes as we approach, and I tie off the tiller so we motor in circles (a first) and then ready the fenders and lines for docking as a cargo train slowly rumbles across the bridge at about the pace of someone casually riding a bicycle. Eventually the creaking iron bridge goes back up and we are once again on our way.

The sun is rising as we near the Ortega River bridge, just in time to illuminate the fishing buoys that I need to avoid in this very last leg of my nearly 2000-nm journey. This bridge also opens on demand. A trawler waits to come through on the other side, and I call them on the VHF, offering to let them through first. When the trawler passes, the couple onboard wave, then get a better look at us in our foul-weather gear and wave enthusiastically, as if they can tell who we are and where we have been, coming in on this early morning dressed for an ocean voyage. Their acknowledgment of our arrival from sea warms my heart. They are our welcoming party, two passing boaters. I need no more.

At The Marina at Ortega Landing, I find my new slip – D-149 – pull in slowly, step off with bow and stern lines in hand, and clumsily pull *Sobrius* to the floating dock, tie her off, and relish the moment of our arrival home. It is done.

*The sunrise was a nice treat at the end of the voyage.*

*I was thoroughly exhausted when we finally pulled into my new slip.*

After docking, I sleep the sleep of the exhausted, totally spent from the all-night river-cruise. But an hour later, I spring from the bunk and leap onto my unstable feet, tormented by a sense of impending disaster. Cristina is looking at me from the port quarterberth, propped up on her elbows reading a book.

"*Where are we?*" I ask, in a state of near panic.

Cristina thinks I am joking around at first, but I'm ready to run up on deck. "Your boat is tied up."

My eyes are intense as I ask the next question "*are we at anchor?*" I'm still completely disoriented.

"No, we are tied up to the dock, at *your marina.*"

The realization slowly dawns on me that all is well, and the sensation that we are drifting into disaster slips away as I lay back down and fall asleep, safely tied up to the dock, at *my marina.*

The End

*As I had hoped, Sobrius retuned with only minor cosmetic damage.*

# Glossary

**AIS** - Automatic Identification System – a system that uses a radio signal to exchange information such as position, course, speed etc. with passing ships; the system also warns of potential collisions

**autopilot** – also referred to as the "tillerpilot" – a device that uses a computer, motion sensors, and a compass to steer the boat by directly moving the tiller. Mine is made by Pelagic.

**back (the wind)** – to change direction counterclockwise

**backstay** – a steel cable or cables, part of the standing rigging, that supports the mast, connecting the transom (the rear of a sailboat) to the top of the mast

**backwind** – (v) to position a sail so that the wind hits it on the opposite side as normal

**bimini** – a canvas roof over the cockpit of a boat, often retractable

**block** – a pulley

**boom topping lift** – a line running from a cleat at the base of the mast to a block at the top of the mast then down to the aft end of the boom. This line supports the boom when the mainsail is down or lifts it to ease the tension on the leech of the sail

**boom vang** – a line and pulley assembly that provides downward tension on the boom, helpful when sailing downwind

**broach** – to heel so far that the rudder comes out of the water and no longer functions

**bow** – the front of a boat

**dorade box** – a vent on the deck of a boat designed to let air pass through without allowing water ingress

**fetch** – the distance wind blows across water and thus creates waves

**foot** – the bottom edge of a sail

**fry** – very young fish

**genoa** – the largest of a collection of jibs; a large headsail

**gunwale** – the raised edge of the deck of a boat

**gybe** – also "jibe," to change course across the wind with the wind coming from behind, necessitating moving the boom from one side of the boat to the other

**heel** – to lean (a sailboat) leeward, pushed by the wind

**heave-to** – a maneuver of tacking without releasing the jib sheet, resulting in backwinding the jib, the tiller is then lashed to leeward and the main is let mostly out, the boat then slows and tends to itself

**hull speed** – the maximum speed of a displacement boat (a boat that won't plane), and a function of the waterline length

**jacklines** – flat nylon webbing, attached at strong-points on the deck, to which a sailor clips his or her tether, resulting in being attached to the boat but maintaining mobility

**jib** – the sail on the front of a sailboat, attached to the headstay (or forestay or jibstay). Jib #1 would be the largest jib or the genoa, and they decrease in size with increasing numbers. Smaller sails are used in higher winds, and the storm jib is the smallest of my 5 jibs.

**kellet** – a weight that holds the anchor rode to the bottom, preventing the keel from snagging the rode

**ketch** – a sailboat with two masts, the aft mast being shorter than the fore mast

**knot (kt)** – one nautical mile per hour (speed)

**lazyjacks** – a system of ropes that run from boom to mast which catch the mainsail when it is taken down, to prevent it from spilling out onto the deck

**lee** – an area where the wind is blocked, as by an island or a structure

**leeward** – away from the wind

**leech** – the trailing edge of a sail

**luff** – the forward edge of a sail

**nm** – nautical mile, 1.1 statutory miles and equal to one minute of latitude

**pelagic** – adjective describing creatures that live in the deep ocean and rarely come into shallow water or near coastlines; also the brand of my tillerpilot

**port** – left facing forward

**preventer** – a line that ties to the boom and pulls it forward, which prevents unintentional gybes.

**quarterberth** – a sleeping berth in the rear of a boat and on one side, typically beneath the cockpit

**reef** – (v) to make a sail smaller, allowing it to handle stronger wind

**rode** – line or chain connecting an anchor to a boat

**scope** – the ratio of anchor-rode length to water depth

**sheet** – a line that controls the trim of a sail

**spreaders** – horizontal struts on the mast about 2/3 of the way up that help support the mast by pushing on the cap shrouds

**stanchion** – a steel post on the edge of the deck of a sailboat that supports the lifeline

**starboard** – right facing forward

**stern** – the rear of a boat

**tack** – (v) 1. to change course across the wind and with the wind coming from ahead, necessitating moving the sails from one side of the boat to the other 2. to attach the lower forward corner of a sail to the boat, (n) the lower and forward corner of a sail

**tether** – a strong short line attached to a lifejacket or harness with a carabiner at the other end, used to attach oneself to the boat and prevent falling overboard

**tillerpilot** – also referred to as the "autopilot" – a device that uses a computer, motion sensors, and compass to steer the boat by directly moving the tiller. Mine is made by Pelagic.

**transom** – the flat rear section of the hull of a boat

**trim** – (n) the angle of a sail relative to the wind, and the shape of a sail; (v) to change the trim of a sail, typically by adjusting a sheet or other line

**veer (the wind)** – to change direction clockwise

## APPENDIX 1, PREPARATIONS AND SUPPLIES

In the year before this Journey, I replaced the electric bilge pump, fixed the manual bilge pump, built a collision bulkhead, built new dorade boxes, bought a new anchor and rode, bought a new (used) jib, acquired a spare tiller, replaced the water pump in the engine, replaced the transmission coupling, replaced the secondary fuel filter, painted the hull and the topsides, varnished the teak, replaced the depth sounder, replaced the VHF radio, added non-skid flooring to the cabin, built a desk organizer, built a tool organizer, added adjustable jib cars, fixed a broken cleat and replaced bolts on three others, added a strong padeye near the bow for a preventer block or a steering sail, bought a shortwave radio receiver, bought charts, bought more jerry cans to up my water storage to 52 gallons, and bought a second 5-gallon jerry can for diesel.

A Garmin InReach satellite communicator provided communications offshore, weather reports, tracking, and SOS capability. A SPOT also provided tracking and SOS capability.

Explorer Charts were a great benefit to navigation.

I use an ICOM MA500-TR AIS transponder, and love it.

My autopilot is a Pelagic Bluefin tillerpilot, and I love it too.

I brought 52 gallons of water and could have been comfortable with this amount for two months, as I used about 5 gallons a week for drinking and rinsing the dishes, which I cleaned in saltwater. For bathing, I swam in the ocean every day (except for the passages to and from The Bahamas) and only rinsed in freshwater once before restocking the water in Clarence Town, after which I rinsed with a quart of fresh water almost every time.

I only burned 5 gallons of diesel in the first five weeks of the journey, as I sailed almost exclusively. I burned much more on the way home, mainly because I decided on going to Miami instead of sailing to wherever the wind dictated. Total fuel usage was about 24 gallons.

## APPENDIX 2, THINGS I DID WRONG:

1) I turned the wrong way when I encountered the *Brooke Chapman*, and then didn't know the meaning of the phrase "one whistle", which means the captain wishes to pass port-to-port.
2) I should have practiced reefing, particularly the second reef, before the journey.
3) I didn't use a preventer often enough, and should have had two rigged, one on each side of the mast.
4) I should not have dropped anchor while hove-to (at the Whale Hole).
5) I should not have been freediving solo.
6) I sailed away from the Whale Hole too soon. I should have waited until my head was straight.
7) Twice I hove-to without looking behind me first.
8) The video camera was once off when I thought it was on, and twice it was on still photo when I thought it was on video, costing me two great shark videos.
9) I probably should not have gone into Lake Worth Inlet at night with the tide coming out while wind and waves were going in, and never having been there before.
10) I should have familiarized myself with all the inlets along Florida's East Coast before sailing home from Miami.
11) I should have had an ICW cruising guide.
12) I should have had a backup method of making coffee.
13) I should have had a life raft.

## APPENDIX 3, THINGS I DID RIGHT:

1) I brought plenty of food and water.
2) I had multiple foul-weather jackets, gloves and hats so I didn't have to wear wet clothes.
3) I had all three Explorer Chart Books.
4) I had a fine anchor (a Vulcan 15kg) and rode, as well as two backup anchors.
5) I used both paper and electronic charts.
6) I studied the charts before each passage.
7) I let the weather dictate my plans (except for going to Miami).
8) I swam every day and appreciated the beauty of my surroundings.
9) I had a shortwave radio receiver and knew how to get weather reports with it.
10) I used an AIS transponder.
11) I never slept for more than 20 minutes while underway. For this I used a Timex Expedition watch with a countdown timer.
12) I chased my dream to its fruition.
13) I wrote a book about the journey and convinced you to buy it (thanks!).

## ACKNOWLEDGEMENTS

Thanks to my family for supporting me on this journey and help editing.

Thanks to Dr. Chris Ruhland , Judy Kahn, and Cristina Vidal Artaud for editing.

Thanks to Don Mack for his advice about Explorer Chartbooks and the Comer Channel.

Thanks to David from the sailboat *Kera Vela* for the advice about getting a shortwave radio and tuning in to the Chris Parker weather forecast.

Thanks to Dorothy and Glenn from the sailboat *Dot's Way* for company, a delicious fish, and advice about the Ragged Islands.

Thanks to Lenny McAneny and McAneny Builders for employment before and after this journey.

Thanks to the Marina at Ortega Landing in Jacksonville, Florida, for providing me with a great place to stay before and after the journey.

Thanks to David Hows of The Ocean Sailing Podcast for helping me promote this book.

Thanks to Michael Wilson for photographs of *Sobrius* at Buenavista Cay

Thank you for reading my book! If you enjoyed it, please take a moment to leave a review at the site where you purchased it.

You can follow me and my adventures on **Facebook** and **YouTube**; both are "**Paul Trammell**."

Look up the "Journey to the Ragged Islands" series of videos on YouTube to see the videos I shot while writing this book in the Bahamas.

To see color versions of all the photos in this book, look up on YouTube the video "Color Photos from the book Journey to the Ragged Islands."

Happy Sailing!

Freedom to roam
On a floating home
Might make me smile
For a little while
If the deep blue sea
Were kind to me
I would follow the wind
Wherever it may send
I would follow the stars
No noise from cars
Sunset and sunrise
Warm colorful skies
Whatever the weather
For worse or for better
Nature by my side
My only bride

Made in the USA
Columbia, SC
29 December 2018